THE SENSES IN PERFORMANCE

The Senses in Performance is the first anthology dedicated to assessing critically the role of the human sensorium in performance.

The seventeen original essays gathered in this volume offer a multifaceted approach to the methodological, theoretical, practical, and historical challenges facing the scholar and the artist interested in studying the subtle actions of the human senses in all sorts of performances: from ritual to theatre, from dance to interactive architecture, from performance art to historical drama and opera.

There are contributions from:
Richard Schechner * Deidre Sklar * Phillip B. Zarrilli * Barbara Kirshenblatt-Gimblett * Denise E. Cole * Mary Fleischer * Stanton B. Garner Jr * Stephen Di Benedetto * Dorita Hannah * Martin Welton * Maya E. Roth * Jennifer Fisher * Kerrie Schaefer * Cobina Gillitt * Allen S. Weiss * Sally Banes and André Lepecki.

This ground-breaking anthology shows how the creative uses of taste, touch, smell, hearing, balance and vision, in Western and non-Western traditions, remain one of the most generative operations for critical and performative inventions and interventions.

Sally Banes is Marian Hannah Winter Professor of Theatre and Dance Studies, University of Wisconsin-Madison. She is author of *Dancing Women: Female Bodies Onstage* (Routledge 1998).

André Lepecki is Associate Professor in Performance Studies at New York University. He is the author of *Exhausting Dance: Performance and the Politics of Movement* (Routledge 2006).

WORLDS OF PERFORMANCE

What is a "performance"? Where does it take place? Who are the participants? What is being enacted? Does it make a difference if the performance is embodied by live performers or represented on film, video, or digital media? How does the performance interact with individuals, societies, and cultures? Not so long ago, many of these questions were settled. But today, orthodox answers are misleading, limiting, and unsatisfactory.

"Performance" as a practice and as a theoretical category has expanded exponentially. It now comprises a panoply of genres, styles, events, and actions ranging from play, sports, and popular entertainments to theatre, dance and music, secular and religious rituals, the performances of everyday life, intercultural experiments, and more. And beyond performance proper is the even more dynamically unsettled category of the performative.

For nearly fifty years, *The Drama Review (TDR)*, the journal of performance studies, has been at the cutting edge of exploring performance. In *TDR*, artists and scholars introduce and debate new ideas; historical documents are published; new performance theories expounded. The Worlds of Performance Series is designed to mine the extraordinary resources and diversity of *TDR's* decades of excellence.

Each Worlds of Performance book is a complete anthology, arranged around a specific theme or topic. Each volume contains hard-to-get seminal essays, artists' notes, interviews, creative texts, and photographs. New materials and careful introductions insure that each book is up to date. Every Worlds of Performance editor is a leader in the field of performance studies. Each Worlds of Performance book is an excellent basic resource for scholars, a textbook for students, and an exciting eye-opener for the general reader.

Richard Schechner
Editor, *TDR*
Series Editor

OTHER TITLES IN THE SERIES

Acting (Re)Considered 2nd edition edited by Phillip B. Zarrilli

Happenings and Other Acts edited by Mariellen R. Sandford

A Sourcebook for Feminist Theatre and Performance: On and Beyond the Stage edited by Carol Martin

The Grotowski Sourcebook edited by Richard Schechner and Lisa Wolford

A Sourcebook of African-American Performance: Plays, People, Movements edited by Annemarie Bean

Brecht Sourcebook edited by Carol Martin and Henry Bial

Re: Direction. A Theoretical and Practical Guide by Rebecca Schneider and Gabrielle Cody

Popular Theatre: A Sourcebook edited by Joel Schnechter

Carnival: Culture in Action – The Trinidad Experience edited by Milla Cozart Riggio

THE SENSES IN PERFORMANCE

Edited by Sally Banes and André Lepecki

Routledge
Taylor & Francis Group

NEW YORK AND LONDON

First published 2007
by Routledge
270 Madison Ave, New York, NY 10016

Simultaneously published in the UK by Routledge
2 Park Square, Milton Park, Abingdon, Oxon OX14 4RN

Routledge is an imprint of the Taylor & Francis Group

Typeset by Fakenham Photosetting Ltd

British Library Cataloguing in Publication Data
A catalogue record for this book is available from the British Library

Library of Congress Cataloging-in-Publication Data
The Senses in Performance/edited by Sally Banes, André Lepecki.
    p. cm. – (Worlds of performance)
    Includes bibliographical references and index.
    1. Performing arts. 2. Senses and sensation. I. Banes, Sally. II. Lepecki, André.
    PN1584.S46 2006
    790.2–dc22
    2006022155

ISBN 10: 0-415-28185-7 (hbk)
ISBN 10: 0-415-28186-5 (pbk)
ISBN 10: 0-203-96592-2 (ebk)
ISBN 13: 978-0-415-28185-0 (hbk)
ISBN 13: 978-0-415-28186-7 (pbk)
ISBN 13: 978-0-203-96592-4 (ebk)

CONTENTS

ILLUSTRATIONS

CONTRIBUTORS

Sally Banes is Marian Hannah Winter Professor of Theatre History and Dance Studies at the University of Wisconsin-Madison. Her books include *Terpsichore in Sneakers: Post-Modern Dance* (Wesleyan University Press, [1980] 1987), *Democracy's Body: Judson Dance Theater 1962–64* (Duke University Press, [1983] 1993), *Writing Dancing in the Age of Postmodernism* (University Press of New England, 1994), *Dancing Women: Female Bodies on Stage* (Routledge, 1998), and *Subversive Expectations: Performance Art and Paratheater in New York 1976–85* (University of Michigan Press, 1998).

Denise E. Cole is a temporary Assistant Professor at Central Michigan University. She often presents at conferences on the topics of English court performance and medieval hospitality. She is currently working on a book about the revels at the court of Henry VIII.

Stephen Di Benedetto is currently an Assistant Professor of Theatre History at the Department of Theatre Arts, University of Miami. His writings on the senses in performance can also be found in *Performance Research*, *Journal of Dramatic Theory and Criticism*, and *New Theatre Quarterly*. He is now actively engaged in research on the body in contemporary performance art and on scenography.

Jennifer Fisher is Assistant Professor of Contemporary Art and Curatorial Studies at York University in Toronto. She is a founding member of the curatorial collaborative DisplayCult, which produced *CounterPoses* (1998), *Vital Signs* (2000), *Museopathy* (2001) and *Linda M. Montano: 14 Years of Living Art* (2003). She co-directed *UnCommon Senses: The Senses in Art and Culture,* an interdisciplinary conference held at Concordia University in Montreal in 2000.

Mary Fleischer is Professor of Theatre Arts and Chair of the Division of Fine & Performing Arts at Marymount Manhattan College. She holds a PhD in Theatre from the Graduate Center of the City University of New York, and her interdisciplinary interests have generated performance and research projects including a forthcoming book, *Embodied Texts: Symbolist Playwright-Dancer Collaborations.*

Stanton B. Garner Jr, Professor of English at the University of Tennessee, is the author of *The Absent Voice: Narrative Comprehension in the Theater* (1989), *Bodied Spaces: Phenomenology and Performance in Contemporary Drama* (1994), and *Trevor Griffiths: Politics, History, Drama* (1999). His recent work explores the intersections of theatre and medicine in the late nineteenth and early twentieth century.

Cobina Gillitt is an independent scholar working on Indonesian performance and contributes frequently to academic journals on this topic. She holds a PhD from the

Performance Studies Department at New York University. Her dissertation analyzed New Indonesia Theatre between 1968 and 1978.

Dorita Hannah is Associate Professor at Massey Unversity College of Design in New Zealand. She has published extensively on architecture and performance and her project "Heart of PQ" received the 2004 National Award for Research from the New Zealand Institute of Architects. She is currently finishing her doctoral dissertation on "Event-space: theatre architecture and the historical *avant-garde*" at the Department of Performance Studies, New York University.

Barbara Kirshenblatt-Gimblett is University Professor and Professor of Performance Studies, New York University. She has written extensively on Jewish cultural performance, aesthetics of everyday life, tourism, museums, and heritage. Her publications include *Destination Culture: Tourism, Museums, and Heritage* (Berkeley: University of California Press, 1998).

André Lepecki is Associate Professor of Performance Studies at New York University. His publications include the anthology *Of the Presence of the Body* (Wesleyan University Press, 2004) and *Exhausting Dance: Performance and the Politics of Movement* (Routledge 2006).

Maya E. Roth is Director of Georgetown University's Theater Program and Artistic Director of the Davis Performing Arts Center. Her published work focuses on feminist performance, space-based criticism, and civic theatre, with particular emphasis on the plays of Timberlake Wertenbaker. Roth received her PhD from the University of California, Berkeley.

Kerrie Schaefer completed her PhD in Performance Studies at the University of Sydney and now lectures in Drama at the University of Newcastle, Australia. Her research interests are in contemporary performance, feminism(s) and performance, place and performance, and performance-based community cultural development and social change.

Richard Schechner is University Professor of Performance Studies, New York University. He has published extensively on performance theory, including *Performance Studies: An Introduction* (London, New York: Routledge, 2002), *Environmental Theatre* (expanded edition) (New York Applause Book, 1994), *The Future of Ritual: Writings on Culture and Performance* (New York: Routledge, 1993), and *Between Theater & Anthropology* (Philadelphia: University of Pennsylvania Press, 1985). He is the editor of *The Drama Review, The Journal of Performance Studies*. He is Artistic Director of East Coast Artists of New York and an Honorary Professor at Shanghai Theatre Academy and at the Institute of the Arts, Havana.

Deidre Sklar is the author of *Dancing with the Virgin: body and faith in the fiesta of Tortugas, New Mexico* (University of California, 2001). Her articles appear in the *Journal of American Folklore, The Drama Review*, and *Dance Research Journal*, among others. She is currently a Research Associate at Oberlin College.

Martin Welton is a Lecturer in Drama at Queen Mary College, University of London. His research interests include perception and performance, acting and performance theory, and actor training systems. He also works as a performer, most recently with Sound and Fury Theatre Company, and Emilyn Claid.

Allen S. Weiss has written or edited over 25 books, including *The Aesthetics of*

Excess (SUNY Press), *Perverse Desire and the Ambiguous Icon* (SUNY Press), *Phantasmic Radio* (Duke University Press), *Sade and the Narrative of Transgression* (Cambridge University Press), *Experimental Sound and Radio* (MIT Press), *French Food* (Routledge), *Breathless: Sound Recording, Disembodiment, and the Transformation of Lyrical Nostalgia* (Wesleyan University Press), and *Feast and Folly: Cuisine, Intoxication, and the Poetics of the Sublime* (SUNY Press). He has recently directed *Theater of the Ears*, a play for electronic marionette and taped voice based on the writings of Valère Novarina. He teaches in the Departments of Performance Studies and Cinema Studies at New York University.

Phillip B. Zarrilli is internationally known for actor training through psychophysical processes and as a director. He conducts intensive training throughout the world, at his private *kalari*/studio in Wales, and as part of BA and MA/MFA programs at the University of Exeter. His books include *Acting Reconsidered, When the Body Becomes All Eyes,* and the forthcoming title, *The Psychophysical Actor at Work: a post-Stanislavskian approach.*

ACKNOWLEDGMENTS

On the way to its completion, this project was faced with an unexpected, scary, but fortunately overcome, adversity. The only reason this book finally reached publication was thanks to the unwavering support and patient dedication of all its contributors. To their steadfastness and commitment, to their scholarship and work, we are deeply thankful. Our thanks also go to our incredibly professional editors at Routledge, Talia Rodgers and Minh Ha Duong, and also to Richard Schechner, who believed in and fostered this project from its very start.

Sally Banes and André Lepecki

1

INTRODUCTION

The performance of the senses

André Lepecki and Sally Banes

"Nothing in man," wrote Michel Foucault in his famous essay on Nietzsche's notion of genealogy, "not even his body – is sufficiently stable to serve as the basis for self-recognition or for understanding other men" (Foucault 1977: 153). Drawing from Nietzsche's understanding of the body as self-differentiating becoming, Foucault reminds us how the body is constitutively unstable, always foreign to itself – an open process of continuous self-estrangement where the most fundamental physiological and sensorial functions endure ongoing oscillations, adjustments, breaks, dysfunctions, and optimizations, as well as "the construction of resistances" (153). The construction of resistances, for Foucault, would be so many ways of reinventing not only subjectivity but also a whole new corporeal project, what he later called "a livable life."[1]

Now, to cast the body as essentially metamorphic within the force field of history is to give to perception and the sensorium central roles that transcend the purely somatic. Neither can be seen any longer as anthropologically stable, historically neutral, or a culturally passive neuro-physiological basis where subjectivities find common ground. On the contrary, perception and the sensorium are to be understood as historically bound cultural agents, constantly being activated and repressed, reinvented and reproduced, rehearsed and improvised. In an intertwining process where the somatic, the physiological, and the neurological criss-cross the historical, the sociological, the political and the imaginary, the profoundly performative interfaces occurring between history, corporeality, power, language, and the sensorial become apparent.

No wonder then that performance practices become privileged means to investigate processes where history and body create unsuspected sensorial-perceptual realms, alternative modes for life to be lived. To carry out the task of analyzing "the senses in performance" is also to carry out bio-political investigations of the many critical thresholds where the corporeal meets the social, the somatic meets the historical, the cultural meets the biological, and imagination meets the flesh.

To these investigations, to the critical exploration of a plethora of performance practices where the instability of perception and the creative activation of the senses are explored, to the identification of those many chiasms intertwining the physiological

1

and the cultural, to the advancement of innovative methodologies in performance analysis focused on a variety of cultural contexts and sensorial organizations, this anthology is dedicated.

In writing history, theory, or criticism of the senses in performance, one is faced with significant challenges. For instance, a descriptive language for tastes, textures, aromas, and sounds (as performance devices) that is as rich and detailed as that for sight and musical or verbal sounds has yet to be developed. Partly for that reason, the tasks of interpretation regarding the uses of alternative, or uncharted, senses in performance (senses that fall outside Western classifications and divisions of the sensorium into taste, vision, smell, touch, and hearing) are complex. Thus, we invited leading and emerging scholars in the fields of theatre studies, performance studies, dance studies, semiotics of the senses, and philosophy to address, through a variety of methodologies and through historical, contemporary, and cross-cultural examples, new strategies to write about, and to rethink, the experiences of the senses in performance.

The seventeen essays gathered in this volume approach the methodological, theoretical, practical, and historical challenges of studying the subtle action of the senses in performance and offer case studies of the uses of taste, touch, smell, and/or hearing (other than dialogue, music, and specific sound effects), as well as other senses, in performance in both Western and non-Western traditions (including drama, dance, opera, and performance art). What we believe comes out of this collection is a multi-faceted vision of how the senses in performance remain a site of unsuspected critical and performative power.

Performances of the senses reveal histories – they propose practices, privilege materials, mirror social conditions, and implement techniques. And in each of these steps a body is constructed – even if momentarily – even if just for the duration of one particular performance. Every performer, every actor, dancer, musician, body artist enduring her or his training knows well how to operate these more or less localized, more or less momentary, more or less material constructions of body and senses, these perennial metamorphoses. Moreover, every performer knows these transformations to be a profoundly psycho-physical fact. Audiences intuit this metamorphic sophistication of the sensorium that the trained performer endures, enacts, and projects. They recognize it, sense it, fall into it, are summoned by it, and then either reject it or applaud it.

But what still needs to be articulated more clearly if we want to build a theory of the performance of the senses is that any such performance generates and reveals subjacent economies and politics of appearing. Indeed, whether this appearing, this stepping of the sensed object or subject into the fore of perception, happens visually, or happens rather as an olfactory, or tactile, or proprioceptive, or gustatory, or aural experience (or as a combination of, or synesthesia between, different sensory organs), the imbrication of sensory perception with language and memory makes the senses a matter of urgency for understanding the conditions under which the body interfaces with and assigns privileges to certain modes of the perceptible while condemning other modes to the shadows of the imperceptible and the valueless.

A performance theory of the senses would allow for an accounting and a critique of whole hegemonic or majoritarian politics of the perceptible and the imperceptible, of the significant and the insignificant, of what emerges within the field of attention and what will remain unremarked. In other words: as the senses shift in relation to social and cultural changes, what they also change are the political conditions of possibility for entities, substances, bodies, and elements to come into a being-apparent. It is in this light that we can talk not only of a performance of the senses but also of a *performative power of the senses*. The political economy of the senses subjacent to any system of presence, to any system of power, by casting a dividing line between the properly perceptible and the imperceptible, impacts on the ontological and political status of any perception by defining it as significant or as insignificant.

This can be read as a rather gloomy rendition of the political agency of the senses. But the same mechanisms allow the senses to trigger acts of resistance. As Nadia Seremetakis reminds us, "the sensory landscape and its meaning-endowed objects bear within them emotional and historical sedimentation that can provoke and ignite gestures, discourses, and acts – acts which open up these objects' stratigraphy" (Seremetakis 1994: 7).

Thus, changes in the perceptual field chronicle a history of sensory disciplining but also of sensory dissent – Foucault's "creation of resistances" – a history of how bodies relate to the world, and a history of how certain stimuli gain symbolic currency and linguistic validation as properly belonging to the realm of the aesthetic. Within the history of theatre and performance, historians, theorists, and critics have either totally ignored certain senses and certain sensorial experiences or, at best, relegated them to the periphery of critical attention and of theoretical investigation. Indeed, besides certain sights (e.g., costumes, sets, lighting, gestures, postures) and sounds (e.g., speech, music, sound effects) usually attached to specific linguistic referents, a whole plethora of sensorial information in performance has been discarded, unnoticed and poorly documented.

However, live performance often does involve the senses in ways that transgress the boundaries of the visually iconic and of the linguistically and musically sonic. Taste, touch, smell, vestibular and kinesthetic senses, pain, and hearing sound *qua* sound are pivotal sensorial experiences in making and experiencing performance across cultures. In the West, modern and postmodern attempts to re-involve audience members in sensory experiences – thought to be part of the total artwork that characterized theatre from ancient Greece up through the European Renaissance – have led to experiments with theatre architecture and technology as well as to new forms of staging theatre, dance, opera, and performance art. For Western critics and scholars, knowledge about regimes of the senses, both traditional and contemporary, in non-European-American cultures often prompts a deep re-evaluation of Western aesthetic and cognitive premises regarding what is experienced sensorially in performances.

The particular cultural force contained in the agential power activated by the senses in performance is revealed in a sentence by North American theatre director Matthew Goulish. He asked: "What is culture?" His own answer: "The formation of attention." Goulish's question and answer summarizes the dramaturgical backbone of much of the staged and video work he has been co-creating with Lin Hixson and the other members of the Chicago-based ensemble Goat Island. But Goulish's sentence captures the privileged relationship that any performance practice has with the manufacture of perceptive-sensorial techniques as culture-making techniques. The different ways through which performance practices create and form a plethora of modes of attention reveal precisely those endless exchanges criss-crossing the body and linking its sensorium to environment, genealogy, soma, culture, and performance practices. This open exchange between the somatic and the cultural begs for new ways to write critically on performance practices, since much of our implied modes of classifying performance are supported by an implicit and unacknowledged sensorial mapping. As

Barbara Kirshenblatt-Gimblett reminds us in her contribution to this anthology (see Chapter 6): "It has taken considerable cultural work to isolate the senses, create genres of art specific to each, insist on their autonomy, and cultivate modes of attentiveness that give some senses priority over others." The modernist fragmentation of artistic practices into self-contained and autonomous genres would correspond to a fragmentation of the senses into self-contained and autonomous "perceptions."

The essays collected in *The Senses in Performance* challenge inherited notions of sensorial performances. Taken as a whole, it could be said that a common thread running throughout this anthology can be found precisely in the realization that any body in a performance situation (be it the bodies of the performers or the bodies of the audience) is an inexhaustible inventor of sensorial-perceptual potentials and becomings. In Chapter 13, Maya Roth, when analyzing the work of the Omaha Magic Theatre in the late 1980s, reminds us precisely how a whole new organization of the senses can actually be transmitted to an audience. Moreover, she tells us that this transmission is a mode "to bring the audiences to their bodies," reminding us that the body is something that may have been stolen from its subject, that the body may not be the full property of its subject's desire and agency. Roth's essay reminds us how transmissibility of the senses is one of performance's most powerful performatives.

Processes of invention and becoming, then, are not only purely corporeal but also dialogically tied to technological developments. Two decades before Foucault published his essay on Nietzsche, Walter Benjamin had already remarked that the historical dynamic of the senses revealed how the sensorial and the technological fabricate each other dialectically. In his famous essay on "The work of art in the age of mechanical reproducibility," Benjamin wrote:

> During long periods of history, the mode of human sense perception changes with humanity's entire mode of existence. The manner in which human sense perception is organized, the medium in which it is accomplished, is determined not only by nature but by historical circumstances as well.
>
> (Benjamin 1988: 219)

This is Benjamin's anthropological view of history – a long durational process where "humanity" gradually changes its modes to perceive and to sense. But within this anthropological view there were also philosophical and political preoccupations. It is the very advent of film and photography that is seen by Benjamin as effecting a profound transformation not only on the nature of the work of art itself but on the nature of our perceptive-sensorial relation to it as well, a political transformation of what we deem to be our most natural mode of relating: our senses, our perceptions. In this way, at the core of any critical analysis of artistic practices in the age of mechanical reproducibility, Benjamin identifies the potential for creating what would be called today a political anthropology of the senses.[2]

What could be the project of a political theory of the senses be when transposed to the broad field of performance studies and of performance practices? What could be the creation of a "political performance studies" of the senses? In many ways, such a project would have to account for both Foucault's notions of history and Benjamin's careful attending to the perceptive-sensorial summons already encapsulated in the art object itself, while keeping in mind Goulish's and Kirshenblatt-Gimblett's remarks on the endless possibilities that performance brings to the formation of unsuspected modes of attention and of attending, and Roth's notion of sensorial transmissibility. It would imply looking at the ways technology, and particularly technologies of representation, create and implement, but also dissolve and disturb, perception. Many of the essays in this anthology reveal this dialogue between the senses and technologies of representation by addressing the implied organization of the senses that sustain and make possible Western theatrical representation. Stanton Garner (see Chapter 9) rethinks the question of theatrical "illusionism" and notes how "attention to sensory address in the theatre can help to illuminate the internal dynamics and representational volatility of realism itself." Kerrie Schaefer's essay (see Chapter 15) probes how theatrical representation holds the senses in a particular economy of theatrical consumption, which she believes is challenged by the figure of the cannibal – a figure she introduces to initiate "a discussion of the efficacy of political theatre in the 'society of the spectacle,' where the audience has been transformed into consumers." Jennifer Fisher (see Chapter 14) thinks of the role of "tactilism" or "tactile synesthesia" as the counter-representational device used by contemporary performance artists (Valie Export, Ron Athey, Vito Acconci, among others) "to interrogate technologies of vision."

But a crucial question remains unanswered: to know what "the senses" would be. It is well known that by positing such a realm, and by apparently isolating "the senses" from other agents that reveal the intertwining between the physiological and the cultural (agents such as "desire," "language," "fantasy," "dreaming," "sexuality"), we could be uncritically participating in a very specific mode of understanding the body that derives directly from Western notions of embodiment and perception. But it is precisely to a critique of Western notions of embodiment – where body functions are compartmentalized within autonomous zones and properly assigned functions – that performance art, since the mid-1960s, and particularly since the early 1970s, with the advent of body art, has been challenging consistently. We can think of Chris Burden performing Velvet Water (1974), a piece where he "breath[es] water, which is the exact opposite of drowning"; we can think of Marina Abramovic and Ulay's relational work in the mid-1970s, highly influenced by Eastern notions of energetic body and "extra-sensorial" perceptions. Richard Schechner, in Chapter 2, draws from his work as practitioner and theoretician to propose a similar critique of how all aesthetics are bound to distinct cultural mappings that define an energetics and a potential for the performing body. Schechner shows how the work of the performer rivals in epistemological depth the work of the scientist and proposes a dialogue between Western cognitive sciences and Eastern systems of emotional mapping – a dialogue based on his performance practice and on his interdisciplinary research on performer training – and encapsulated in his notion of "rasaesthetics."

The intercultural model is a central one to consider the agential power of sensory invention and transmission. In Chapter 4, Deidre Sklar "unearths kinesthesia" in order to analyze "groping" as an intriguing mobilization of touch that could allow for a cross-cultural model of sensorial performance (see Chapter 4). The political undertones of the sensorium are explored by Cobina Gillit in Chapter 16 when she notes how "the hyperstimulation from excessive sensory experience" dramaturgically structures Putu Wijaya's "Theatre of Mental Terror," thus unleashing unsuspected political readings of his work.

In Western theatre, the breaking down of body and meaning through sensorial over-stimulation can be found in Antonin Artaud's Theatre of Cruelty – a project at the same time theatrical and sensory-corporeal. In Chapter 17, Allen S. Weiss offers a careful dissection of Artaud's "body without organs" to reveal how Artaud's "anatomy" exposes the unsustainable contiguities between the anatomy of the bourgeois spectator and the architecture of traditional theatre. The relationships between architecture's tacit organization of the audience's sense is creatively explored in Chapter 11, where Dorita Hannah not only describes and theorizes how architecture has an implied anatomy of the senses that keep in place a certain mode of intersubjective relationality but also describes a specific architectural project developed by her and built in order to offer new sensorial experiences.

The intimate history of how the senses, political power, and theatre fuse only to be transmitted as normative modes of perception and signification is told in three historically focused chapters. Denise E. Cole writes in Chapter 7 of how "edible and human performances shared the same theatrical conventions" in early Tudor entertainment "precisely because they were both threads in the complex design of regal hospitality." In Chapter 8, Mary Fleischer explores how smell is a particularly appropriate sense in Symbolist theatre due to "its inherent formlessness" and "its transgressive ability to permeate the atmosphere and to dissolve boundaries." The transgressive particularities of smell carry with them methodological and epistemological challenges, which are explored by Sally Banes in Chapter 3. Banes identifies an "'olfactory effect' in theatrical events" and maps those effects throughout the history of Western theatre and ritual in order to identify how "the deliberate use of 'aroma design' to create meaning in performance" demands from the performance theorist new methodological tools for addressing signification in performance.

It is with this methodological demand that we can see how the recent history of performance art privileges a dialogue with the Western philosophical tradition most in tune with perception: phenomenology. Particularly relevant in recent performance and theatre studies has been the phenomenology advocated by Maurice Merleau-Ponty, which tried to account for how perception informs and is informed by subjectivity and how subjectivity is always embodied perception.[3] In Chapter 10, Stephen di Benedetto proposes a reading of recent performance art and body art (Franko B, Stelarc, Roca, La Ribot) "deriving from phenomenology" and where the question of language's interface with the bodily and the non-verbal are explored. In Chapter 12, Martin Welton also proposes intriguing exchanges between vision and voice, thus between image (or its absence) and word (and its polysemic activations), when he writes on War Music by Sound and Fury Theatre Company. Welton's text suggests how the whole sensory apparatus, when subverted, also displaces the stability of interpretation and verbal meaning. Phillip Zarrilli, in Chapter 5, theorizes the question of silence in actor training even further in an essay highly influenced by Merleau-Ponty's rare yet telling observations on voicing.

Merleau-Ponty's phenomenology, by binding perception to language, and both to memory, allowed consideration that "the senses" are not well-defined, isolated, autonomous organs of perception. Merleau-Ponty would famously posit that, first, perception always happens laced with temporality and language: perception is fraught with the anticipation of a future and the memory of a past and with the linguistic materiality of the human body. Moreover (and here Heidegger's own particular project for phenomenology, the one exposed in *Being and Time*, is key for Merleau-Ponty), phenomenology proposes that perception happens only when the senses (already constituted by language, just as language is already constituted by the senses) find themselves to be in deep entanglement with the sensed phenomena. Thus, there would be no such thing as a purely perceptive, or purely sensorial, realm. Rather, language, memory, affect, sensation, perception, and historical and cultural forces find themselves in a deep chiasmatic intersubjective relationality, where each element in the relation is continuously crossing and being crossed by all the others. This is an important development that the reader should keep at hand when reading the essays comprising this volume: between the senses and language the difference is often one of degree, not one in kind.

It is within such an understanding of perception that one can posit the senses as pertaining simultaneously to the realms of somatic and physiological adaptations and to the realms of aesthetic, cultural, political, and economic transformations. Each particular, historically defined sensorial system would delimit what could be called a particular "system of presence" with its particular subjectivity and "system of perception." We believe that it is within the formation of these systems of presence and perception that the essays gathered in *The Senses in Performance* become of particular interest not only for the creation of new sensorial experiences but also to more creative modes of theorizing performances and living life.

REFERENCES

Benjamin, Walter. 1988. The work of art in the age of mechanical reproduction. In *Illuminations*, edited by H. Arendt. New York: Schocken Books.

Butler, Judith. 1990. *Gender Trouble: Feminism and the Subversion of Identity. Thinking Gender*. New York: Routledge.

——. 2004. *Precarious Life: The Powers of Mourning and Violence*. London and New York: Verso.

Feldman, Allen. 1991. *Formations of Violence: The Narrative of the Body and Political Terror in Northern Ireland*. Chicago: University of Chicago Press.

Foucault, Michel. 1977. Nietzsche, genealogy, history. In *Language, Counter-Memory, Practice*, edited by D.F. Bouchard. Ithaca, NY: Cornell University Press.

——. 1988. *The History of Sexuality*. 1st Vintage Books edn. New York: Vintage Books.

——. 1995. *Discipline and Punish: The Birth of the Prison*. 2nd Vintage Books edn. New York: Vintage Books.

Garner, Stanton B. 1994. *Bodied Spaces: Phenomenology and Performance in Contemporary Drama*. Ithaca, NY: Cornell University Press.

Jones, Amelia. 1998. *Body Art/Performing the Subject*. Minneapolis: University of Minnesota Press.

Seremetakis, Nadia, ed. 1994. *The Senses Still. Perception and Memory as Material Culture in Modernity*. Chicago: University of Chicago Press.

Taussig, Michael T. 1992. *The Nervous System*. New York: Routledge.

——. 1993. *Mimesis and Alterity: A Particular History of the Senses*. New York and London: Routledge.

NOTES

1   See Foucault (1988, 1995). For a recent use of Foucault's notion, see Butler (1990, 2004).

2   On different propositions on a political anthropology of the senses, see Seremetakis (1994), Taussig (1992, 1993), Feldman (1991).

3   See particularly Jones (1998), Garner (1994).

Part I

THEORY AND PRACTICE

2

RASAESTHETICS

Richard Schechner

Where in the body is theatricality located? What is its place? Traditionally in Western theatre, the eyes and, to some degree, the ears are where theatricality is experienced. By etymology and by practice, a theatre is a "place of/for seeing." Seeing requires distance; engenders focus or differentiation; encourages analysis or breaking apart into logical strings; privileges meaning, theme, narration. Modern science depends on instruments of observation, of ocularity: telescopes and microscopes. Theories derived from observations made by means of ocular instruments define the time–space continuum. From super-galactic strings on the one hand to molecular and subatomic wave/particles on the other we "know" the universe by "seeing" it. See = know; speed = space; distance = time; diachronicity = story. However, in other cultural traditions there are other locations for theatricality. One of these, the mouth, or better said, the snout-to-belly-to-bowel – the route through the body managed by the enteric nervous system – is the topic of this essay. The mouth-to-belly-to-bowel is the "where" of taste, digestion, and excretion. The performance of the snout-to-belly-to-bowel is an ongoing interlinked muscular, cellular, and neurological process of testing/tasting, separating nourishment from waste, distributing nourishment throughout the body, and eliminating waste. The snout-to-belly-to-bowel is the "where" of mixing, intimacy, sharing of bodily substances, mixing the inside and the outside, emotional experiences, and gut feelings. A good meal with good company is a pleasure; so is foreplay and lovemaking; so is a good shit.

THE *POETICS* AND THE *NATYASASTRA*

Aristotle's *Poetics* and Bharata-muni's *Natyasastra*, a Sanskrit manual of performance and performance theory, occupy parallel positions in European and Indian performance theory (and by extension, throughout the many areas and cultures where European-derived or Indian-derived performing arts are practiced). Both ancient texts continue to be actively interpreted and debated, theoretically and in practice. Both are at or near the "origins" of their respective performance traditions; both have evoked "after-texts" or "counter-texts" aimed at enhancing, revising, or refuting their basic principles.

Similar as they are in some ways, however, the two texts differ profoundly. Aristotle was a historical figure (384–322 BCE), the author of many key philosophical texts affecting, even determining, Western thought in various fields as far-ranging as the physical sciences, politics, social thought, aesthetics, and theology. The Macedonian Greek philosopher's writings have been actively debated for nearly two and a half millennia. He specialized in dividing knowledge into knowable portions; he formulated the syllogism. Bharata-muni is a mythic-historical figure, the name of the author or compiler of a very detailed compendium concerning the religios-mythical origins and practices of *natya*, a Sanskrit word not easily translatable but reducible to dance–theatre–music. The precise date of the *NS* remains in question – scholars have placed it anywhere from the sixth century BCE to the second century CE. Exactly how much of the *NS* was the work of one person and how much the lore of many will probably never be known. Bharata-muni, whoever he was, if he was at all, wrote only the *NS*.

Furthermore, the *NS* is a *sastra*, a sacred text, authorized by the gods, full of narration, myth, and detailed instructions for performers. The *Poetics* is secular, focused on the structure of drama and dependent on the logical thinking that its author helped to invent. The *Poetics* is so laconic, running in English translation to about thirty pages, that some believe it to be lecture notes compiled by Aristotle's students after his death rather than the philosopher's own finished work. The *NS* takes the form of an extended disquisition (345 pages in the Rangacharya translation) by Bharata in answer to sages who asked him to explain *natya*. Bharata begins with the story of how *natya* came about, what its proper subjects are, and for whom it was made.[1] Then he goes on to detail everything from theatre architecture to how to perform the various emotions to the structure of dramas, and more.

Some centuries after it was completed, the *NS* was "lost" – fragmented, submerged, misplaced, and unread. The *NS* comes to modern Indians not directly and not as a single text. The *NS* comes down in performance practice and as a series of interpretations. The most important interpreter is the tenth-century Kashmiri Saivite (worshipper of Shiva), Abhinavagupta. Through Abhinavagupta scholars discern earlier interpreters of the *NS* such as Bhatta Lollata, Srisankuka, Bhatta Nayaka, and Bhatta Tauta. As for the *NS* itself, according to Kapila Vatsyayan, "not many texts have been systematically collated and edited and published. Hundreds … lie as manuscripts in public or private collections, in India and abroad, and an equal or larger number are in fragments" (1996: 115). But this fragmentation ought not to be read as "neglect." The *NS* tradition is active, oral, and corporeal. It is present in performers, their teachers, and their performances. We must distinguish the absence of the *NS* as a text (a book brought to light in modern times mostly by Western orientalists[2]) from its presence in actual performances, where it has been absorbed into, and forms the core of, a multiplicity of genres such as *kathak*, *kathakali*, *odissi*, and *bharatanatyam*, which, taken together, comprise Indian classic theatre-dance. The *NS* is much more powerful as an embodied set of ideas and practices than as a written text. Unlike the *Poetics*, the *NS* is more danced than read.

Thus the *NS* and the *Poetics* are different in style, intent, and historical circumstance. The *Poetics*, written nearly a century after Greek tragedy's heyday, constitutes only a small portion of Aristotle's enormous output. The *Poetics* lacks descriptions of actual performances; it is mostly about drama, not theatre, focusing on one play, *Oedipus*, which Aristotle offers as a model for the right way to write plays. Framed as "rational" and "historical," the *Poetics* is not regarded as sacred, although it has been, and remains, remarkably influential. On the other hand, the *NS* is a hybrid of myth and down-to-earth performance knowledge, far-ranging and detailed. Its author and protagonist, the semi-divine Bharata-muni, is almost certainly a pseudonym for a collective oral tradition.

But the greatest difference between the *Poetics* and the *NS* is that the Indian book deals in detail with performance: emotional expression as conveyed by specific gestures and movements, role and character types, theatre architecture, and music. The *NS* considers drama (chapters 20–1), but that analysis is not the core of the *sastra*. Many Indian artists subscribe to the ideal of a theatre that integrates drama, dance, and music. Traditional genres accomplish this integration in ways that do not privilege plot (as Aristotle advised) over dance, gesture, and music. And then there is *rasa*.

RASA: FIRST TAKE

Of *rasa*, the *NS* says:

> There is no *natya* without *rasa*. *Rasa* is the cumulative result of *vibhava* [stimulus], *anubhava* [involuntary reaction], and *vyabhicari bhava* [voluntary reaction]. For example, just as when various condiments and sauces and herbs and other materials are mixed, a taste is experienced, or when the mixing of materials like molasses with other materials produces six kinds of taste, so also along with the different *bhavas* [emotions] the *sthayi bhava* [permanent emotions experienced "inside"] becomes a *rasa*. But what is this thing called *rasa*? Here is the reply:
>
> Because it is enjoyably tasted, it is called *rasa*. How does the enjoyment come? Persons who eat prepared food mixed with different condiments and sauces, if they are sensitive, enjoy the different tastes and then feel pleasure; likewise, sensitive spectators, after enjoying the various emotions expressed by the actors through words, gestures, and feelings feel pleasure. This feeling by the spectators is here explained as the *rasas* of *natya*.
>
> (Bharata-muni 1996: 54–55)

There is a lot going on here, and I do not intend at this time to go into a detailed explication of *rasa* theory. I want here to outline an overall theory of flavor as it pertains to performance, what I call "rasaesthetics."

Rasa is flavor, taste, the sensation one gets when food is perceived, brought within reach, touched, taken into the mouth, chewed, mixed, savored, and swallowed. The eyes and ears perceive the food on its way – the presentation of the dishes, the sizzling. At the same time, or very shortly after, the nose gets involved. The mouth waters in anticipation. Smell and taste dissolve into each other. The hands convey the food to the mouth – either directly as in the traditional Indian way of eating with the fingers or somewhat indirectly by means of utensils (a latecomer everywhere). The whole snout is engaged. In the snout, all the senses are well represented. The lower part of the face contains the mouth, in the center is the nose, above are the eyes. The ears are side-center, but focused forward.

Rasa also means "juice," the stuff that conveys the flavor, the medium of tasting. The juices of eating originate both in the food and from the body. Saliva not only moistens food, it distributes flavors. *Rasa* is sensuous, proximate, experiential. *Rasa* is aromatic. *Rasa* fills space, joining the outside to the inside. Food is actively taken into the body, becomes part of the body, works from the inside. What was outside is transformed into what is inside. An aesthetic founded on *rasa* is fundamentally different from one founded on the "theatron," the rationally ordered, analytically distanced panoptic.

ETYMOLOGIES AND DISTANCED KNOWING

Before going into more on rasaesthetics, here is something on Western notions of theatre. The word "theatre" is cognate with "theorem," "theory," "theorist," and such, all from the Greek *theatron*, itself from *thea*, "a sight," and from *theasthai*, "to view"; related to *thauma*, "a thing compelling the gaze, a wonder; and *theorein*, "to look at" (Partridge 1966: 710). *Theorein* is related to *theorema*, "spectacle" and/or "speculation" (Shipley 1984: 69). These words are thought to be related to the Indo-European root *dheu* or *dhau*, "to look at" (Partridge 1966: 710). The Indo-European root of "Thespis" – the legendary founder of Greek theatre – is *seku*, a "remark" or "saying," but with the implication of a divine vision; and from *seku* derive such English words as "see," "sight," and "say" (Shipley 1984: 353). Greek theatre, then, and all European types of theatre derived from it, are places of/for seeing and saying. What marks this kind of theatre (and after it, film, TV, and possibly the Internet) is its specularity, its strategies of "gazing."

These etymologies reveal the tight bond linking Greek theatre, European epistemology, and seeing. This binding of "knowing" to "seeing" is the root metaphor/master narrative of Western thought. If the humans in Plato's cave were ignorant, it was because all they saw of "truth" were shadows cast on the wall. True reality was so much brighter even than the sun that no human viewer could look at it directly. What Plato said could be known through dialectics, scientists since the Renaissance have tried to do by devising finer and finer instruments of observation. A single net holds Plato's allegory, Galileo's observations, the Hubble Space Telescope, electron microscopes, and the CERN particle accelerator. Where does seeing take place? Only at a distance from what is being seen. Both a logical and a practical difference are necessary to keep what is observed separate from the observing instrument (and/or observer). "Objectivity" can be understood as the desire to keep things at enough distance from the eyes to allow whatever it is to "take shape" perceptually: to see things "in perspective," to "focus on" them. The "uncertainty principle" linking the instrument of observation to what is observed does not dissolve the distance between observer and observed so much as it asserts that what is observed is indissolubly linked to the means of observing. What "moves" the particle is the light that is needed to observe it.

At a more everyday level, as an object is brought close to the face, one loses focus and finally the object blurs, losing its visual shape. And one must not put things into one's eyes. Poking out the eyes is a terrible thing, both legendarily (Jocasta, Oedipus, Gloucester *et al.*) and actually. But a child learns early to see something, focus on it, reach for it, grasp it, and bring it to the mouth. The mouth replaces the eyes as the end point of exploring the "outer" world and relating it to the "inner" world. The "transitional object" (see Winnicott 1971) is how the infant first experiences the sameness/difference between the world outside itself and the world inside itself:

from the breast, to the fingers, to the grasped-tasted-chewed whatever, to the security blanket, to the favorite object. Even before birth, as seen in Lennart Nilsson's well-known *in utero* photographs, the pre-born suck their fingers and toes (see Nilsson's *A Child Is Born*, 2004). Can we doubt that the pre-born enjoy this activity? Nor is the mouth a singular conduit connected solely to the brain (as the eye is via the optic nerve). The mouth opens to the nasal cavity and the whole digestive system; the mouth – including lips and tongue – intimately engages the senses of touch, taste, and smell. The ocular system is extraordinarily focused, while the snout system is wide open, combining rather than separating.

The Greek theatre that Aristotle based his theories on was fundamentally a seeing place. Architecturally – as is evident from what is left of the Theatre of Dionysus on the hillside of the Akropolis, the almost wholly intact theatre at Epidaurus, and from other sites and restorations – the Greek theatre was immense. Most scholars place the number in the audience at the ancient festivals at between 14,000 and 17,000. And although Aristotle favored the drama over the theatre, the actual experience of being in a classical Greek theatre strongly includes the spectacle – dancing, singing, and reciting. The Greek theatre was also, and perhaps mostly, a focus of competition. The Athenians were an intensely competitive people. The *agon* was for them the motor, source, and energy of creation, a model of becoming.[3]

Whatever Aristotle may have wanted, the living heart of Greek tragedy was not plot as such but a particular kind of storytelling, the *agon*. To sort winners from losers, the judges (and those judging the judges, the spectators) had to see clearly and base their opinions on "objectivity." There may have been all kinds of politicking and pressure, maybe even bribes and cheating, but, as in today's spectator sports (with or without instant replays), clarity in presentation and reception was absolutely essential. The goal of the shows was to determine winners and losers – both in the dramas and in the competitions between actors and poets.

RASIC PERFORMANCE IS DIFFERENT

Rasic performance has as its goal not separating winners from losers but extending pleasure – as in an endless banquet or an always-deferred "almost" sexual orgasm. It accomplishes this in a way comparable to cooking: the combination/transformation of distinct elements into something that offers new and/or intense and/or favorite flavors or tastes. Rasic performance values immediacy over distance, savoring over judgment. Its paradigmatic activity is a sharing between performers and partakers (a more accurate term than "audiences" or "spectators," words that privilege ear or eye). The rasic performance event is more a banquet than a day in court. The *NS* puts it this way:

> Those who are connoisseurs of tastes enjoy the taste of food prepared from (or containing) different stuff; likewise, intelligent, healthy persons enjoy various *sthayi bhavas* related to the acting of emotions.
>
> (Bharata-muni 1996: 55)

The Sanskrit word that is translated as "connoisseur" is *bhakta*, which can also mean a person ecstatically devoted to a god, particularly Krishna, who is celebrated by means of singing, dancing, and feasting. The *sthayi bhavas* are the "permanent" or "abiding" or indwelling emotions that are accessed and evoked by good acting, called *abhinaya. Rasa* is experiencing the *sthayi bhavas*. To put it another way, the sweetness "in" a ripe plum is its *sthayi bhava*; the experience of "tasting the sweet" is *rasa*. The means of getting the taste across – preparing it, presenting it – is *abhinaya*. Every emotion is a *sthayi bhava*. Acting is the art of presenting the *sthayi bhavas* so that both the performer and the partaker can "taste" the emotion, the *rasa*.

In chapters 6 and 7, the *NS* gives the eight *rasas* and their corresponding *sthayi bhavas*:

rasa	sthayi bhava	English
sringara	*rati*	love, desire
hasya	*hasa*	humor, laughter
karuna	*soka*	pity, grief
raudra	*krodha*	anger, rage
vira	*utsaha*	vigor, energy
bhayanaka	*bhaya*	fear, shame
bibhasta	*jugupsra*	disgust, revulsion
adbhuta	*vismaya*	surprise, wonder

Abhinavagupta added a ninth rasa: *shanta*, "peace" or "bliss." From Abhinavagupta's time onward, many Indians speak of the "nine *rasas*." But *shanta* does not correspond to any particular *sthayi bhava*. Rather, like white light, *shanta* is the perfect balance/mix of them all; or *shanta* may be regarded as the transcendent *rasa*, which, when accomplished, absorbs and eliminates all the others. A perfect performance, should one occur, would not transmit or express *shanta* (as it could transmit or express any of the other *rasas*), but allow *shanta* to be experienced simultaneously and absolutely by performers and partakers.

It is not my aim in this essay to investigate the many connections between the *sthayi bhavas* and the *rasas*. It is enough to note that "emotions" in the Indian aesthetic performance system, far from being personal – based on individual experience, or locked up and accessible only by means of an "emotional memory" exercise or a "private moment" (Stanislavsky and his disciples) – are to some degree objective, residing in the public or social sphere.

In the rasic system, there are "artistically performed emotions" that comprise a distinct kind of behavior (different, perhaps, for each performance genre). These performed emotions are separate from the "feelings" – the interior, subjective experience of any given performer during a particular performance. There is no necessary and ineluctable chain linking these "performed emotions" with the "emotions of everyday life." In the rasic system, the emotions *in the arts, not in ordinary life*, are knowable, manageable, and transmittable in roughly the same way that the flavors and presentation of a meal are manageable by following recipes and the conventions of presenting the meal.

When I spoke to *kathakali* actors, for example, some told me they felt the emotions they performed. Others did not feel the emotions. There is no yes or no answer to Diderot's question, "Do actors feel the emotions they communicate?" Feeling the emotions is not necessary, though it is not a bad thing either. Whether it happens or not to any particular performer does not necessarily make the performance better or worse. What is relevant is making certain that each "partaker" receives the emotions; and that these emotions are specific and controlled. The emotions, the *sthayi bhava*, are objective; the feelings (what an individual performer or partaker experiences) are subjective. What is shared are the *rasas* of a single emotion or combination of emotions.

It is not easy to differentiate clearly "emotions" from "feelings." Basically, emotions are communicated by means of *abhinaya*; feelings are experienced. So the *rasas* themselves (as flavors of moods) are feelings, but what is communicated or transmitted by means of *rasas* are emotions. One "has" emotions, even if one is not feeling them; one "experiences" feelings even if sometimes disconnected from emotions ("I don't know why I am feeling the way I feel"). The links between emotions and feelings are usually manifest, but not always. When an actor's *abhinaya* is strong, the emotions are communicated, audience members feel feelings – whether or not the actor is feeling something. In expressing the emotions by means of *abhinaya*, one may or may not create feelings in oneself, but a good actor always creates feelings in the partakers (audience). In order for *rasas* to be shared, performers must enact the *abhinaya* of a particular emotion or concatenation of emotions according to the traditions of a specific genre of performance. The feelings aroused may be personal, intimate, and indescribable; but the emotions enacted are consciously constructed and objectively managed.

According to Stanislavsky-based Euro-American acting, one does not "play an emotion." One plays the "given circumstances," the "objectives," the "through line of action," the "magic if." If this is done right, "real" feelings will be experienced and "natural" emotions will be displayed. But according to my interpretation of the *NS* rasic system, one can work *directly* on the emotions, mixing them according to "recipes" known to the great acting *gurus* (which means, simply, "teachers") – or even by devising new recipes. From a Stanislavskian vantage point, such direct work on the emotions will result in false or mechanical acting. But anyone who has seen performers thoroughly trained in the *NS* rasic system knows that these performers are every bit as effective as performers trained in the Stanislavsky system.

If performing rasically is to offer emotions to partakers in the same way that a chef offers a meal to diners, then the effectiveness of the performance depends very much on an active response from the partakers. The *NS* is very emphatic in its insistence that *natya* appeal to people of all stations in life, affecting different people differently.[4] The more knowledgeable the partakers, the better the experience. To respond to the fullest, partakers need to be connoisseurs of whatever performance genre they are taking in, as wine tasters need to know vintages, bottling procedures, and ways of sampling in order to fully appreciate a wine. There is a sliding scale of how much one needs to know. In the rasic system, each person enjoys according to her abilities; the higher the level of knowledge, the greater the enjoyment (or disappointment, if the performance is not up to standard). Japanese *noh* actors study the audience immediately before entering the stage and then adjust their performances to the particular partakers on hand. All performers know this. The best performers save their best performances for the most discerning partakers, and those who know the most expect the best. In India, at least, the active response of the partakers is expected. At dance or music concerts people quietly beat out the *tal,* or rhythm, sing under their breath, and sometimes move their hands in harmony with the *mudras,* or hand-gesture system. At the *Ramlila* of Ramnagar, many persons carry texts of Tulsidas's *Ramcaritmanas,* following along, even singing, as the Ramayanis chant. The same is true of sport or pop music connoisseurs. The "home team advantage" is a direct measurement of how the active participation of the crowd can impact the level of performance.

ORAL PLEASURES, RASICALLY

Fundamentally, the attainment of pleasure and satisfaction in a rasic performance is oral – through the snout, by combining various flavors and tastes; and the satisfaction is visceral, in the belly. How can this be, since the Indian theatre, like the Western theatre, is presented visually and sonically? First, the Indian theatre, both in earlier times and today, is not based on the *agon*, on formally determining winners and losers, either within the dramas (in classical Indian plays often everyone wins) or in terms of competitions between dramatists and actors. In that ancient theatre of India, there were no judges formally ensconced on front marble benches as in the Theatre of Dionysus. Thus there was no attempt to quantify the performing experience, to bring it under the theatron's aegis of visuality. Second, many performances were part of the feasts of the rich or royal and continue to be offered at weddings or other happy celebrations. Religion itself has a feasting quality interweaving performing, worshipping, and eating. Separating work from play, and the sacred from the profane, has always been more a Western than an Indian phenomenon. Third, until the arrival of Islam and then the English, there was no anti-theatrical prejudice or Puritanism in India. Far from it, the arts infused with intense sexual pleasure were often part of the religious experience.

India today is less open to the rasic mix of art, sensuousness, and feasting than before the advent of the Mughals and the British. But imagining performances from the period of Sanskrit drama (fourth–eleventh centuries CE) as indicated by sculptures and paintings at such sites as Khajuraho, the shore temple of Mamallapuram, and the "theatre caves" of Ajanta can get us closer to the kind of experience I am talking about.

> The Ajanta style approaches as near as it is likely for an artist to get to a felicitous rendering of tactile sensations normally experienced subconsciously. These are felt rather than seen when the eye is subordinate to a total receptivity of all the senses. ... The seated queen with the floating hand is drawn so that we obtain information which cannot be had by looking at her from a single, fixed viewpoint. ...The logic of this style demands that movements and gestures can only be described in terms of the area or space in which they occur; we cannot identify a figure except by comparing its position with others around it. ... It could be said that the Ajanta artist is concerned with the order of sensuousness, as distinct from the order of reason.
>
> (Lannoy 1971: 48–49)

Richard Lannoy argues that Sanskrit drama – some form of which is described and theorized in the *NS* – is like the Ajanta paintings:

> The structure and ornamentation of the caves were deliberately designed to induce total participation during ritual circumambulation. The acoustics of one Ajanta *vihara*, or assembly hall (Cave VI), are such that any sound long continues to echo round the walls. This whole structure seems to have been tuned like a drum.
>
> (*Ibid.*: 43)

This tuning was not fortuitous. The Ajanta caves are human-made, excavated and carved out of solid rock. Lannoy continues:

> In both cases [the caves, the theatre] total participation of the viewer was ensured by a skillful combination of sensory experience. The "wrap-around" effect [of] the caves

was conveyed on the stage by adapting the technically brilliant virtuosity of Vedic incantation and phonetic science to the needs of the world's most richly textured style of poetic drama.

(*ibid*.: 54)

What the *NS* supplies are the concrete details of that style, which at its core is not literary but theatrical, not plot-dominated or -driven. Indian classical theatre and dance does not emphasize clear beginnings, middles, and ends but favors a more "open narration," a menu of many delectables – offshoots, sidetracks, pleasurable digressions – not all of which can be savored at a sitting. The performances that the *NS* refers to took place over periods of days or weeks. They were festivals, part of multifaceted celebrations that also featured feasting and audience participation integral to the whole performance complex. Some of this continues today, as experienced in such popular religious festive forms as Ramlila, Raslila, and *bhajan* – singing/dancing, with their circumambulations, hymn singing, trance dancing, food sharing, and wrap-around or environmental theatre staging.

It is not all one way or the other. There is a lot of movement – actual and conceptual – from one kind of action to another. There are phases of these festive performances where partakers stand back and watch or listen and other phases where they participate. This blending of theatre, dance, music, eating, and religious devotion is to many participants a full, satisfying, and pleasurable experience that cannot be reduced to any single category – religious, aesthetic, personal, or gustatory. This kind of event yields experiences that dissolve differences, if only for a little while. This kind of experience is hard to measure from the inside or observe from the outside. It is this experience of an "all-is-inside" theatricality that most sharply distinguishes rasaesthetics from orthodox Western aesthetics derived from the Greek theatre and its reinterpretations in the Renaissance and variations in the drama-based proscenium or frontal-stage work of today. Rasaesthetics is experienced "in the gut," a formulation involving the enteric nervous system.

THE ENTERIC NERVOUS SYSTEM

Take a step into neurobiology. According to recent studies, there is a brain in the belly, literally. The basic research in this area has been conducted by Michael D. Gershon (see his *The Second Brain*, 1998), whose work was summarized in *The New York Times* by Sandra Blakeslee:

> The gut's brain, known as the enteric nervous system [ENS], is located in sheaths of tissue lining the esophagus, stomach, small intestine, and colon. Considered a single entity, it is a network of neurons, neurotransmitters, and proteins that zap messages between neurons, support cells like those found in the brain proper and a complex circuitry that enables it to act independently, learn, remember, and, as the saying goes, produce gut feelings.

(Blakeslee 1996: C1)

The ENS derives from the "neural crest," a bunch of related cells that forms in mammals and birds early in embryo genesis: "One section turns into the central nervous system. Another piece migrates to become the enteric nervous system. Only later are the two nervous systems connected via a cable called the vagus nerve" (*ibid.*: C3). According to Gershon:

> The ENS resembles the brain and differs both physiologically and structurally from any other region of the PNS [peripheral nervous system].[5] ... Both the avian and mammalian bowel are colonized by émigrés from the sacral as well as the vigil level of the neural crest. ... The PNS contains more neurons than the spinal cord and, in contrast to other regions of the PNS, the ENS is capable of mediating reflex activity in the absence of central neural input. In fact, most of the neurons of the ENS are not directly innervated by a preganglionic input from the brain or spinal cord. The functional independence of the ENS is mirrored in its chemistry and structure.
>
> (Gershon *et al.* 1993: 199)

And again, as summarized by Blakeslee:

> Until relatively recently, people thought that the gut's muscles and sensory nerves were wired directly to the brain and that the brain controlled the gut through two pathways that increased or decreased rates of activity. ... The gut was simply a tube with simple reflexes. Trouble is, no one bothered to count the nerve fibers in the gut. When they did [...], they were surprised to find that the gut contains 100 million neurons – more than the spinal cord has. Yet the vagus nerve only sends a couple of thousand nerve fibers to the gut.
>
> (Blakeslee 1993: C3)

What this means is that the gut – esophagus, stomach, intestines – has its own nervous system. This system does not replace or pre-empt the brain. Rather, it operates alongside the brain, or – evolutionarily speaking – "before" or "underneath" the brain:

> The enteric nervous system is ... a remnant of our evolutionary past that has been retained. [It] has been present in each of our predecessors through the millions of years of evolutionary history that separate us from the first animal with a backbone. ... The enteric nervous system is a vibrant, modern data-processing center that enables us to accomplish some very important and unpleasant tasks with no mental effort. When the gut rises to the level of conscious perception, in the form of, for example, heartburn, cramps, diarrhea, or constipation, no one is enthused. Few things are more distressing than an inefficient gut with feelings.
>
> (Gershon 1999: xiv)

But what about emotional feelings? In December 2000, I emailed Gershon about "rasaesthetics" and the ENS. He replied:

> Thank you for your letter. You touch a bit of raw nerve. You are certainly correct in that we in the West who consider ourselves "hard" scientists have not taken Eastern thought very seriously. The problem with a great deal of Eastern thought is that it is not based on documentable observation. You cannot quantify ideas about strong feelings or deep power. We, therefore, either ignore Eastern ideas about the navel, or take them as metaphors, which are not very different from our own metaphors about "gut feelings." On the other hand, I have recently become aware of quantifiable research that establishes, without question, that vagus nerve stimulation can be used to treat epilepsy and depression. Vagus nerve stimulation also improves learning and memory. Vagus nerve

stimulation is something physicians do and is not natural, but 90 per cent of the vagus carries ascending information from the gut to the brain. It is thus possible that vagus nerve stimulation mimics natural stimulation of the vagus nerve by the "second brain." This relationship is particularly important in relation to the human condition of autism. Autism affects the gut as well as the brain. It is thus conceivable that autism could be the result in whole or in part of a disturbed communication between the two brains.

In short, I now take the possibility that the gut affects emotions very seriously. This seems much more likely to me now than it did when I wrote my book. A dialogue between us might be of mutual interest.

The dialogue has not yet progressed beyond the email quoted, but it is destined to.

Let us suppose, in light of ENS research, that when someone says "I have a gut feeling," they actually are experiencing a feeling, a neural response, but not one that is head-brain-centered. Let us suppose that the feeling is located in, or emanating from, the "second brain," the brain in the belly. When expressed, this feeling is an emotion. Can such feelings be trained? That is, what are the systems converting "gut feelings" into expressible emotions? Gershon is interested primarily in the therapeutic value of vagus nerve stimulation, of causing or evoking feelings in autistics, who suffer from lack of affect or lack of range of affect. The rasaboxes exercise is a kind of ENS training suitable for "normal" or "artistic" uses.

The presence and location of the ENS confirms a basic principle of Indian medicine, meditation, and martial arts: that the region in the gut between the navel and the pubic bone is the center/source of readiness, balance, and reception, the place where action and meditation originate and are centered. A related place is the base of the spine, the resting spot of *kundalini*, an energy system that can be aroused and transmitted up the spinal column. Gaining an awareness of and control over the gut and lower spine is crucial to anyone learning various Asian performances, martial arts, or meditations.

Phillip Zarrilli has for many years researched both in a scholarly and in a practical way the relationship between what in the Keralan martial art *kalarippayattu* is called the *nabhi mula* (root of the navel) and performance art training, psychophysical centering, and ayurvedic medicine. According to him:

> When impulses originate from the *nabhi mula* ... [they] are "grounded," "centered," "integrated," "filled out," "dynamic." The *nabhi mula* of kalarippayattu is identical to the *svadhisthanam* of classical yoga. Its location is two finger widths above the anus and two finger widths below the root of the navel. It is at this center that both breath and impetus for movement into and out of forms originate.
>
> (Zarrilli 1990: 136)

Zarrilli emphasizes that the *nabhi mula* is important "psychophysically" as the source of feeling and movement, a kind of "gripping" (*piduttam*) or firmness of body, spirit, and feelings that affect the whole human being. The Chinese notion of *ai* and the Japanese "activating force" *ki* are closely related to the *nabhi mula* and the sense of *piduttam*. In *noh* theatre, the *tanden*, located "in the belly two inches below the navel" (Nearman 1982: 346) is the energy center. The point is that this "center" is a radiating spot:

> The actor is engaged in his total being in a psychophysical process where his internal energy, aroused in his vital center below the navel, then directed into and through the

embodied forms of external gesture (body and voice) is of course fundamentally the same [in noh] as the interior process of the kathakali actor. This despite the fact that the exterior manifestation of the interior process is different.

(Zarrilli 1990: 143)

I could cite many more examples, but it all comes down to what Zarrilli so nicely summarizes:

> In all such precise psychophysical moments, the "character" is being created – not in the personality of the actor but as an embodied and projected/energized/living form between actor and audience. These Asian forms assume no "suspension of disbelief," rather the actor and spectator co-create the figure embodied in the actor as "other." The "power of presence" manifest in this stage other, while embodied in this particular actor in this particular moment, is not limited to that ego. That dynamic figure exists between audience and actor, transcending both, pointing beyond itself.

(*ibid.*: 144)

The rasic system of response does not preclude the eye and ear during actual performance, but during training especially, it works *directly and strongly* on the ENS, which, under different names, has been very important and well theorized in various Asian systems of performance, medicine, and the martial arts, all of which are tightly related in Asian cultures. Thus, when I say that the rasic aesthetic experience is fundamentally different from the eye-dominant system prevalent in the West, I am not speaking metaphorically.

THE "RASABOXES" EXERCISE

But if not metaphorically, how? Let me answer that first in terms of training, then in terms of public performances. Over the past five years, I and several of my colleagues at East Coast Artists,[6] especially Michele Minnick and Paula Murray Cole, have been developing the rasaboxes exercise, which is an application of some of the ideas in this essay.[7] It is based on the assumption that emotions are socially constructed, while feelings are individually experienced.

The rasaboxes exercise takes many hours to complete; in fact, it is open-ended. It can not be done in one session. It continues from one day to the next. The exercise proceeds as an orderly progression of steps:

1. Draw or tape a grid of nine rectangular boxes on the floor. All rectangles are the same; and each ought to be about 6' × 3'.
2. In variously colored chalk, inside each rectangle write the name of one *rasa*. Use chance methods to determine which *rasa* goes where. Write the names in roman-alphabetized Sanskrit. Leave the center or ninth box empty or clear.
3. Very roughly "define" each *rasa*. For example, "*raudra*" means anger, rage, roaring; "*bibhasta*" means disgust, spitting up/out, vomiting.
4. Have participants draw and/or describe the *rasas*. That is, ask each person to interpret the Sanskrit word, to associate feelings and ideas to it. Emphasize that these "definitions" and associations are not for all time, but just "for now." Also emphasize that drawings, abstract configurations, or words can be used. In moving from one box to another, people must either "walk the line" at the edge of the boxes or step outside the rasabox area entirely and walk around to

the new box. There is no order of progression from box to box. A person may return to a box as often as they like, being careful not to overwrite someone else's contribution. Take as much time as necessary until everyone has drawn their fill. When a person is finished, they step to the outside of the rasaboxes area. This phase of the exercise is over when everyone is outside the rasaboxes area. Sometimes this takes several hours.

5. When everyone is standing at the edge of the rasabox area, time is allowed for people to "take in" what has been drawn/written. Participants walk around the edge of the rasaboxes. They read to themselves and out loud what is written. They describe what is drawn. But they cannot ask questions; nor can anything be explained.

6. Pause. Silence.

7. Self-selecting, one person at a time enters a box. The person takes/makes a pose of that *rasa*: for example, the pose of *sringara* or *karuna*, or whatever. The person can do as few as a single *rasa* or as many as all eight named *rasas*. (Remember that the ninth or center box is "clear.") A person can move from box to box either along the edge or on the lines – in which case the movement is "neutral." But if a person steps into a box, they must take/make a rasic pose. This phase continues until everyone has had at least one chance to enter and pose within the rasaboxes.

8. Same as 7, but now the pose is supplemented by a sound.

In steps 7 and 8, there is no "thinking." Just take/make a pose and/or a sound, whatever is "there" in association with the *rasa*. Move rather quickly from one rasabox to the next. Do not worry how "pretty," "true," or "original" the pose/sound is. Just do it. But once you are outside the boxes, reflect on how you composed your *rasa* and what it felt like to be in a composed *rasa*. In other words, begin the exploration of the distinction between feelings (experience) and emotion (public expression of feelings). Do not worry which came first. It is a chicken-and-egg question with no correct answer.

In fact, the first poses/sounds often have the quality of social clichés – of the "already known" that fit the *rasas* as casually understood: big laughs for *hasya*, clenched fists for *raudra*, weeping for *karuna*, and so on. The distance between stereotype and archetype is not great. Sooner or later, the social stereotype/archetype will be augmented by gestures and sounds that are more intimate, personal, quirky, unexpected. Practice leads one toward these. The road from outer to inner = the road from inner to outer.

9. Move more rapidly from one box to the next. Quick changes, no time for thinking it out in advance.

Here we are beginning to grapple with Antonin Artaud's call for actors who are "athletes of the emotions." Actual athletic competitions come to mind. A basketball player sits on the sidelines, quiet, a towel draped over his shoulder. But when called on to enter the game, he explodes with energy, performs at a high level of skill, and is entirely focused on his task. A whistle blows, and the athlete relaxes. The time out over, he jumps back into the game. One of the goals of the rasabox exercise is to prepare actors to move with the same mastery from one emotion to another, in a random or almost random sequence, with no preparation between emotional displays, and with full commitment to each emotion. What happens at the feelings level is left indeterminate; as with the performers in India, some doers of the rasabox exercise will "feel" it, others will not.

10. Two persons enter, each one in his or her own box. At first, they simply make the *rasas* without paying attention to each other. But then they begin to "dialogue" with the rasas and shift rapidly from one box to another. So, *sringara* confronts *vira* and then *vira* moves to *adbhuta*; after a moment *sringara* rushes along the line to *bibhasta*, and *adbhuta* jumps to *bhayanaka*.

At step 10, many new combinations appear. People begin to find things that are far from the social clichés. Those on the outside are often amused, sometimes frightened, or moved. "Something" is happening, although it cannot be reduced to words. A few people are hesitant about going into the boxes at all. The exercise is both expressive and a scalpel that cuts very deeply into people. Paradoxically, in performing different emotional masks, the participants discover aspects of their beings that had remained hidden – sometimes even from themselves.

11. Participants bring in texts from outside – that is, monologues from known plays or stuff written just for the exercise. Scenes from dramas are enacted by two or even three people. The text remains fixed, but the *rasas* shift – with no preplanning. So, for example, Romeo is all *sringara*, but Juliet is *karuna*; then suddenly Juliet springs to *bibhasta* and Romeo to *adbhuta*. And so on – the possible combinations are nearly endless. Occasionally, Romeo and Juliet are in the same box.

At this stage, actors test out the many different possibilities of any given text. Or, rather, the texts are revealed as not being fundamental, but permeable, open, wildly interpretable.

12. Scenes are enacted with one underlying *rasa*, on top of which are bits played in different *rasas*.

Here one begins to see how a whole production could be mapped as a progression of *rasas*. The progression could be scored or improvised each performance.

There are even more possibilities. The rasabox exercise is designed to be unfinishable. It is not intended to be a "true example" of an *NS*-based performance. Indeed, what comes from the rasabox exercise is not at all like what one sees at any traditional Indian performance. The exercise actually points to the creative possibilities suggested by the underlying theory of the *NS*. It "comes from" rather than "is an example of" that theory.

THE EMPTY BOX

What about the empty box at the center? Historically, there was no "*shanta rasa*" until Abhinavagupta added it some centuries after the *NS* was compiled. In the exercise, as in the historical development of *rasa* theory, the "ninth rasabox" is special. What happens there? In the exercise, a person can enter that box – the *shanta* space – only when the person is "clear." What that means is not for the one directing the exercise to say. Each person will have their own criteria for total, whole clarity. In the years that I have directed the rasabox exercise, *shanta* has been occupied very rarely, once or twice. There can be no challenge to such a position. So what if it is "not really so" that the person is "clear"? How can another person tell? And maybe it is so, maybe the participant has surpassed all *samsara*, all the clutter of feelings, the confusion of mixed emotions, the noise of change. I will not judge.

RASAESTHETICS IN PERFORMANCE

Now let me turn from training to performance. Indian theatre, dance, and music are not banquets. In *odissi*, *bharatanatyam*, *kathakali*, *kathak*, and so on performers dance, gesture, impersonate, and sometimes speak and sing. Occasionally, there is burning incense thickening the air with odor. But for the most part, the data of the performance is transmitted from performer to partaker in the same way as in the West (and elsewhere): through the eyes and ears. How is this rasic? Watching traditional Indian genres, one sees the performer looking at their own hands as they form different *hastas* or *mudras* – precise gestures with very specific meanings. This self-regarding is not narcissism in the Western sense. *Abhinaya* literally means to lead the performance to the spectators – and the first spectator is the performer herself. If the self who is observing is moved by the self who is performing, the performance will be a success. This splitting is not exactly a Brechtian *verfremdungseffkt*, but neither is it altogether different. Brecht wanted to open a space between performer and performance in order to insert a social commentary. The rasic performer opens a liminal space to allow further play – improvisation, variation, and self-enjoyment.

The performer becomes a partaker herself. When she is moved by her own performance, she is affected not as the character but as a partaker. Like the other partakers, she can appreciate the dramatic situation, the crisis, the feelings of the character whom she is performing. She will both express the emotions of that character and be moved by her own feelings about those emotions. Where does she experience these feelings? In the ENS, in the gut – inside the body that is dancing, that is hearing music, that is enacting a dramatic situation. The other partakers – the audience – are doubly affected: by the performance and by the performer's reaction to her own performance. An empathic feedback takes place. The experience can be remarkable.

In orthodox Western theatre, the spectators respond sympathetically to the "as if" of characters living out a narrative. In rasic theatre, the partakers empathize with the experience of the performers playing. This empathy with the performer rather than on the plot is what permits Indian theatre to "wander," to explore detours and hidden pathways, unexpected turns in the performance. Here *rasa* and *raga* (the classical Indian musical form) are analogous. The partakers' interest is not tied to the story but to the enacting of the story; the partakers do not want to "see what happens next" but to "experience how the performer performs whatever is happening." There is no narrational imperative insisting on development, climax, recognition, and resolution. Instead, as in *kundalini* sexual meditation, there is as much deferral as one can bear, a delicious delay of resolution.

I am here expounding a theory of reception – even to the extent that the performer's self-regarding is a reception of her own performance. This needs further elaboration. One treatise on *abhinaya* instructs the dancer to sing with her throat, express the meaning of that song with her hand gestures, show how she feels with her eyes, and keep time with her feet. And every performer knows the traditional adage: Where the hands go, the eyes follow; where the eyes go, the mind follows; where the mind goes, the emotions follow, and when the emotions are expressed, there will be *rasa*. Such a logically linked performance of emotions points to the "self," not the self as personal ego but the *atman* or profound absolute self, the self that is identical to the universal absolute, the *Brahman*.

Eating in a traditional manner in India means conveying the food directly to the mouth with the right hand. There is no intermediary instrument such as a fork or spoon. Sometimes a flat bread is used to mop up or hold the food; sometimes rice is used to sop up a curry. But in all cases, the food on the index and third finger is swept into the mouth by an inward motion of the thumb. Along with the food, the eater tastes his own fingers. The performer regarding her *mudras* is engaging in a kind of "theatre feeding." As with self-feeding, the emotions of a performance are first conveyed to the performer and the partakers by means of the hands.

Orthodox Western performing arts remain invested in keeping performers separated from receivers. Stages are elevated; curtains mark a boundary; spectators are fixed in their seats. Mainstream artists, scholars, and critics do not look on synchronicity and synesthesia with favor. Eating, digestion, and excretion are not thought of as proper sites of aesthetic pleasure. These sites – aside from rock concerts, raves, and sports matches – are more in the domain of performance art. In early performance art there were Carolee Schneemann, Allan Kaprow, Shiraga Kazuo, Hermann Nitsch, Chris Burden, Stelarc, Paul McCarthy, and others. Later came Mike Kelley, Karen Finley, Annie Sprinkle, Ron Athey, and Franko B., all of whom insisted on making "the body" explicit (see Schneider 1997; Jones 1998). Their work began to elide differences between the interior and the exterior; to emphasize permeability and porosity; to explore the sexual, the diseased, the excretory, the wet, and the smelly. Performances used blood, semen, spit, shit, urine – as well as food, paint, plastics, and other stuff drawn from the literal rather than the make believe. This work is not very Asian on the surface, but at an underlying theoretical level, it is extremely rasic.

These kinds of performance need to be studied in terms of rasaesthetics. That means paying attention to the increasing appetite for arts that engage visceral arousal and experience; performances that insist on sharing experiences with partakers and participants; works that try to evoke both terror and celebration. Such performances are often very personal even as they are no longer private.

What I am asking for goes beyond performance art. Rasaesthetics opens questions regarding how the whole sensorium is, or can be, used in making performances. Smell, taste, and touch are demanding their place at the table.[8] Thus I am making a much larger claim – and sending out a more general invitation. I am inviting an investigation into theatricality as orality, digestion, and excretion rather than, or in addition to, theatricality as something only or mostly for the eyes and ears. I am saying that performance practice has already moved strongly into this place, and now is the time for theory to follow.

REFERENCES

Bharata-muni. 1967. *The Natyasastra*, translated and edited by Manomohan Ghosh. Calcutta: Manisha Granthalaya.

—— 1996. *The Natyasastra*, translated and edited by Adya Rangacharya. New Delhi: Munshiram Manoharlal.

Blakeslee, Sandra. 1996. "Complex and hidden brain in the gut makes cramps, butterflies, and Valium." *The New York Times*, 23 January: C1–3.

Byrski, Christopher. 1973. *Concept of Ancient Indian Theatre*. New Delhi: Munshiram Manoharlal.

Classen, Constance. 1998. *The Color of Angels*. London: Routledge.

Gershon, Michael D. 1999. *The Second Brain*. New York: Harper Perennial.

——. 2000. Personal email correspondence. December.

Gershon, Michael D., Alcmene Chalazonitis, and Taube P. Rothman. 1993. "The neural crest to bowel: development of the enteric nervous system." *Journal of Neurobiology* 24, 2: 199–214.

Howes, David, ed. 1991. *The Varieties of Sensory Experience*. Toronto: University of Toronto Press.

Jones, Amelia. 1998. *Body Art: Performing the Subject*. Minneapolis: University of Minnesota Press.

Lannoy, Richard. 1971. *The Speaking Tree*. London: Oxford University Press.

Nearman, Mark J. 1982. "*Kakyo* Zeami's fundamental principles of acting," *Monumenta Nipponica* 37, 3: 333–74.

Nilsson, Lennart and Lars Hamburger: 2004. *A Child is Born* (revised edition). New York: Delacorte Press.

Partridge, Eric. 1966. *Origins: A Short Etymological Dictionary of Modern English*. London: Routledge & Kegan Paul.

Schneider, Rebecca. 1997. *The Explicit Body in Performance*. London: Routledge.

Shipley, Joseph T. 1984. *Origins of English Words: A Discursive Dictionary of Indo-European Roots*. Baltimore: Johns Hopkins University Press.

Spariosu Vatsyayan, Kapila. 1996. *Bharata: The Natyasastra*. New Delhi: Sahitya Akademi.

Winnicott, D.W. 1971. *Playing and Reality*. London: Tavistock.

Zarrilli, Phillip. 1990. "What does it mean to 'become the character': power, presence, and transcendence in Asian in-body disciplines of practice." In *By Means of Performance*, edited by Richard Schechner.

NOTES

1   At the very start of the text, Bharata claims for the *NS* the status of a veda – the most sacred of ancient Indian texts. This is not all that unusual. Such claims to being the "fifth *veda*" were used to validate and strengthen a text. Tradition finally assigned the rank of *sastra* to the *NS*, a position well down the hierarchical ladder of sacred writings. As for the framing origin myth itself, which is told in chapter 1 – the story of Brahma's composition of the "fifth *veda*," its transmission to Bharata and his sons, and their performance of the "first *natya*" on the occasion of the Mahendra's flag festival (the victory celebration of Indra's triumph over *asuras* and *danavas* [demons]) – much can be made of it. The demons are enraged by the performance of their defeat, they rush the stage and magically freeze "the speeches, movements, and even the memory of the performers" (Bharata-muni 1996: 3). Indra intervenes, thrashing the demons with a flagpole, which is then installed as a protective totem. Brahma instructs the gods' architect Visvakarman to construct an impregnable theatre, well guarded by the most powerful gods. This having been done, the gods say that it is better to negotiate with the demons than to exclude them forcibly. Brahma agrees, approaches the demons, and inquires why they want to destroy *natya*. They reply: "You are as much the creator of us as of the gods, so you should not have done it" (omitted them from *natya*) (ibid.: 4). "If that is all there is to it," Brahma says, "then there is no reason for you to feel angry or aggrieved. I have created the *Natyaveda* to show good and bad actions and feelings of both gods and yourselves. It is the representation

of the entire three worlds and not only of the gods or of yourselves" (ibid.: 4). Thus *natya* is of divine origin, all-encompassing, and consisting of actions both good and bad. For an extended and highly sophisticated interpretation of the *NS* framing myth, see Byrski (1974).

2 According to Kapila Vatsyayan (1996: 32–6) and Adya Rangacharya, whose recent English translation of the *NS* is the most readable, in 1865 American Fitz Edward Hall unearthed and published several chapters. In 1874, German Wilhelm Heymann (or Haymann, as Vatsyayan spells it) wrote an influential essay that stimulated further translations of several chapters by French scholar Paul Reynaud (or Regnaud as Vatsyayan spells it). But it was only in 1926 that the Baroda critical edition was commenced. The whole text – in Sanskrit – was not in print until 1954.

> In spite of all these results, the final text is contradictory, repetitive and incongruent; there are lacunae too, but, what is worse, there are words and passages that are almost impossible to understand. … It is not only modern scholars who suffer this inability to understand; even almost a thousand years ago … Abhinavagupta … displayed this tendency.
>
> (Vatsyayan 1996: xviii)

Vatsyayan provides a "Database of the *Natyasastra*" locating and listing all 112 known extant texts and fragments. All the texts are Sanskrit but transcribed in a variety of scripts: Newari, Devanagari, Grantha, Telugu, Malayalam, Tamil, Kanarese. Thus we know that from an early time that the *NS* was widely distributed across the subcontinent.

3 "In Presocratic thought the prerational notion of agon is used to describe the natural world as a ceaseless play of forces or Becoming" (Spariosu 1989: 13).

4 According to the first chapter of the *NS*, Brahma created the *natyaveda*:

> to show good and bad actions and feelings of both gods and yourselves [humans]. It is the representation of the entire three worlds [divine, human, demonic] and not only of the gods or of yourselves. Now *dharma* [correct living], now *artha* [warring], now *kama* [loving], humor or fights, greed or killing. *Natya* teaches the right way to those who go against *dharma*, erotic enjoyment to those who seek pleasure, restraint to those who are unruly, moderation to those who are self-disciplined, courage to cowards, energy to the brave, knowledge to the uneducated, wisdom to the learned, enjoyment to the rich, solace to those in grief, money to business people, a calm mind to the disturbed. *Natya* is the representation of the ways of the worlds using various emotions and diverse circumstances. It gives you peace, entertainment, and happiness, as well as beneficial advice based on the actions of high, low, and middle people.
>
> (Bharata-muni 1996, chapter 1; English adapted from Ghosh and Rangacharya translations)

5 The peripheral nervous system (PNS) consists of the many nerve cells throughout the body connected to the brain via the spinal cord. The PNS receives sensory input, which is then transmitted to the brain, where it is "interpreted" as various kinds of touch – hot/cold, pain, tickling, etc. Signals are sent back from the brain resulting in bodily movements, and so on. The ENS is part of the PNS, but both structurally and operationally very different from the rest of the PNS. The ENS, for the most part, operates independently of the brain, although it is connected to the brain via the vagus nerve.

6 East Coast Artists is a company I formed in New York in the early 1990s. Productions I have directed with ECA are *Faust/Gastronome* (1992), *Three Sisters* (1997), and *Hamlet* (1999). The rasabox exercise was developed both during ECA rehearsal workshops and at workshops I ran at NYU in the 1990s. In the late 1990s, I worked very closely with Michele Minnick and Paula Murray Cole in relation to rasaboxes. Minnick and Cole have led several rasabox workshops in New York and elsewhere. The exercise is dynamic. It continues to change.

7 The exercise is not based on the theory, exactly; nor does the theory result from the exercise, exactly. Rather, there is a convergence and an interplay between what I am thinking and what I am doing. This interplay is open – that is why both the exercise and the theory are "in development" and not "finished."

8 The work of Constance Classen and David Howes and the group of scholars associated with them is well worth noting. They are developing an anthropology and an aesthetics of the senses. See *The Variety of Sensory Experience* (1991) edited by Howes, and Classen's *The Color of Angels* (1998). In April 2000, Classen, Howes, Jim Drobnick, and Jennifer Fisher convened "Uncommon Senses: An International Conference On the Senses in Art and Culture" at Concordia University in Montreal with 180 presenters.

3

OLFACTORY PERFORMANCES[1]

Sally Banes

The smells of Western culture were attenuated throughout much of the twentieth century; modern sanitation reduced "bad" odors in daily life, while changing values diminished the rich use of scents for special occasions, such as religious rituals and theatrical events (see Classen *et al.* 1994). The beginnings of Western theatre in ancient Greek festivals like the Eleusinian mysteries (in modern times considered the prototype of the modern *Gesamtkunstwerk*) were suffused with intense aromas of all kinds: including fruit, floral, grain, and animal offerings; blood and burning animal flesh; wine, honey, and oil libations; and the burning of incense and other materials in sacred fires (see Burkert 1985). In our times, the use of incense in Catholic churches constitutes a diminished survival of the ritual use of smell in religious performances. Scented theatre programs and perfume fountains were only two of the nineteenth-century olfactory devices in Western theatres (see Haill 1987), but during most of the twentieth century, the "fourth wall" conventions of realism generally divided the spectator from the mainstream stage and permitted only sight and sound to cross its divide.[2]

Historically, the cultural uses of aromas in the West diminished with the hygiene campaigns of the late nineteenth and early twentieth century, since the spread of disease was linked to foul odors. Perhaps the deodorization of the theatre was in some ways connected to the scientific ambitions of naturalism, to an idea of the theatre as a sanitized laboratory (whereas odor could be precisely described in the pages of a naturalistic novel, safely distanced from the body of the reader).[3] The deodorization of the modern theatre may also be one facet of a conscious move away from – even an antagonism toward – religious ritual. In that context, it is not surprising that the Symbolists, hostile to naturalism and fascinated by religious mysteries, restored aroma to performance in the late nineteenth century.

Over the course of the twentieth century, various artists (both mainstream and *avant-garde*) repeatedly attempted to renew the sense of smell as part of the theatrical experience (including drama, dance, opera, and performance art) using aroma both to challenge and to expand the realist aesthetic. In the 1990s, olfactory effects in performance became particularly pronounced. And yet, the use of aroma onstage has received surprisingly little critical or scholarly attention; there is no published history of olfactory performances, nor have most theatre semioticians included smells in their analyses of theatrical signs. Thus there exists a largely unexplored rhetoric of what I will call the "olfactory effect" in theatrical events – that is, the deliberate use of "aroma design" to create meaning in performance.[4] Perhaps this is because so often the use of smell seems merely iconic and illustrative, a weak link in a chain of redundancy across sensory channels that does nothing more than repeat what is already available visually and aurally. However, I contend that smell has been used and may be used in a wide variety of ways; that on closer analysis even the seemingly elementary use of smell as illustration proves more complex than at first glance; and that it is useful to the history and criticism of both theatre and aroma to anatomize these distinctions. (Although throughout the history of Western performance there have been all sorts of accidental and/or unintended smells in the theatre, from the food spectators eat to the odor emanating from urine troughs, in this article I am concerned only with olfactory effects through aroma design.)

Jim Drobnick has noted the "ambiguous semiological status" of smell – the way it is situated, as Alfred Gell puts it, "somewhere in between the stimulus and the sign" (in Drobnick 1998: 14). Perhaps this ambiguity (and also the technical difficulty of controlling scent in the theatre) has served as a deterrent to the elaboration of aroma design. Yet despite its low aesthetic status,[5] aroma is not simply part of nature but does carry cultural meaning, and certainly the conscious use of aroma design in the theatre – a place characterized, as Roland Barthes has put it, by a "density of signs" ([1964] 1972: 262) – is a mode of communication that, like any other element in the *mise en scène*, can be used for artistic effects and thus analyzed and interpreted.

In his 1964 essay "Rhetoric of the image," Barthes analyzes how visual images (like advertisements) communicate meaning (*ibid.*). I find Barthes's "spectral analysis" of the visual image useful for my project for a number of reasons, in particular because he separates out the various components of images according to their communicative channels (linguistic as well as visual). This can be useful by analogy for separating out and then reassembling the various components of the theatrical *mise en scène*, including the olfactory.

My project of anatomizing a rhetoric of aroma in theatrical representations begins with the premise that there is a total, integrated sensory image (or flow of images) created in the theatre, of which the olfactory effect may be one component. Thus in analyzing meanings conveyed by aroma design in the theatre, one needs to discuss the use of odors in relation to the dominant sensory channels of theatre – the visual and the aural – and not simply as isolated sensory events. The aroma may work in concert with the other sensory channels to reinforce meaning, or it may complement or conflict with the other channels. Moreover, keeping in mind C.S. Peirce's semiotic triad, icon – index – symbol (1991), will be useful in distinguishing between various representational strategies, especially in understanding how aroma either enhances or departs from realism.

I begin my poetics of theatrical aroma design with a taxonomy that is structured according to the representational function that the odors in the performance are intended to discharge. I should point out that my categories in this taxonomy are not mutually exclusive, since these olfactory effects may perform more than one function (and the functions are not all parallel in nature). There are six categories so far: (1) to illustrate words, characters, places, and actions; (2) to evoke a mood or ambience; (3) to complement or contrast with aural/visual signs; (4) to summon specific memories; (5) to frame the performance as ritual; and (6) to serve as a distancing device. (There is also a seventh category, that of unrecognizable smells, which remains to be explored further.)

The most common use of aroma onstage is to illustrate words, characters, places, or actions. For instance, in *The Governor's Lady* (1912), director David Belasco enhanced the realistic effect by creating an onstage replica of a Childs' Restaurant, complete with the aroma of actual pancakes, which were cooking during the play; in *Tiger Rose* (1917), he scattered pine needles on the floor to create the proper scent for the forest setting; and in *The First Born* (1897), set in San Francisco's Chinatown, he burned Chinese incense (Marker 1974: 61–3). Often (but not always), the technological mode of dissemination of odor in this category of illustration involves cooking food, either onstage or offstage – for instance (in various recent productions): bread, toast, bacon and eggs, hamburgers, soup, spaghetti sauce, omelettes, popcorn, onions, garlic, artichokes, mushrooms, panela (caramelized cane sugar), hazelnut cookies, risotto, jasmine-scented rice, fish and chips, curry, sausages, sauerkraut and kielbasa, kidneys, boiled beef, Cajun shrimp, and Australian barbequed meats of all kinds.[6]

But there are many other illustrative aromas besides those derived from food: for example, the smells of manure, diesel, and citronella in Ivo van Hove's 1999 production of *India Song* (Wilson 1999: 8); of rose perfume in the Persian Garden scene of the 1952 Paris Opéra revival of Rameau's opera-ballet *Les Indes Galantes* (Guest 1976: 201); of various "unhygienic" eighteenth-century smells in Mark Wing-Davey's 1995 production of *The Beaux' Stratagem* (Winn 1995: 35); of marijuana in various productions of *Hair*; and of cigarette smoke in countless performances.

Related to the illustrative function, but operating more generally, is the use of olfactory effects to evoke a mood or ambience, as in Vsevolod Meyerhold's 1910 production of *Don Juan*, when "proscenium servants" sprayed perfume to create an aura of luxury (Leach 1989: 89–90). Similarly, but more recently, Graeme Murphy's ballet *Shéhérazade* for the Sydney Dance Company (1979) incorporated perfume smells wafting from the silken canopies of the set (Cargher 1979: 47). In Valentine de St.-Point's "métachorie" dance performances in Paris in 1913, the dancer burned large pots of incense, according to her theory of correspondences – no doubt derived from Baudelaire and also the Symbolist staging of *The Song of Songs* at the Théâtre d'Art in 1891[7] – governing the scent, predominant color, musical environment, and central poetic idea for each dance (Moore 1997). In Le Théâtre La Rubrique's 1993 production of *Cendres de Cailloux* by Daniel Danis, "the audience was put in darkness during most of the two hours' performance. During the course of the play, the actors used ... natural essences to recreate, through smell, the feeling of being in the forest of Northern Quebec" (Lavoie 1999). A 1996 New York production of Joe Orton's *Entertaining Mr Sloane*, directed by David Esbjornson, used strawberry-scented room spray to create a tacky ambience (Brantley 1996).

By far the most frequent use of aroma design, where it does occur, seems to fall into these first two categories: to illustrate the dramatic or visual text specifically or, more generally, to create a mood. But it is significant to note that, more rarely but perhaps more pointedly, directors, choreographers, and performance artists sometimes engage the use of odors for exactly the opposite function to illustration: to complement or contrast with what is happening in the rest of the performance.

That is, rather than creating redundancy along all the channels of the message, in this category of our taxonomy, the odor introduces new or even conflicting information.

A striking example of the contrastive use of aroma took place during the British performance artist Cosey Fanni Tutti's performance *Women's Roll* (1976), in which Tutti slashed her clothing and created artificial wounds using both stage make-up and crushed berries. Tutti has remarked that she wanted the spectators to get "an unpleasant visual stimulus but a pleasant olfactory stimulus" (in MacGregor 1999b), thus perhaps unsettling their views of how to interpret this display of a woman's body (see also MacGregor 1999a; Goldberg 1998: 118). In another mode entirely, Shaun Lynch's *Clean Smell Opera* (1980) used so many cleaning products – as the performer showered, washed her hair, cleaned dishes, and laundered and bleached clothes – that their smells became overpowering and repugnant, thus commenting punningly as well as ironically on the soap opera and the advertisements being broadcast by the television that was present onstage during the performance (see Carroll 1980).

Several theatre artists have used aroma design to focus particularly on what is often said to be a unique, or at least striking, quality of the sense of smell – its power vividly to summon up memories. The contemporary magician/performance artist Aladin has discussed the way he uses "his 'magic' abilities to create a very localized scent of jasmine in various parts of the audience, using this device to conjure some sense of remembrance" (in Hewitt 1999). In *El Hilo de Ariadna* (*Ariadne's Thread*, 1992), by the group Imagen (Taller de Investigación de La Imagen Dramática de la Universidad Nacional de Colombia), participants were led blindfolded through a labyrinth, entering rooms with distinctive scents (such as those associated with a schoolroom or a child's nursery) that were meant to evoke distant memories (Nascimento 1999). And in Theresa May's site-specific performance *Dragon Island* (1993, produced by Theatre in the Wild), a priestess instructed the spectators to crush herbs that she passed to them. The scent of the *pot-pourri* was meant to take them back in time; they were invited to narrate their memories, casting a "magic spell" that brought them into the play's events to help Arthur to find the dragon (May 1999).

Finally, my last two categories have less to do with aroma design as part of the work's representational strategies than with the framing and contextualization of those representations. First is the use of aroma to frame the performance as a ritual. Here odor functions not strictly as a representation itself but as a contextualizing condition for appreciating the other representations that the performance creates. The constant burning of incense throughout Peter Brook's *Mahabharata* (1985) may on the one hand fall into the illustrative category as an olfactory icon of Indian culture, but on the other hand, it shapes the ways in which the audience understands and experiences the performance: it suggests that this is a sacred, not a secular, event, and not only because it is based on a sacred Hindu text.

In the final category, the olfactory effect serves as a distancing device (or, in Russian formalist terms, as a mode of defamiliarization) by calling attention to itself as a theatrical effect, thus foregrounding its own operation as a semiotic system.[8] For instance, in the Irish troupe Barrabas's production of *The Whiteheaded Boy* (1997), aroma calls attention to the artifice of theatre (and perhaps of representation altogether) when an actor holds a piece of bread up to a patently fake fireplace and suddenly, magically, the smell of toast wafts through the theatre (see Marks 1999).

If in some sense the use of odors onstage, even as a mode of enhancing realism, always calls attention to itself in Western theatre as unusual, even a gimmick, several other productions have also used aroma design for this function of distantiation, not only foregrounding the olfactory effect but also underscoring its use as always potentially excessive and therefore bordering on camp. These productions flamboyantly exploit what might be called AromaRama or Smell-O-Vision (to borrow terms from the short-lived cinematic experiments with smell in the late 1950s). And, as in *The Whiteheaded Boy*, olfactory effects here, while illustrative on one level, function deliberately to undermine, not enhance, realism. A notable example of this combination of illustration and distantiation – which I call ostentatious illustration – is Richard Jones's staging of Prokofiev's opera *The Love for Three Oranges* (for the English National Opera in 1989), which used scratch-and-sniff cards (like those used at screenings of John Waters's 1981 film *Polyester*). The cards could, when scratched, release one of six different smells at specific points in the performance, ranging from (according to one writer) "oranges, … 'an exotic perfume,' … and 'a cross between bad eggs and body odour' for the entrance of Farfarello, a demon noted for his bad breath and wind" (Reynolds 1989: 3).[9] Through aroma design, directors, choreographers, and performance artists use different representational strategies that may also be categorized not according to this taxonomy of function but along another grid, that of Peirce's semiotic triad of icon–index–symbol, taking into account the relation of the signifier (in this case smell) to the signified. Recall that in Peirce's system, an icon resembles that which it signifies; an index has a natural relation to it, such as cause or effect; and a symbol has no natural relation to its signifier but represents it through social (or here, we can also say artistic) convention (Peirce 1991). Adding this semiotic system to the taxonomy of functional analysis I have just sketched gives us a deeper insight into the poetics of aroma onstage.

Aroma was an important part of the 1999 New York production of Ayub Khan-Din's play *East Is East*, a bittersweet comedy about an Anglo-Pakistani working-class family in England in the 1970s; both of the published reviews of the play's production start by discussing the smell of fish and chips that pervades the theatre even before the play begins (see Kuchwara 1999: D3; Brantley 1999: C13).[10] It is the smell of the family business, a chip shop owned by the Pakistani father, in which his English wife and most of their kids work. Taken purely as a separate component, the smell operates indexically, as an "effect" or natural sign of cooking fish and chips (in the way that smell will always serve indexically to "point to" its source and therefore signify it, first and foremost). But taken as part of the total representation, here the aroma operates iconically, as one element in a gestalt or ensemble of theatrical means that creates a realistic representation of a particular, localized setting through principles of resemblance.

It is interesting to note in the case of this particular play that the smell effect creates an ironic aspect. The aroma of fish and chips is strongly associated with a particular ethnicity – that is, British (Anglo) ethnicity. Yet in *East Is East* this aroma works incongruously and ironically along several dimensions: on the one hand, the olfactory effect connotes (through the strong cultural meaning of the fish-and-chips odor) that the former colonial (the Pakistani patriarch) has appropriated the smells of the colonizer, while on the other hand, in the play's action the father refuses to assimilate into British culture, even while his business smells like he has.

As I have noted, the most frequent use of aroma design is iconic and illustrative. But there are cases that fall into Peirce's second category, the indexical, where the olfactory effect, as part of the theatrical ensemble, either foreshadows what is to come (as in the case of another scene in May's site-specific *Dragon Island*, when the spectators passed a smelly stream, which alerted them that they were about to reach the lair of the "odorous dragon") or, more poetically, sets conceptual categories of association in motion through metaphor and other literary tropes. In Jenny Strauss's 24-hour ritual performance piece *Idio/Passage: Private Vernacular, Public Catharsis* (1996), rotting meat mixed with other items (including honey, urine, and dirt) in order, according to the artist, to create a "provocative/nauseating smell" and to "mark time in a nonlinear way" as the odors intensified during the course of the performance (Strauss 1999). The sweet smell of honey and the fresh smell of dirt (indices of nonhuman nature) mixed with the putrescence of meat (working metaphorically here to stand for human flesh) and acrid urine (an index of the human body), suggesting a view of human substance as both repulsive and yet part of an attractive natural world.

There are also uses of aroma that are purely symbolic and conventional – that is, not linked in any natural way, whether analogous or causal, to what they represent. For instance, Michael Dempsey, in his 1999 production of Thomas Kilroy's *Talbot's Box*, burned laudate incense to suggest the obsession of the main character, a recovering alcoholic, with religion and prayer. In what is probably the best-known use of aroma in performance, the Symbolist production *The Song of Songs*, author/director Paul Roinard posited a mystical correspondence between speech, music, color, and scent. For instance, in one section, the vowels $i - e$, illuminated with o, corresponded to music in the key of D, the color pale orange, and the scent of white violets (Roinard [1891] 1976: 131).

The symbolic use of olfactory effects often suggests (without directly illustrating) liturgical uses of incense and other aromas, but there are symbolic uses that fall into other cultural categories than the religious. For instance, Bobby Baker's *Cook Dems* (1992) – in which the performance artist made a pizza-dough breastplate, antlers, and a bread-ball skirt – used the smell of baking dough as a metaphor for the female body. In Robbie McCauley's *Food Show* (1992, with Laurie Carlos and Jessica Hagedorn), the performers made and served to the spectators various foods with particular ethnic resonances and associations.

Two aspects of the use of olfactory effects in recent performances are noteworthy. One is that aromas are often used effectively to telegraph a stereotype of class or nationality or ethnicity, as in McCauley's work, Tim Miller's grilling hamburgers in *Postwar* (1982), the use of incense in *India Song*, or the real spaghetti dinner eaten by the Italian family in various productions of Eduardo de Filippo's *Saturday, Sunday, Monday* (such as Franco Zeffirelli's at the National Theatre in 1973). To return to Barthes's rhetorical analysis of images, one could say that what is being strongly indicated associatively by the aroma in these cases is not suburbia, India, or Italy, but suburbanicity, or Indianicity, and so on – that is, the aroma contributes not to an illustration of those specific geographical sites but to a condensed, culturally embedded association of those cultural sites instantly recognizable to that particular audience (Barthes [1964] 1977: 48).

The second striking aspect, related to the first, is that often the ethnicity or nationality invoked by the olfactory effect is an exotic "Other" – that is, the exotic "Other" is represented precisely as possessing a smelly (or fragrant) identity. The intense use of aromas in van Hove's *India Song*; in the Tamasha Company's London production of Sudha Bhuchar and Shaheen Khan's *Balti Kings* (2000) (see Marsh 2000; Nightingale

2000); in a recent Toronto adaptation of *The Arabian Nights* (1995) directed by William Lane (see Wagner 1995); in Kai Tai Chan's 1982 dance *One Man's Rice*, performed by his One Extra Dance Company in Sydney (see Lester 2000); in the French equestrian theatre company Zingaro's production *Chimère* (see Holden 1996); and in so many other productions in the West that make use of non-Western themes, implies that the East (or subaltern culture in the West) is suffused with aromas, both pleasant and unpleasant, and, in doing so, creates an ideological representation of the West as odorless and therefore neutral and the norm.

The question arises as to why smell has returned to the theatre with a vengeance at the turn of the twenty-first century. I would like to advance two possible answers. One is that in recent years, mainstream Western culture has in fact turned away from its prior deodorizing trajectory; indeed, our culture has become obsessed with experiencing smells intensely, from incense to herbal *pot-pourris* to perfume and aromatherapy. And surely the current fascination with olfactory effects in the theatre is itself part of this Western renascence of scent. But also, it may well be that the recent rash of olfactory performances in the West is yet another plot turn in the continuing narrative of the theatre's anxiety toward the mass media, of its reaction first to movies and then to television, which ironically can produce realism even better than live theatre. Perhaps the olfactory effect in performance is a way to engender an impression of authenticity, a way to supply the spectator with a vivid slice of "the real," whether or not the theatrical style is realistic, and thus a way to carve out a niche for theatre where "liveness" makes a difference.

REFERENCES

Barthes, Roland. 1972 [1964]. "Literature and signification." In *Critical Essays*, translated by Richard Howard, 261–7. Evanston, Ill.: Northwestern University Press.

——. 1977 [1964] *Image–Music–Text*, translated by Stephen Heath. New York: Hill & Wang.

Brantley, Ben. 1996. "A house guest inspires not so maternal feelings." *The New York Times*, 22 February: C13.

——. 1999. "Pungent life with father, serving love and chips." *The New York Times*, 26 May: E1.

Burkert, Walter. 1985. *Greek Religion: Archaic and Classical*, translated by John Raffan. Cambridge, Mass.: Harvard University Press.

Cargher, John. 1979. "Reports: foreign, Sydney." *Ballet News* 1, 6: 47.

Carroll, Noël. 1980. "Cleaning Up Her Act." *The Soho Weekly News*, 27 July.

Classen, Constance, David Howes, and Anthony Synnott. 1994. *Aroma: The Cultural History of Smell*. London: Routledge.

Deák, Frantisek. 1976. "Symbolist staging at the Théâtre d'Art." *The Drama Review* 20, 3 (T71): 120–2.

Drobnick, Jim. 1998. "Reveries, assaults, and evaporating presences: olfactory dimensions in contemporary art." *Parachute* 89: 10–19.

Elam, Keir. 1980. *The Semiotics of Theatre and Drama*. London: Methuen.

Goldberg, RoseLee. 1998. *Performance: Live Art Since 1960*. New York: Harry N. Abrams.

Greenfield, Edward. 1989. "Arts: review of 'Love for Three Oranges' at the Coliseum." *The Guardian* (London), 8 December.

Guest, Ivor. 1976. *Le Ballet de l'Opéra de Paris*. Paris: Opéra de Paris/Gallimard.

Haill, Cathy. 1987. "Buy a Bill of the Play!" *Apollo 126* (New Series 302): 284.

Henry, Georgina. 1989. "Media file." *The Guardian* (London), 18 December.

Hewitt, Christopher. 1999. Email correspondence. 9 November.

Holden, Stephen. 1996. "Magical world of man and beast." *The New York Times*, 19 September: C13.

Kuchwara, Michael. 1999. "'East Is East' Might Play Better on TV." *The Washington Times*, 29 May: D3.

Lavoie, Bernard. 1999. Email correspondence. 9 November.

Leach, Robert. 1989. *Vsevolod Meyerhold*. Cambridge: Cambridge University Press.

Lester, Garry. 2000. "Kai Tai Chan: a different path." PhD dissertation, Deakin University.

MacGregor, Catherine. 1999a. "Abject speculation: refiguring the female body in the performance work of Cosey Fanni Tutti." Paper delivered at Performance Studies International 5, Aberystwyth, 10 April.

———. 1999b. Email correspondence. 23 November.

Marker, Lise-Lone. 1974. *David Belasco: Naturalism in the American Theatre*. Princeton, NJ: Princeton University Press.

Marks, Peter. 1999. "An Irish classic given cartoon form." *The New York Times*, 8 October: E3.

Marsh, Tim. 2000. "Hot ticket." *The Times* (London), 15 January.

May, Theresa. 1999. Email correspondence. 9 November.

Moore, Nancy. 1997. "Valentine de St.-Point: 'La Femme Intégrale' and her quest for a modern tragic theatre in L'Agonie de Messaline (1907) and La Métachorie (1913)." PhD dissertation, Northwestern University.

Nascimento, Claudia. 1999. Interview with author. Madison, Wis., 18 November.

Nightingale, Benedict. 2000. "Balti Kings." *The Times* (London), 17 January.

Peirce, Charles S. 1991. *Peirce on Signs: Writings on Semiotic*, edited by James Hoopes. Chapel Hill, NC: University of North Carolina Press.

Reynolds, Nigel. 1989. "Opera lovers smell after scratching through Prokofiev." *The Daily Telegraph*, 7 December: 3.

Roinard, P.N. 1976 [1891]. "The Song of Songs of Solomon (script)," translated by Leonora Champagne and Norma Jean Deák. *The Drama Review* 20, 3 (T71): 129–35.

Shepherd-Barr, Kirsten. 1999. "Mise en scent: the Théâtre d'Art's 'Cantique des cantiques' and the use of smell as a theatrical device." *Theatre Research International* 24, 2: 152–9.

Strauss, Jenny. 1999. Email correspondence. 7 November.

Wagner, Vit. 1995. "Arabian Nights weaves together ancient tales." *Toronto Star*, 14 September: H5.

Wilson, Sue. 1999. "Tales of passion, obsession and tragic isolation." *The Independent* (London), 4 September: 8.

Winn, Steven. 1995. "Smells like old times." *San Francisco Chronicle*, 10 September, Sunday Datebook: 35.

Zgutowicz, Monica. 1980. "A study of the use of odor in Western performance." MA thesis, New York University.

NOTES

1 Originally published in *TDR: The Drama Review* 45.1 (2001) 68–76.

2 This article is an expanded version of a paper delivered at the Uncommon Senses Conference, Montreal, 27–29 April 2000.

3 Although André Antoine used sides of beef that must have exuded a strong odor in his 1888 production of Fernand Icres's *The Butchers*. But for the most part, by the twentieth century, realism had opted for a deodorized stage.

4 A recent exception, pointing to a new scholarly interest in aroma design onstage, is Shepherd-Barr (1999). Also see Zgutowicz (1980).

5 See Drobnick (1998: 10–14) for an overview of philosophical views about smell in relation to art.

6 For the various examples in this essay, I have collected anecdotal information about theatrical aroma design from a large number of people who either responded to my email queries on various theatre, performance, and dance studies listservs or corresponded (or spoke) with me privately. I will not cite those unpublished sources here unless quoting directly from them (although I am extremely grateful to all those individuals). Where available, I will supply citations for published documentary references to the performances.

7 On *The Song of Songs*, see Roinard ([1891] 1976) and Deák (1976).

8 Keir Elam discusses this aspect of foregrounding in terms of what the Prague structuralists called *aktualisace*, which, as he points out, is closely related to the Russian formalist idea of *ostranenie* (defamiliarization, making things strange) and also to Brecht's *Verfremdungseffekt* (1980: 16–19).

9 The scratch-and-sniff cards were created by Givenchy, a renowned perfume house (Greenfield 1989). When the opera was broadcast on television by the BBC on Boxing Day 1989, *The Listener* (circulation 60,000) distributed the cards in its Christmas issue for viewers to use at home (Henry 1989).

10 *East Is East* was originally commissioned by the Anglo-Asian theatre company Tamasha, which produced it in London in 1996. The 1999 New York production, directed by Scott Elliott, was co-produced by the Manhattan Theatre Club and the New Group. A film based on the play and directed by Damien O'Donnell was released in 1999.

4

UNEARTHING KINESTHESIA
Groping among cross-cultural models of the senses in performance

Deidre Sklar

"I shall now close my eyes, I shall stop my ears, I shall call away all my senses," Descartes declares, and sits down to discover what is left. He still exists: "I exist, I am, that is certain." Later, he rewrites: *cogito ergo sum*, "I think, therefore I am" (Descartes 1973: 151, 157, quoted in Synnott 1991: 70). Descartes has made a jump. He now equates the awareness of existence to "thinking." But from where did Descartes' awareness of existing come? Had the European tradition of excluding from the "five senses" proprioception, the perception of one's own sensations, tricked Descartes into believing that he could think without benefit of sensation and its traces? "What if there exist different forms of reasoning, memory, and attention for each of the modalities of consciousness (seeing, smelling, speaking, hearing, etc.) instead of reasoning, memory, and attention being general mental powers?" asks sensory anthropologist, David Howes (1991a: 10). The "what if" is unnecessary. Richard Bandler and John Grinder, students of linguistic anthropologist Gregory Bateson (and originators of the popular therapy "neurolinguistic programming"), discovered that not only do different people think in terms of different "representational systems" (such as internally seeing images, hearing sounds/talking to themselves, or feeling kinesthetic sensations), the same individual is likely to rely on one sensory modality to "go after" information (visually searching, aurally questioning, kines-thetically groping) and another to "check out" what comes up (looks good, sounds true, feels right) (Bandler and Grinder 1979: 14). There can be no "thinking" that does not depend on one or another or a combination of sensings.

Not reason but imagination is the essential meaning-making operation.[1] As philosopher Mark Johnson (1987) writes, in a Cartesian understanding of meaning-fulness, cognitive operations are divided between the formal, conceptual, and intellectual work of reason and the material, perceptual, and sensible work of the body; constructed this way, the body provides us with sensory perceptions, while the mind conceptualizes these as representations. Kant hypothesized that the mediating factor between sensation and conceptualization was imagination. But Kant "couldn't draw the reasonable conclusion that imagination is both bodily and rational" (xxvii–xxviii). Imagination, Johnson argues, works not merely reproductively to duplicate or reflect experience but productively, as an ongoing activity that structures experience by organizing perceptions, figuratively, into patterns. Johnson calls these patterns "image schemata" or "embodied schemata," for they emerge from and give structure to bodily experience.[2]

Embodied schemata are neither percepts nor concepts, but "mediating representations" (152) drawn from bodily experience. We share innate structures of embodiment – arms, legs, tongue, teeth, ears, skin, eyes – that both enable and limit the possibilities of embodied experience (Sheets-Johnstone 1990: 17). We also share sensory potential and the innate capacity to "transfer perceptual experience from one sensory modality to another"(Stern 1985: 47). Before infants recognize specific sights, touches, and sounds, or that impressions "belong" to a particular sense, they make global abstractions of structures across the senses. They can recognize, for example, the sight of a ball they had only previously known by touch. They can translate levels of sound intensity to levels of visual intensity and recognize temporal patterns, such as duration and rhythm, across all the modalities (47–9). This process of extrapolating from sensation, organizing by structural likeness, and abstracting into global patterns parallels the work of imagination that Johnson describes for building embodied schemata. It is the basis on which the senses are developed differentially, and symbolically, in different cultural communities.

Sensations, occurring in an "intersubjective milieu," are inevitably intersubjective, anthropologist Tom Csordas writes (1993: 138); our bodies are from the beginning in and part of the world. He enjoins his colleagues to follow "a phenomenology that will lead to conclusions both about the cultural patterning of bodily experience, and also the intersubjective constitution of meaning through that experience" (140–1). In the European philosophical tradition, bodily experience has been patterned as "the five senses" and further divided into "intellectual" or distanced senses (sight and hearing) and affective and proximate ones (smell, taste, touch) (Howes 1991b: 177). Aristotle called touch and taste, in particular, "animal senses," the other three "human" ones (Synnott 1993: 63). But other cultures offer other "sensory profiles," to use David Howes' term. He and his colleague, Constance Classen, suggest that these sensory orders may be gleaned by asking, for example, which senses are emphasized in talk, in performance, in artifacts and body decoration, in childraising, in media of communication, in the natural and built environment, and in mythology and its representations (Howes and Classen 1991). A few examples from the anthropological literature illustrate.

Songhay sorcerers, anthropologist Paul Stollers writes, learn about power and history by "eating it," ingesting odors and tastes, savoring textures and sounds (1997: 3). The stomach, he explains, is the site of personality and agency, and social relations are conceived in terms of eating (7). To say that one eats another person is to say that one knows him so well, one ingests his being. To eat the market is to master it. To eat the words of the ancestors and be eaten by them is to transform both (7). Knowledge apparently occurs by a process of ingestion or, more broadly, by taking something into one's body and transforming and being transformed by it. Eating becomes a metaphor for processes of incorporation, and also transformation.[3] In performance, the music, praise poetry, perfumes, and dancing entice spirits to enter and possess people's bodies (56). In the relationship with what is ingested, the Songhay person is momentarily replaced.

Eating and being eaten is also the subject of east Indian *prasad*, the sacred ritual in which food is offered to and tasted by the gods, with the leftovers going to humans.

Sylvain Pinard[4] writes that "to achieve *moksa* [liberation], the individual 'soul' or *atman*, which is called 'food' in the Upanishads, must be sacrificed to Brahma, himself conceived as food" (226). In what he calls a "digestive theology," Pinard imagines the dynamic exchange of "society and cosmos as a huge digestive system" (228). Coarse and refined are separated out "in the digestive system of the Supreme Being" (229). *Rasa*, literally taste, but inclusive of both savor and essence, is "not released until that (digestive) process is complete" (229). The absorption of the audience in *rasa* is the aim of the performing arts in India.[5] Apparently, where performers are eaten in a Songhay world, the audience is also eaten in India.

Divinity is eaten in both cases, as it is in Catholic Christianity. In the Hispano-Catholic community of Tortugas, New Mexico, where I did long-term fieldwork, communion was at the heart of people's experience of God. When I asked one of the elders if she could experience God during the annual pilgrimage as she did in church, she reminded me that "You can't take communion without going to church." Then she added, with a self-enclosing hug, "Maybe it's the place, the enclosed space, maybe it's the mass." It was not so much the taste of the host that was important as its ingestion, a kinesthetic-tactile experience.

The theme of separating out food for humans and food for the gods recurs throughout the literature on sacrificial offerings. Carl Kerenyi writes: "The invention and first offering of the characteristic sacrifice of a religion may well be regarded as an act of world creation or at least as an act establishing the prevailing world order" (1963: 43). In the pre-Platonic sacrificial offering that established the change from Titan to Olympian world orders, Prometheus, the ritual specialist in charge, tricked the Olympian Zeus, giving the edible meat of the ox to humans and the dry bones and smoke to the gods. But the deception worked against humans, for meat, unlike the dry bones and smoke that went to the gods, established the human imperative of having to feed the body in order to survive. Gods do not eat, and animals eat their meat raw, but humans must cook to eat. And when they cook, they must also acknowledge, through sacrificial offerings, the superior, non-corporeal gods (Vernant 1981a, 1981b).[6] Is this story the precursor to Aristotle's designation of eating as a lower, "animal" sense and smelling as a higher one? The Greek gods do not eat earthly food, but apparently, taking in the sacrificial smoke, they can smell it.

Smell occurs through the medium of air but includes the odorous by-products of corporeality. It is, in this sense, a combination of breathing and eating. It is less proximate, therefore less "animal" than taste, but less distanced than sight and hearing. In contemporary US popular culture, smell's "animal" aspect, as in the smell of bodies, is covered up. Smell's food-for-the-gods aspect is present (as incense) in the Catholic Church and in New Age spiritual practices borrowed from Asia. Smell is rarely a subject of scholarly attention.[7] Is its absence more a reflection of scholars' values in a secular academy than of the values of those whom scholars write about?

Through breathing, one can incorporate spiritual otherness without eating it. For Pueblo people along the New Mexico Rio Grande, breathing rather than eating is the model for spiritual (and social) exchange, and air rather than food is the medium that carries meaning. After a dance, Puebloans lift the evergreens they carry to their mouths, breathing in their life-renewing properties, then breathing them out to the world. Breath carries the life force between self and world. It also carries words, which derive not from the head but from the heart.[8] Speaking (words that ride the breath from the heart) is a kind of praying, and therefore one must be careful what one says.

The drum is the heartbeat of Pueblo dancing. A Pueblo friend once explained that dancers "ride the drum," letting awareness be carried out and in on its pulse. The strong beat sends one out to the land, the echo beat brings one back into the body. Out and in, other and self. Thoughts ride the pulse of the drum, like breath, dispersing and re-gathering. The sensory emphasis is kinesthetic, tactile, and auditory.

Robert Coles, who recorded the drawings and stories of children from many cultural communities, discovered that Pueblo children learned to "see" by metaphorically bringing themselves close to what they looked at. They were taught to notice in a kinesthetic and participatory way, to "capture" a sight while at the same time giving themselves to it. Describing her drawing of the land, one girl explained: "It gets so dry for so long; the earth *cracks*, and when you *walk* over it, you can *hear* it *cry* for water. Even a cactus plant seems to be *saying* that it would like a little drink. I could *have a cloth over my eyes* and know if I was *walking* over some very *thirsty* land: the *noises, the feel of the earth* under my feet. It is like *rubbing* your skin with your hand when you've hurt yourself and the cut is just beginning to heal" (Coles 1977: 435). I have added italics to point up the emphasis on kinesthetic, tactile, auditory, and even gustatory sensing, as well as the emphatic de-stressing of the visual.

I have been inching toward a hole in the sensorium. Kinesthesia, the proprioceptive sense of movement, has been omitted from the "five senses." It is the most proximate sense, related to touch (since movement can be felt only in the tactile relationship between parts), but the other senses depend on it as well. As Sheets-Johnstone writes, "(The living body) is first and foremost the center of a tactile-kinesthetic world that, unlike the visual world, rubs up directly against things outside it and reverberates directly with their sense. The tactile-kinesthetic body is a body that is always in touch, always resounding with an intimate and immediate knowledge of the world about it" (Sheets-Johnstone 1990: 16). Kinesthesia is like the missing acknowledgment of the emperor's body without his clothes.[9]

The significance of kinesthesia to thinking is illustrated in a 1940s study designed by anthropologist David Efron (1972), a student of Franz Boas. To refute Nazi notions about the inheritance of so-called "racial gestures," Efron examined and compared the conversational gestures of Jewish immigrants from the ghettos of Lithuania and Poland with those of Neapolitan and Sicilian peasant immigrants, both in New York city. He then studied the gestures of their children, the second generation in America, to determine what became of these differences under the impact of assimilation. His findings, that differences in gestural patterns are not determined by inherent physiological, psychological, or mental differences, but by the interaction between learned traditions and social conditions, were predictable even in 1940. But Efron also found something less predictable, that gestures were an intrinsic part of the thinking process (105 fn48). Furthermore, differences in gestural style embodied differences in *ways* of thinking. The Italian immigrants used gestures to embody the *content* of their thought, like a sign language. They carried, so to speak, "a bundle of pictures" in their hands (123). The Jewish immigrants used gestures to embody the *process* of theirs, to "link one proposition to another, trace the itinerary of a logical journey, or to beat the tempo of mental locomotion" (98). Efron's findings point not only to different sensory profiles (an emphasis among the Italian immigrants on the visual, among the Jewish on the auditory and tactile/kinesthetic) but also to differences in the qualitative aesthetics of their thinking. In Laban movement analysis terms, the Italian immigrants emphasized shape, the Jewish, rhythm and spatial direction.

Once we entertain the inclusion of kinesthesia, a second kind of "profile" emerges that can be crosshatched with the sensorium. It concerns aesthetic structures and dynamics. Along with the discovery that infants extrapolate across sensory modalities to abstract structural patterns like shape, Daniel Stern found that they also extrapolate "vitality effects" (1985: 55), complex qualities of animation. These feeling qualities are not emotions (happiness, sadness, anger, etc.) but kinetic dynamics (rushing, ambling, smoothing). They combine what Laban movement analysts call "efforts," including temporal pattern and speed, intensity of effort or force, quality of weight, and amount of flow or tension. Inherent in all activity, vitality effects are the way that life manifests as qualities of energy, related to what Sheets-Johnstone calls "originary kinetic liveliness" (1999: xxiv). In their changing patterns, vitality effects are the "activation contours" (Stern 1985: 57) of experience. I am suggesting that vitality effects are inherent to both embodiment and thinking, and that they interweave with the sensorium in the cultural construction of meaning. Admitting profiles of these aesthetic structures and dynamics into the analytical mix would enable a more multidimensional cultural reckoning than the sensorium alone can provide.

Anthropologist Edward Hall (1977), writing in the 1960s, insisted that the first step in communicating across cultural differences was to move into "synch" with the rhythms of another's speech and movement. "If you want to fit in, move to the same rhythm" (79). Hall was thinking in particular of European-Americans' difficulty fathoming African-Americans' communications. But both groups would surely be even more challenged to move into synch with the *dulugu ganalon*, the "lift-up-over sounding" Steven Feld describes for Kaluli rhythms in Papua New Guinea. Here, a *gisalo* dancer wears long fluid feathers from the back of his belt and a string of shells hanging from each side. As the dancer bobs up and down in a subtly undulating motion, the shells hit the ground slightly later than the dancer's feet, "in-synchrony yet out-of-phase" (8). Over this, the feathers make a more sustained swishing sound. The sounds of feet, shells, and feathers have an overlapping, dense pulse, more like a wave than like the "beat" of either Afrocentric or Eurocentric musical sonance. The sound of the feathers, Feld writes, resembles, intentionally, the sound of the local waterfalls, the shells a voice at the waterfall. Here, more than the sensory emphasis on hearing and kinesthesia, the particular dynamics of time (in-synchrony yet out-of-phase) and space (lift-up-over) are the openings to cultural significance.

Perhaps in some cross-cultural encounters, synching would be less fruitful than moving into formation, or getting in touch. Dance anthropologist Brenda Farnell (1999) tells a story of mistaking the significant features of Assiniboine Plains Indian sign-talk because of the assumptions she brought to fieldwork. Trained in a culture whose movement aesthetics emphasize body shape, as in ballet, she looked for meaning in the shapes of people's signing gestures. Eventually, she recognized that the significant element was not shape but the path and direction of movement in space. This structural preference related to an Assiniboine metaphysical principle concerning the importance of "that which gives motion to everything that moves" (154). Farnell tells the story to illustrate the absurdity of the idea that "the language of the body transcend(s) all cultural and linguistic boundaries" (146). Furthermore, within the same culture, trends in body gestalts change and can be sore spots of contestation, as they currently are in the politicized polarization of opinion in the USA about the "touchy-feely" 1960s.[10]

How then, does an audience sensitized to one modality learn to move into synch with a performance that emphasizes another? And how does a stage director or choreographer invite apprehension in a different modality from the audience's habitual one? The regulars at my local coffee shop have suggested putting rocking seats into Broadway theatres and serving freshly baked bread, but I am less interested in cutting and pasting excerpts of the "other senses" onto stage performances than in awakening a somatic mode of attention in general. Consider, for example, the excruciatingly slow movements of Butoh master Kazuo Ohno performing for an American audience habituated to the barrage of quick short images and sound bites of television news. I could not "see" his performance until I stopped looking at it as a visual spectacle and moved into a kinesthetic mode, joining the rhythm of my attention to that of his movements. I experienced a similar demand in the 1960s, in the medium of sound, at one of the first minimalist music concerts of the era, LaMonte Young performing at the Museum of Modern Art. I responded to the repeated monotones with intense boredom until my expectation of an impending change was pushed to its limit and snapped. Where the shift to join Kazuo Ohno was intentional, here I did nothing. The drone itself pushed my attention to slow and open. The sound then took up more space, so to speak, no longer an annoying insect buzz but an encompassing auditory environment in which multiple layers and transformations of sound became apparent. Rodney Needham (1967) discusses the potential of sharp percussive sound to shock the body into opening up a space of attention.[11] Perhaps the theatre tradition of three claps before the curtain rises intends this same clearing of the sensory palate.

What then? To what purpose instigate a qualitative shift to somatic attention? From a somatically awake state, a kind of "thinking" different from the automatic everyday mode is possible. Pierre Bourdieu (and many after him) have asserted that we are conditioned to a habitual *modus operandi*, "possessed by" a socio-cultural habitus that "functions at every moment as a matrix of perceptions, appreciations, and actions" (1977: 83). Translating into Mark Johnson's terms, the embodied schemata by which we think and act in the world are unconscious. But, since we are continually and creatively participating in schema building, we are at least potentially capable of being aware of doing so. A call to somatic attention can loosen customary "thought" patterns and also set them in relief. If, as I have argued, aesthetic patterns are as formative of thinking as symbolic ones, then a shift in the way we configure aesthetic information can jostle the whole epistemological structure, and performance becomes a kind of insight meditation. I am making a large claim for somatic awareness, nothing less than declaring its potential for interrupting automatic responses.

A performance that does this can be an act of generosity, as Lawrence Sacharow writes. In a *New York Times* essay on Thomas Richards, the inheritor of Jerzy Grotowski's theatre laboratory, Sacharow describes the experience of being in this audience as like "being in the presence of people who are unconditionally generous" (*New York Times*, 20 August 2000, Arts, p. 5). He continues, "This seeking of inner transformation, *rooted in the vibrations of sound and corporeal awareness*, raises the level of self-awareness – of being in the body – both for those observing and those being observed" (my emphasis). As Sacharow points out, Grotowski borrowed techniques from ritual traditions to enact a theatre whose emphasis was more on transformation than on selling tickets. Herein lie the possibilities for generosity.[12]

I end with a point concerning the relation of somatic and verbal modes. In mathematics and propositional thinking, as well as much of everyday mental chatter, words and symbolic representations are split off from the immediacy of sensation and worked as abstractions in relation to each other. It is common enough to discuss abstract theories without feeling the somatic reverberations of words. But it is also possible to bid words to participate in the somatic schema they represent. Then the process of thinking with words becomes a process of evoking their somatic reverberations. For example, if I say to myself "ball," I recognize the letters to refer to a ball, but I can also summon what I saw or felt or remembered when I said the word: the dirtied pink Spalding (pronounced spal-*deen*) we threw against apartment building walls in Brooklyn, its chalky texture, the exciting rebound of a "good" ball, the thud of a "dead" one, the friend I played with whose grandfather owned the grocery store where we stuck our hands into the brine of a barrel of sour pickles. These are all part of my version of the embodied schema, "ball." Words in the intimate space of sensual aliveness reverberate with somatic memory. One feels their meaning as rhythm, texture, shape, and vitality as well as symbol. Their object is made subject. This awakening of bodily intelligence, and its potential for disrupting the soporific power of the automatic verbal flow, is the point of engaging the proximate senses.

Acknowledgment

I am grateful to Sally Banes for organizing the original ASTR symposium on "The Other Senses in Performance," to Sally and to André Lepecki for their perseverence in seeing this volume to press, and to Mary Hayne for her editorial suggestions on my manuscript.

REFERENCES

Bandler, Richard and John Grinder. 1979. *Frogs into Princes*. Moab, Utah: Real People Press.

Banes, Sally. 1994. "Power and the dancing body." In *Writing Dancing in the Age of Postmodernism,* 43–50. Hanover, New Hampshire: Wesleyan University Press.

Bourdieu, Pierre. 1977. *Outline of a Theory of Practice*. Cambridge: Cambridge University Press.

Bull, Cynthia Cohen. 1997. "Sense, meaning, and perception in three dance cultures." In *Meaning in Motion. New Cultural Studies of Dance,* edited by Jane Desmond, 269–88. Durham, NC, and London: Duke University Press.

Classen, Constance, David Howes and Anthony Synnott. 1994. *Aroma: The Cultural History of Smell*. New York and London: Routledge.

Coles, Robert. 1977. *Eskimos, Chicanos, Indians.* Volume IV of *Children of Crisis.* Boston and Toronto: Little, Brown.

Descartes, René. 1973. *The Philosophical Works of Descartes*, Vol. 1, translated by E. Haldane and G.R.T. Ross. Cambridge: Cambridge University Press.

Desmond, Jane C. 1994. "Embodying difference: issues in dance and cultural studies." *Cultural Critique*, Winter 1993–94: 33–63.

Eck, Diane. 1985. *Darsan: Seeing the Divine Image in India*. Chambersburg, Pennsylvania: Anima Books.

Efron, David. 1972 [1941]. *Gesture, Race* and *Culture. A tentative study of some of the spatio-temporal and "linguistic" aspects of the gestural behavior of eastern Jews and southern*

Italians in New York City, living under similar as well as different environmental conditions. The Hague and Paris: Mouton.

Farnell, Brenda. 1999. "It goes without saying – but not always." In *Dance in the Field: Theory, Methods and Issues in Dance Ethnography*, edited by Theresa J. Buckland, 145–60. London: Macmillan and New York: St Martin's Press.

Feld, Steven. 1982. *Sound and Sentiment. Birds, Weeping, Poetics, and Song in Kaluli Expression.* Philadelphia: University of Pennsylvania Press.

——. 1990 "Aesthetics and synesthesia in Kaluli ceremonial dance." *UCLA Journal of Dance Ethnology* 14: 66–81.

Hall, Edward. 1977. "Rhythm and body movement." In *Beyond Culture*, 71–84. New York: Anchor.

Howes, David. 1991a. "Introduction: to summon all the senses." In *The Variety of Sensory Experience. A Sourcebook in the Anthropology of the Senses*, edited by David Howes, 3–24. Toronto: University of Toronto Press.

——. 1991b. "Sensorial anthropology." In *The Variety of Sensory Experience. A Sourcebook in the Anthropology of the Senses*, edited by David Howes, 167–91. Toronto: University of Toronto Press.

Howes, David and Constance Classen. 1991. "Sounding sensory profiles." In *The Variety of Sensory Experience. A Sourcebook in the Anthropology of the Senses*, edited by David Howes, 257–88. Toronto: University of Toronto Press.

Johnson, Mark. 1987. *The Body in the Mind. The Bodily Basis of Meaning, Imagination, and Reason.* Chicago and London: University of Chicago Press.

Kerenyi, Carl. 1963. *Prometheus. Archetypal Image of Human Existence*, translated by Ralph Mannheim. New York: Bollingen Series LXV. Archetypal Images in Greek Religion Vol. I.

Lex, Barbara. 1979. "The neurobiology of ritual trance." In *The Spectrum of Ritual: A Biogenetic Structural Analysis*, edited by Eugene G. d'Aquili *et al.*, 117–51. New York: Columbia University Press.

Needham, Rodney. 1967. "Percussion and transition." *Man* (n.s.) 2, 606–14.

Novack, Cynthia. 1990. *Sharing the Dance: Contact Improvisation and American Culture.* Madison: University of Wisconsin Press.

Pinard, Sylvain. 1991. "A taste of India: on the role of gustation in the Hindu sensorium." In *The Variety of Sensory Experience. A Sourcebook in the Anthropology of the Senses*, edited by David Howes, 221–30. Toronto: University of Toronto Press.

Reed, Susan A. 1998. "The politics and poetics of dance." *Annual Review of Anthropology* 27: 503–32.

Sheets-Johnstone, Maxine. 1990. *The* Roots *of Thinking.* Philadelphia: Temple University Press.

——. 1999. *The Primacy of Movement.* Amsterdam and Philadelphia: John Benjamins.

Sklar, Deidre. 1997. "Passing through the oblique: the embodied thinking of Etienne Decroux." *Words on Decroux 2. Mime Journal*: 58–77.

——. 2001. *Dancing with the Virgin: Body and Faith in the Fiesta of Tortugas, New Mexico.* Berkeley: University of California Press.

Stern, Daniel N. 1985. *The Interpersonal World of the Infant. A View from Psychoanalysis and Developmental Psychology.* New York: Basic Books.

Stoller, Paul. 1989. *The Taste of Ethnographic Things. The Senses in Anthropology.* Philadelphia: University of Pennsylvania Press.

——. 1997. *Sensuous Scholarship.* Philadelphia: University of Pennsylvania Press.

Synnott, Anthony. 1991. "Puzzling over the senses: from Plato to Marx." In *The Variety of Sensory Experience. A Sourcebook in the Anthropology of the Senses*, edited by David Howes, 61–78. Toronto: University of Toronto Press.

Vernant, Jean-Pierre. 1981a. "The myth of Prometheus in Hesiod." In *Myth, Religion and Society. Structuralist Essays by M. Detienne, L. Gernet, J.-P. Vernant and P. Vidal-Naquet*, edited by R.L. Gordon, 43–56. Cambridge: Cambridge University Press.

———. 1981b. "Sacrificial and alimentary codes in Hesiod's Myth of Prometheus." In *Myth, Religion and Society. Structuralist Essays by M. Detienne, L. Gernet, J.-P. Vernant and P. Vidal-Naquet*, edited by R.L. Gordon, 57–79. Cambridge: Cambridge University Press.

Wikan, Unni. 1991. "Toward an experience-near anthropology." *Cultural Anthropology* 6(3): 285-305.

NOTES

1   Sections of the following argument concerning schema building have been abstracted from Sklar (2001), Chapter 9.

2   "Image" here is not limited to visual representation but includes the full possible range of sensory media – movement, sound, image, taste, smell, etc. – through which we experience and represent knowledge. To counter the visualist bias and to emphasize the full sensorial nature of "imagination," I prefer the term "embodied schemata."

3   Eating gave the clue for tool making, according to anthropologist Maxine Sheets-Johnstone. Stone tools are like teeth. Both are hard: they do not give way. "The concept of a stone serving as an instrument for cutting, scraping, skinning, and other such actions – as an instrument capable of differentially transforming another object – is analogically latent in the everyday experience of eating"(1990: 27–8).

4   Pinard argues that in the Hindu sensorium, *prasad* is as significant as *darsan,* visual witnessing of the deities. Pinard is responding to Diane Eck's *Darsan: Seeing the Divine Image* (Eck 1985).

5   See Richard Schechner, Chapter 2 in this volume, for a more complex treatment of *rasa.*

6   See also Sklar (1997) for an analysis of Etienne Decroux's corporeal mime as a twentieth-century version of the Prometheus myth.

7   See, however, Barbara Kirshenblatt-Gimblett, Chapter 6 in this volume, and Classen *et al.* (1994).

8   See also Wikan (1991) on the heart as the seat of thinking in Bali.

9   Sometimes, the tactile/kinesthetic lurks beneath a seeming visual emphasis. Stella Kamrisch, writing about east Indian *darsan*, the auspicious witnessing of the Hindu divinities, likewise finds in sight a deeper attention to touch. She writes, "Seeing, according to Indian notions, is a going forth of the sight towards the object. Sight touches it and acquires its form. Touch is the ultimate connection by which the visible yields to being grasped" (quoted in Pinard 1991: 230). As Pinard succinctly summarizes, "sight is conceived on the analogy of touch" (230).

10   In the last ten years, scholars in cultural studies in dance have addressed the political dimensions of movement practices in depth. See, for example, Desmond (1994), Banes (1994), Reed (1998). For a treatment of the socio-kinesthetic ambience of the USA in the 1960s, focused through an analysis of contact improvisation, see Novack (1990). Novack, aka Bull (1997) has also compared ballet, contact improvisation, and Ghanaian dance in terms of their sensory profiles.

11   See also Lex (1979) on the effect of rhythm and other sensory elements in facilitating ritual trance.

12   I cannot help but consider the opposite possibility – the potential for danger as well as generosity inherent in interrupting somato-sensory habits. Longstanding ritual traditions engage normative values as well as aesthetic structures. There is certainly evidence that one can call an audience to somatic attention and fill the opening with propaganda and worse.

5

SENSES AND SILENCE IN ACTOR TRAINING AND PERFORMANCE[1]

Phillip B. Zarrilli

"a story is told as much by silence as by speech. Like the white spaces in an etching, such silences render form.

(Susan Griffin, *A Chorus of Stones*, 1992: 172)

QUESTIONS OF THEORY AND PRACTICE

How can the contemporary actor's body and experience in performance be theorized?[2] What methodological tools are most useful in an attempt to better understand the embodied work and sensory experience of the actor? What are the implications for actor training and practice of such (re)considerations of the embodied experience of the actor? What techniques and approaches to training, rehearsal, and performance allow the actor to more fully inhabit one's body-mind and experience when rendering the "white spaces" and "silences" that constitute theatrical form, thereby creating the possibility of experience and meaning for an audience?

Drawing on the work of post-Merleau-Ponty phenomenologists, this essay explores one model of the actor's embodied modes of experience and then elaborates a few of the practical implications of the model for training and performance.[3] Like all accounts of embodiment and experience, this one is necessarily limited by "our propositional modes of representation," since it is extremely difficult "to express the full meaning of our experience" (Johnson 1987: 4). In spite of such limitations, this essay is intended to contribute to phenomenological studies of embodiment by extending their focus from exclusive concern with the everyday to such non-everyday practices as acting, and to build on the earlier uses of phenomenology in the analysis of theatre. Previous studies by Bert O. States (1971), Bruce Wilshire (1982), Alice Rayner (1994), and Stanton Garner (1994) have contributed much to our under-standing of the theatrical event and redressed the critical disappearance of the (lived) body and embodiment in the creation of meaning and experience within the theatrical event[4]; however, the focus is this essay is specifically on the actor's modes of embodiment *per se*.

MERLEAU-PONTY AND THE "PROBLEM" OF THE BODY

Beginning in the seventeenth century, Western philosophers came to identify the body as a physical object much like other material objects – as having certain anatomical and functional properties that could be characterized as following certain scientific principles. Among those systematically challenging this understanding of the body during the 1960s, a series of three books by Maurice Merleau-Ponty – *Phenomenology of Perception* (1962), *The Primacy of Perception* (1964), and *The Visible and the Invisible* (1968) – marked a paradigm shift in Western thinking about the role of the body in the constitution of experience when he raised the fundamental philosophical problem of the body's role (or lack thereof) in constituting experience. He critiqued the hitherto static, objective nature of most representations of the body and experience:

> Thinking which looks on from above, and thinks of the object-in-general must return to the "there is" which underlies it; to the site, the soil of the sensible and opened world such as it is in our life and for our body – not that possible body which we may legitimately think of as an information machine but that actual body I call mine, this sentinel standing quietly at the command of my words and acts.
>
> (1964:160–1)

Rejecting the exclusive assumption of the natural sciences and modern psychology, which treated the physical body (*Korper*) as a thing, object, instrument, or machine under the command and control of an all-knowing mind, and thereby challenging the Cartesian *cogito*, Merleau-Ponty (re)claimed the centrality of the lived body (*Leib*) and embodied experience as the very means and medium through which the world comes into being and is experienced. He demanded an account of the "actual body I call mine," that is, the body as "an experienced phenomenon … in the immediacy of its lived concreteness," and "not as a representable object … for the abstractive gaze" (Schrag 1969: 130). He thereby rejected mind–body dualism and (re)claimed the centrality of the body and embodied experience as the locus for "experience as it is lived in a deepening awareness" (Levine 1985: 62). For Merleau-Ponty, the focus of philosophical inquiry shifted from "I think" to an examination of the "I can" of the body, i.e., sight and movement as modes of entering into intersensory relationships with objects, or "the world" (1964: 87). Dermot Moran summarizes Merleau-Ponty's contribution as undoubtedly producing "the most detailed example of the manner in which phenomenology can interact with the sciences and the arts to provide a descriptive account of the nature of human bodily being-in-the-world" (2000: 434).

THE PROBLEM OF THE CONTEMPORARY ACTOR'S BODY/BODIES

We organize "the world" we encounter into significant gestalts, but "the body" I call mine is not *a* body, or *the* body, but rather a process of embodying the several bodies one encounters in everyday experience as well as highly specialized modes of non-everyday or "extra-daily" bodies of practices such as acting or training in psychophysical disciplines to act. This notion of embodiment as a process of encounters opens up "the body" not as an object and "carries us past the inveterate tendency to reify what we are trying to think and understand and engage" (Levin 1999: 128). As Stanton Garner points out, "embodiedness is subject to modification and transformation, multiple and varying modes of disclosure, and … the forms of ambiguity that characterize the phenomenal realm represent experience in flux, oscillating within and between modes of perceptual orientation" (1994: 51).

This essay begins with an examination of Drew Leder's post-Merleau-Ponty account of one of the most vexing problems of the body – corporeal absence, i.e., the "question of why the body, as a ground of experience … tends to recede from direct experience" (1990: 1) and thereby becomes absent to us. Leder provides an extensive account of the modes of bodily absence characteristic of the everyday surface and recessive bodies. Given my focus on the contemporary actor's modes of bodily being-in-the-world, I build upon Leder's account by proposing two additional extra-daily modes of embodiment, experience, and absence characteristic of acting: an aesthetic "inner" body-mind discovered and shaped through long-term, extra-daily modes of practice such as yoga and martial arts and an aesthetic "outer" body constituted by the actions/tasks of a performance score – that body offered for the abstractive gaze of the spectator. I supplement my reading of Leder by drawing upon Japanese philosopher Yasuo Yuasa's (1987) complementary analysis of body schema, *ki* energy, and awareness.

In the final part of the essay, I explore how very specific images and metaphors can assist practitioners in remaining attentive to their bodies, i.e., in learning how to thematize the body by directing their awareness/attention to and through the absent body and negative space. My hypothesis is that "thematizing" the body-mind allows one's awareness to be more fully "present" within an act of embodiment. Once this approach is sufficiently embodied and internalized through work on breath, body, and environment, the actor can then tactically deploy this heightened sensory "attentiveness" to specific performance scores, each with its unique dramaturgy.

A FUNDAMENTAL PARADOX: "THE ABSENT BODY"

Drawing upon but attempting to address some of the inadequacies in Merleau-Ponty's phenomenological account of the everyday experience of the body, Drew Leder's *The Absent Body* addresses a fundamental problem and paradox:[5]

> While in one sense the body is the most abiding and inescapable presence in our lives, it is also essentially characterized by absence. That is, one's own body is rarely the thematic object of experience. When reading a book or lost in thought, my own bodily state may be the farthest thing from my awareness. I experientially dwell in a world of ideas, paying little heed to my physical sensations or posture.
>
> (1990: 1)[6]

Such forgetfulness is not "restricted to moments of higher-level cognition" but equally characterizes our engagement in activities such as sports, physical labor, or the performing arts – dance, acting, live performance, etc. When "engaged in a fierce sport, muscles flexed and responsive to the slightest movements of my opponent … it is precisely upon this opponent, this game, that my attention dwells, not on my own embodiment" (*ibid.*: 1).

How are we to account for this bodily absence? For Leder, the lived body (*Leib*) is not a homogeneous thing but rather "a complex harmony of different regions, each operating according to indigenous principles and incorporating different parts of the world into its space" (*ibid.*: 2). Leder provides a lengthy description of two modes of embodiment through which our everyday experience is usually constituted – the *surface body* and the *recessive body* (see Table 5.1), each of which is characterized by its own mode of bodily absence.[7]

The "ecstatic" surface body

We intersubjectively engage the world around us through our sensorimotor *surface body*, such as when we use a hand to explore, touch, or relate to the world. This body encompasses the most prominent functions that shape our experiential field, such as the power of the gaze. The basic stance of the surface body *vis-à-vis* the world it encounters is "ecstatic" in that the senses open out to the world. This is the body of "flesh."[8] Unless disturbed or interrupted in some way, our experience is usually characterized by a certain degree of ongoing spatio-temporal continuity. "My eyes can scan a visual world that is without sudden gaps or crevices. If I abandon one sense, perhaps closing my eyes, the other senses help to maintain the continuity of the world" (Leder 1990: 42). Physiologically, the surface body is characterized primarily by *exteroception*, i.e., the outer-directed five senses open us out to the external world, usually "without immediate emotional response" (*ibid.*: 43).

> However, the lived body always constitutes a nullpoint in the world I inhabit. No matter where I physically move, and even in the midst of motion, my body retains the status of an absolute "here" around which all "theres" are arrayed. … Precisely as the center point from which the perceptual field radiates, the perceptual organ remains an absence or nullity in the midst of the perceived.
>
> (*ibid.*: 13)

Given that the body constitutes a null point in our perceptual field, we experience *from* the body, and the sensory world "involves a constant reference to our possibilities of active response" (*ibid.*: 18). It is precisely in the ecstatic nature of our corporeality that the first reason that the body is forgotten, i.e., "the body conceals itself precisely in the act of revealing what is Other" (*ibid.*: 22). This primordial absence is correlated with the very fact of being present in/to the world we experience. "The surface body tends to disappear from thematic awareness precisely because it is that *from* which I exist in the world," i.e., "my organs of perception and motility are themselves transparent at the moment of use" (*ibid.*: 53). When we fix our visual focus "upon that which lies spatially and temporally ahead, the back of the body is comparatively forgotten. It is absorbed in background disappearance" (*ibid.*: 29).

This commonplace disappearance of our surface body is made possible in part by the operation of a second mode of perception – *proprioception* – the "sense of balance, position, and muscular tension, provided by receptors in muscles, joints, tendons, and the inner ear" (*ibid.*: 39). Proprioception allows our surface body to adjust our limbs, muscles, etc. appropriately to any motor task; therefore, we do not usually have to think about how to walk up a set of steps.

The sensorimotor repertoire of the lived body is in a constant state of transformation that is most evident when learning a new skill. Skill acquisition is at first extrinsic, where one acts "*to* the skill qua thematized goal" (*ibid.*: 31). For example, when first learning the lion pose in the Indian martial art, *kalarippayattu* (see Figure 5.1), a beginner must learn how to assume the pose "correctly" by placing one foot facing forward and the other foot at ninety degrees while keeping the two heels in line

Table 5.1 The actor's embodied modes of experience

	First body	Second body	Third body	"Fourth body"
	surface body	recessive body	aesthetic inner body-mind	aesthetic "outer" body [the "body" constituted by actions/tasks in performance, e.g., the "character" in drama, offered for the gaze of the audience]
	sensorimotor	visceral	subtle	fictive
Stance in relation to the world	ecstatic	recessive	hidden/then ecstatic in practice	once created as score then ecstatic or recessive
Fundamental direction	outward	inward	once awakened: outward/inward as a dialectic	once created as score that to and from which one acts
Mode of disappearance	focal & background disappearance	depth disappearance recedes	absent once cultivated	absent once created
		modes of disappearance are both focal/background and recessive		
Mode of perception	exteroception [plus proprioception]	interoception	attentiveness to exteroception, proprioception, interoception	"as if"

Table 5.1 Continued

	that from which I exist in the world	the inner depths	that through which I may heighten or cultivate my relationship to subtle modes of "interiority" and/or the "world" [voluntary]	that through which I "appear" to act in a 'world'
Mode of operation/ awareness				
Mediated/marked primarily by	"flesh"	"blood"	"breath"	"appearance"

Note: Also drawing upon Merleau-Ponty, Japanese philosopher Yasuo Yuasa in his *Ki Shugyo Shintai* (*Ki-Energy, Self-Cultivation, and the Body*) proposed his own version of a "body-scheme" in order to describe and analyze the dynamic lived relationship between "the lived and living body" (Nagatomo 1992: 49). For a brief summary of Yasuo Yuasa's body scheme, see Appendix.

Figure 5.1 The lion pose from *kalarippayattu*: an intensive training workshop held at Gardzienice Theatre Association, Poland, in May 1999, led by the author in the center forward position. In the lion pose, the heels should be in line with one another, the external gaze straight ahead, hands crossed right over left, hips forward, and spine lengthened. As this is a beginning workshop, not all participants display the "correct" form. For some, the heels are not fully in line, or the hips are displaced slightly to the right so that one is not fully "centered." Eventually, as one attunes the body toward "correct" practice, the "internal eye" keeps an awareness and link to the "negative" space from the lower abdomen down through the rear foot and into/through the floor, along the lengthened spine, and out through the palms to the right and left. Photograph by Przemek Sieraczynski.

with one another, the knees directly above the feet providing support, the external focus ahead, and the spine lengthened. Skill acquisition is often at first characterized by a volitional shift of attention prompted either by a teacher's instruction to, for example, "check the alignment of the heels" or a self-conscious shift of one's attention to check one's own alignment. The "to" over time becomes the "from," i.e., as one acquires skill in taking the lion pose and moving to and from it. What was extrinsic becomes intrinsic and "intuitive." The practitioner has *incorporated* the lion pose and its steps to the point of mastery in which he/she can now act on and operate on the world *from* a place of knowing how to move to and from the lion pose. The individual's proprioceptive sense allows them to make subtle, minor adjustments to the very act of placing the foot without thematizing the adjustment, i.e., one's body-mind "intuitively" adjusts as one moves. In this sense, the body disappears.

The "recessive" visceral body

The second body that Leder describes is the *recessive body*, i.e., the deep, inner, visceral body of corporeal depths, which in physical terms includes the mass of internal organs and processes enveloped by the body surface, such as digestion and sensations such as hunger. Physiologically, our experience of our internal viscera and organs is characterized by *interoception*. Compared with the surface body, "interoception does not share the multidimensionality of exteroception" (Leder 1990: 40). Leder provides the example of taking a bite of an apple, which, before swallowing, is experienced through sight, touch, smell, and taste. But once swallowed, "these possibilities are swallowed up as well" (*ibid.*: 39). Except for the occasional and often unpleasant evidence of digestive activity or dysfunction, "the incorporation of an object into visceral space involves its withdrawal from exteroceptive experience" (*ibid.*: 39). The withdrawal of the visceral body is a form of "depth disappearance" in that the viscera are "part of the body which we do *not* use to perceive or act upon the world in a direct sense" (*ibid.*: 53). Lacking the specificity of the surface body, visceral sensations are therefore often vague and anonymous – we experience this body as "recessive," i.e., going or falling into the background. Characterized by its recession, the visceral body is therefore much more difficult to thematize.[9] This is the (metaphorical) body of "blood," suggesting that depth dimension of experience "beneath the surface flesh" (*ibid.*: 66) and suggesting our temporal emergence into life at the moment of birth.

The normative disappearance of both surface and recessive bodies is reversed when we experience pain or dysfunction. In pain, sensory intensification in the body demands direct thematization (*ibid.*: 77ff). Pain is an affective call that has the "quality of compulsion", i.e., the pain seizes and constricts our attention. I must act now *to* the body to relieve the discomfort. If I begin to lose my balance when walking up a set of steps, my proprioceptive sense thematizes the dysfunction in my normally "good" balance, and I automatically attempt to regain my balance before falling. In both cases, I involuntarily act toward the body, not from it.

Our everyday experience of the lived body is a constant intermingling and exchange of "flesh and blood", i.e., "we form one organic/perceptual circuit" inhabiting the surface/recessive body as a gestalt that moves between ecstatic and recessive states – projecting out into the world and falling back (*ibid.*: 160). The body's disappearance and absence thereby mark our "ceaseless relation to the world" (*ibid.*: 160). Leder's account concludes that the lived body's ecstatic and recessive nature provides an "ambiguous set of possibilities and tendencies that take on definite shape only within a cultural context" (*ibid.*: 151). The West has tended to valorize "immaterial reason," and this dissociation of mind from body has encouraged us to "abandon sensorimotor awareness for abstracted mathematical or linguistic forms," in contrast to more positive modes of cultivating the types of bodily awareness often required of the actor/performer (*ibid.*: 153).

The "aesthetic" "inner" body-mind

Since my interest is in constructing a phenomenological analysis of the lived body that takes account not only of the everyday surface and recessive bodies but also the non-ordinary, extra-daily lived body, I propose adding to the surface and recessive bodies an equally important (third) mode of awareness and experience – the "aesthetic" inner body-mind. This body is that realm of extra-daily perception and experience associated with long-term, in-depth engagement in certain psychophysical practices or training regimes – yoga, the martial arts, acting/performing *per se*, or similar forms of embodied practice that engage the physical body and attention (mind) in culti-vating and attuning both to subtle levels of experience and awareness. This process of cultivation and attunement is "aesthetic" in that it is non-ordinary, takes place over time, and allows for a shift in one's experience of the "body" and "mind" aspects from their gross separation, marked by the body's constant disappearance, to a much subtler, dialectical engagement of body-in-mind and mind-in-body. It is, therefore, marked as "aesthetic" since experience is gradually refined to ever-subtler levels of awareness, and "inner" since this mode of experience begins with an exploration from "within" as the awareness learns to explore the body.

I take as an example the well-documented paradigm of the body-mind developed in Indian yoga and the closely related Indian martial art *kalarippayattu,* where a subtle level of inner awareness is often accessed through attentiveness to the breath.[10] In contrast to the involuntary, everyday modes of disappearance and absence, or the sudden attention given to the body in pain, these positive, voluntary modes of refined self-presencing allow the practitioner to explore realms of embodiment that, while always bound by certain phenomenal constraints, nevertheless allow one to (re)negotiate the terms and quality of engagement of the lived body-mind in its encounter with itself in the world – at least during optimal moments of psycho-physical practice or engagement.[11]

At first, this subtle inner body-mind is "hidden," unknown, and therefore funda-mentally absent from experience. Since this body-mind and mode of experience is not necessary for the survival of the everyday body, it is understood to lie "dormant" within, available only to and through certain modes of psychophysical practice that engage the awareness. When an individual undergoes assiduous practice of particular embodied disciplines like yoga and related martial arts, this body has the potential to be "awakened," i.e., this mode of experience and perception through the body is opened and can become available to the experience of the practitioner as the body-mind.

To awaken the subtle inner bodymind, one must first attend directly to a particular embodied activity. In the practice of yoga and the martial arts, such attentiveness is often achieved by means of attentiveness to the breath. This inner body is therefore literally as well as metaphorically marked by the "breath" – the inner circulation of wind/energy/life-force identified in non-Western paradigms of the body as *prana* or *prana vayu* in India, in Chinese practices as *qi*, and in Japanese as *ki*. For Buddhists and Hindus, this inner body-mind is fully mapped as the subtle body of yoga where the breath or life-force travels along channels (*nadi*) and activates wheels (*chakras*) along the line of the spine.[12] For Chinese Daoists, this mode of inner experience of the viscera is pictured "as centers along greater and lesser pathways for the circu-lation of *qi*" (ibid.: 182).

Over long-term practice, the result is that one's experience of the body and mind aspects of experience can be fundamentally altered, i.e., a subtle inner body-mind is revealed and can be cultivated aesthetically through specific practices. Once awakened, this body-mind or mode of awareness becomes "ecstatic" and can be directed inward and/or outward through one's practice. The ecstatic nature of this "inner" experience is often manifest in non-Western paradigms as extremely subtle vibrations and/or heat. It can operate from the body, to the interior of the body, or between the from and the to. In some disciplines, especially inwardly directed forms of meditation intended to take the practitioner away from engagement with the everyday world and away from the body toward renunciation or self-transcendence, the direction is inward, and the body therefore intentionally recedes. These modes of practice are ecstatically recessive. But in other disciplines, especially martial arts or those modes of meditation intended to enliven and alter one's encounter with the immediate environment, the direction is outward toward this encounter with the environment and world as one meets it. It is in these outwardly oriented practices that one's stance ecstatically modulates between the inner and outer – the inner/depth core and the outer world one encounters.

Of all the processes of the recessive visceral body, respiration – the act of breathing, which involves surface exchanges several times each minute – is the most accessible of our visceral processes to intentional control. Our breathing responds instantaneously to shifts in emotion; therefore, "breathing is 'based in existence more than any other physiological function'" (*ibid*.: 183). It is through the breath that the aesthetic inner body reaches and touches both the surface body of exteroception and the depth ("blood") body of our inner recesses.

The fundamental state of absence of this third, aesthetic inner body-mind is witnessed in our everyday relationship to breathing. The act of breathing, like other visceral domains, normally disappears unless a particular physical condition such as a heart problem, or a non-normative mode of exertion such as climbing 200 stairs quickly, calls our attention to difficulties or pain in breathing. Alternatively, focusing our attention in and on the act of breathing in a particular way, and in relation to the body, provides one means by which to both work against the recessive disappearance of the breath in order to cultivate the breath and our inner awareness toward a heightened, "ecstatic" state of engagement in a particular practice and/or in relation to a "world." For example, some masters of *kalarippayattu* teach simple breathing exercises at the beginning of training (see Zarrilli 1998: 128–39). Individuals stand with feet shoulder width apart, external gaze fixed on and through a point ahead at eye level. They are instructed to keep the mouth closed and to breath through the nose, simultaneously (and literally) following with their "inner eye" the breath as it travels in and down along the line of the spine down to the lower abdominal region about two inches below the navel (in Sanskrit, the root of the navel, *nabhi mula*). Sensing the completion of the in-breath, and keeping the inner eye fixed on the breath, on the exhalation they follow the breath on its journey back up and out through the nose. The practitioner's attention is directed simultaneously outward with the external eye, and inward and down with the "inner eye."

Japanese philosopher Yasuo Yuasa discusses how it is "possible to correct the modality of the mind by correcting the modality of the body" (Nagatomo 1992: 56) through the use of breathing exercises:

> Physiologically, the respiratory organ is regulated and controlled by the autonomic nerves and motor-nerves; the respiratory organ has an ambiguous character of being linked both to the voluntary and involuntary muscles. This means that one can consciously control the rhythm and pattern of breathing, and in turn affect the physiological functions governed by the autonomic nervous system.
>
> (*ibid*.: 56)

The experiential circuit developed through such practices is the "unconscious quasi-body" that corresponds to the *ki* meridian system or network beneath the skin covering the entire body and used in acupuncture (*ibid.*, *passim*). It is roughly equivalent to the subtle body of yoga.

Such attentive breathing can gradually shift one's awareness to the breath in the here and now as it traverses its way to the visceral depths of the body below the navel. Eventually, with long-term practice, the sensory awareness of following the breath can be extended from the lower abdomen downward through the lower body and out through the soles of the feet, up through the torso along the line of the spine and out the top of the head, and out through the arms/hands/fingers or palms as the "inner wind or energy" travels through the body. It is a process of what Yasuo Yuasa calls developing "*ki* awareness" (*ibid.*, *passim*). Although it is normal for a beginner to at first "space out" or experience the mind wandering away from staying attentive to the simple task of following the breath to and from the lower abdomen – keeping the "eyes in the gut" – over long-term practice such attentiveness to breath works against the normative disappearance of the body.

Although I have focused here on the example of the subtle body of yoga and *kalarippayattu* because this particular interior map of the subtle body has been well documented ethnographically, the existence of an "aesthetic inner body-mind" marked by this particular map is not, I would argue, exclusive to these particular practices. Rather, numerous modes of traditional as well as contemporary actor/dancer training, such as Japanese *noh,* LeCoq, Meyerhold's biomechanics, Grotowski-based work, *butoh,* Suzuki training, and *kathakali* dance-drama, provide practitioners with modes of deep, assiduous training in which they have the potential to develop an "aesthetic inner body-mind." Each particular cultural, historical, or artistic/pedagogical practice over time develops a version of this aesthetic inner body-mind. The mature practitioner ideally develops the ability to voluntarily thematize the body through use of the breath so that one "stays [more] present" in the moment of practice. Although this type of "self-presencing" experience is not one of the primary, everyday "ways in which most of us live out the body" (Leder 1990: 153), for the actor, martial artist, or meditator, such attending to bodily activity itself is practically cultivated through long-term training and/or long-term experience on stage *per se*, where one is able to attain a non-ordinary, optimal "inner" awareness to be deployed in one's practice.[13]

To summarize the discussion thus far, one's experience of the gestalt body as a whole is usually within the context of experiential disappearance; however, for the individual practicing some type of psychophysical discipline or through long-term embodied practice, the experience of surface and recessive bodies can be enhanced and modulated by the gradual awakening and attunement of a third, inner aesthetic inner body-mind.

The aesthetic "outer" body

In performance, the actor enacts a specific performance score – that set of actions/tasks that constitute the aesthetic "outer" body offered for the abstractive gaze of the spectator – often read and experienced as "character" in a conventional drama. The actor's "body," therefore, is dually present for the objective gaze and/or experience of an audience and as a site of experience for the actor *per se*. The actor's "body," therefore, is a site through which representation as well as experience are generated for both self and other. The actor undergoes an experience that is one's own and is therefore constitutive of one's being-in-the-world, and simultaneously constitutes a "world" for the other. Stanton Garner describes this as the "irreducible twinness of a field that is – from all points – simultaneously inhabited and seen" (Garner 1994: 51). For spectators attending the enactment of a drama, this fourth body is conventionally read and experienced as a particular "character."

During performance, the actor ideally embodies, attends to, and inhabits an experiential field structured by the set of actions/tasks immediately at hand that collectively constitute the performance score and does so with a mode of embodied inhabitation fulfilling the qualities and constraints of the aesthetic conventions received or constructed for that particular performance. For the actor operating at virtuoso levels, once the score is created through rehearsals or a period of devising, it presents itself to the actor as potentially both ecstatic and recessive, i.e., that structure to and/or from which one "acts" or bodies forth the performance. The fundamental direction is both "to" and "from," i.e., the actor's performance is a modulation or oscillation in relation to that score. As a constructed/fictive score, this set of tasks or actions is "absent" until it is created and bodied forth in performance. Once created and present for the actor as a score, the modes of disappearance are both focal/background and recessive.

For the actor within the enactment of the score "in" a role, their perception operates between exteroception, proprioception, and interoception, i.e., adjustments are made as necessary to/with/for the immediate demands of the four "bodies." Ideally, the actor thematizes the score as it unfolds, inhabiting as fully as possible each action within the score and linking each action as its moment of enactment arrives. However, constant adjustments must be made to and within the moment of enactment – to one's balance, to the action of another actor, to a cough or laugh from the audience, etc. The experiential field of the actor is, as Garner explains, "subject to ambiguity and oscillation. At the center of this ambiguity is the tension between inside and outside" (Garner 1994: 51). The actor, therefore, operates with a "dual consciousness" in a process of constant modulation of the four bodies with all their ambiguities and tendencies, always ideally thematizing the unfolding score. The actor is inhabiting and embodying a score through which he appears to act "in a world." The actor's breath "appears" to be the character's breath, i.e., the actor's breath both *is* his own and simultaneously "is" the breath of the character.

For the actor as self, the "organic/perceptual circuit" experience knits together all the "bodies" as a gestalt within which there is constant dialectic movement between ecstatic and recessive states with respect to each of the bodies (Leder 1990: 160). None of these "bodies" is settled or absolute but always in a constant state of ambiguity. Therefore, the actor's "lived" experience within the "world" of performance engages a constant dialectic between these four "bodies" or experiential "circuits." Yuasa calls this kind of "knowledge" somatic – "knowledge gained *through the body*" and not "knowledge of the body."

> Such knowledge may be contrasted with "intellectual" knowledge. Intellectual knowledge is that mode of cognition which results from objectifying a given object, which propositionally takes a subject–predicate form, and which divorces the somaticity of the knower from "the mind" of the knower. For these reasons, intellectual knowledge circumscribes its object; it is incapable of becoming one with the object. Somatic knowledge in its immediate, everyday occurrence lacks this objectification. There is a "feeling-judgment"

operative in somatic knowledge. In feeling-judgment, "knowing that" and "feeling that" are one and the same in the constitutive *momentum* of forming a judgment. In this experience, there is an attunement of mind and body, of "I" and other, and of human nature *qua* microcosm and physical nature *qua* macrocosm.

(Nagatomo 1992: 63)

Optimally, in heightened extra-daily activities such as performance the surface and recessive bodies may recede further into the background, but they are always present. The lived body as a gestalt is present as an intersecting, intertwining, "chiasm" of multiple bodies.

The actor's "body" as the "chiasmatic body"

The notion that the experience of the lived body may best be described as a "chiasm" – braiding, intertwining, or criss-crossing – originated with Merleau-Ponty's early description of the intertwining that characterizes the body's fundamental relationship to the world through the surface body (Merleau-Ponty 1968, *passim*). In the model proposed here, the chiasmic nature of experience as a braiding and intertwining is more complexly elaborated in the modulation of the four modes of bodily experience described above: the ecstatic surface, the depth/visceral recessive, the subtle inner bodies, and the fictive body of the actor's score. Leder's analysis adds to Merleau-Ponty the dimension of "depth" or verticality associated with our deep visceral experience (Leder 1990: 62–3). Such verticality is most evident in the voluntary modes of psychophysical practice that awaken experience through the subtle inner body-mind. In yoga and selected martial arts like the yoga-based *kalarippayattu*, when one "exercises" the body-mind through the various forms, one is understood to be literally "braiding," interweaving, or tying "knots" within the inner body. As the practitioner repeats over and over again a form like the lion pose, they move from one lion into another by sliding the rear foot along the earth and inside "through the centre" (or abdomen) before sliding the foot forward. When performed "correctly" with the hips forward and a lengthened spine, the repetitious action of bringing the foot/leg in (to one's centre), and then out (from the centre) constitutes a form of "churning" or "knotting" that literally exercises the lower abdominal region. This act of "tying" or "braiding" creates a constant opposition – the type of opposition we experience when we tie a tight knot in a rope, pulling with our two hands on both ends of the rope simultaneously in opposite directions to tighten the knot. Here the results of long-term exercise of the body as chiasm can be manifest as a grounding "energy" circulated "out" from the lower abdomen, through the feet (the ends of the rope), along the spine, and available to/in the hands (the ends of the rope).

In such heightened modes of psychophysical practice, one is able to experience a "bidirectional incorporation" where "the boundaries between inner and outer … become more porous" (*ibid.*: 165). The lower abdominal region is the activated inner "depth" to and from which one's attentive thematization of the body can travel along the line of the spine outward through the rear foot, out the top of the head, and through the palms. Ideally, within a South Asian paradigm, one's ability to engage and encounter the world is heightened and attuned to the point where "the body becomes all eyes" with an ability to respond immediately through the body-mind to the sensory surround.[14]

The chiasmic model of experience and embodiment outlined here points not to a mode of subjectivity that is unitary in its self-presencing but, rather, the operation of subjectivity as a constantly shifting tactical improvisation modulating between one's body-mind and its modes of engaging its own deployment in the score (physical and textual) during training and performance. One is in a constant process of making adjustments to one's presence and/or absence in relation to the bodies as they encounter *this particular* moment of enactment of a score. Each of these "bodies" might be thought of as a "circuit" of experience. Within the phenomenological model explored here, the actor's complex subjectivity is never settled or fixed within a "present" or a "body" but rather is continuously engaged in a process of its own play with the to's and froms that are characteristic of each mode or circuit of embodiment/experience. The structure of the actor's score provides the actor with one set of tasks or actions to be "played," i.e., to be corporeally engaged with and through one's body-mind.

PSYCHOPHYSICAL TRAINING OF THE SENSES AND KINESPHERE THROUGH ABSENCE

I return now to the earlier discussion of the simple fact that when we fix our visual focus "upon that which lies spatially and temporally ahead, the back of the body is comparatively forgotten. It is absorbed in background disappearance" (Leder 1990: 29). Using *kalarippayattu,* yoga, and *taiqiquan* provides actors with an intense, long-term exposure to training through which their awareness has the possibility of shifting from normative, everyday modes to a more open, heightened kinesthetic mode in which the body "becomes all eyes." As seen in the earlier example of the lion pose, rather than the "back" of the body being forgotten and disappearing, the "negative" or absent space furthest away from the point of external focus can be as fully inhabited as the place of the gaze – one "looks from behind," one "sees" from/through one's feet, keeping an awareness of the feet as the foot moves along the surface of the floor. As the gestalt of the body as a whole expands beyond the surface and recessive bodies to include this inner body-mind, it is possible for the actor to voluntarily thematize both the body and the space around and behind the body that usually disappears.

The simple habitual repetition of a physical form like the lion does not necessarily lead to a discovery of the inner body or an expansion of one's awareness. In the training I provide, I have intentionally developed a language and set of metaphors that assist the practitioner to develop the ability to inhabit an attentive awareness in and through the body-mind. To take another example from *kalarippayattu,* I will explain how I begin to teach the elephant pose (Figure 5.2).

Over time, this process leads to a dialectical thematizing of the "to" and the "from," or a heightening of one's embodied awareness of movement as one moves. Deane Juan explains how tactile/bodily-based sensation can provide "two streams of information ... one that gives me impressions about the object [of touch], and another that gives me impressions about the body part that is doing the contacting and its relationship to the rest of me" (in Johnson 1995: 375).

As described earlier, the lower abdominal, visceral region is that place "to" and "from" which the intertwining extensions of attention/awareness are circulated, thereby enhancing the chiasmatic nature of one's relationship to both self and

Figure 5.2 The beginning position for assuming the elephant pose from *kalarippayattu*: with eyes focused ahead on a specific point, I instruct participants to keep the point of external focus ahead (from the gut) but to also have an awareness of the "negative" space above from the spinal column upward through the top of the head and simultaneously downward from the lower abdomen through the soles of the feet, filling the "negative" space below. Over long-term training, the awareness of the practitioner gradually expands to include the ahead through the external gaze, the behind, and the periphery, as well as the up-and-down vertical emphasized in this photograph. In my own teaching, I constantly side-coach participants to direct their awareness in and through particular parts of the body as we practice, thereby assisting them to internalize the process of thematizing the body and negative space while moving through complex forms. From an intensive training workshop held at Gardzienice Theatre Association, Poland, in May 1999. Photograph by Przemek Sieraczynski.

environment in the process of engaging both. This can easily be seen in yoga *asanas* as well (Figure 5.3).

Through such training, one gradually experiences a state of fuller attentiveness in which one is "physically alert, physically prepared" (Hamilton 2000: 27) to respond or react to something. Learning to "attend to" with the body-mind creates an additional mode and quality of self-presencing within the relationship between oneself and what is being attended to. Acting requires attunement to the subtler qualities and modes of such fully embodied acts of awareness when attending to. It also requires the ability to sustain a fully engaged body-mind relationship between one moment of attending to and the next. This active state of awareness or attending to is not restricted to the visual mode of awareness but is a rendering of the practitioner into a state of body-mind awareness and readiness to respond through the entire range of senses to the environment. It is the engagement of both surface and depth bodies in the voluntary process of chiasmic exercise that renders the possibility of such open engagement both to the depths within and to

Figure 5.3 A demonstration of the extension of breath/energy simultaneously through the top of the head and soles of the feet while executing a yoga *asana*. Like the other poses/movements described above, this simultaneous extension of energy in two directions creates a dynamic opposition from the lower abdomen up and out, and from the lower abdomen out through the feet, thereby "filling" absent or "negative" space. From an intensive training workshop held at Gardzienice Theatre Association, Poland, in May 1999. Photograph used by permission of Przemek Sieraczynski.

the world outside the body.[15] Although hearing, taste, and smell are not overtly engaged in the training, the attuning of the body-mind as a whole to voluntary thematization allows the actor to focus their attention as necessary in the embodied act of tasting, hearing, or smelling as necessary to the realization of a particular performance score. If the attention "drops out," the actor "fails" to maintain the type of awareness that will be sufficient to attract the audience's attention. What differentiates the requirements placed on the actor is precisely the mode of attending to in which the audience engages (*ibid.*, passim) – a gap in the fully embodied attentiveness of the actor can lead to a gap in the audience's attention. The actor's self-presencing engagement is therefore both a to–from for himself and for others.

"ATTENDING TO" IN PERFORMANCE: BRINGING THE ABSENT BODY INTO THE PERFORMATIVE MOMENT

I turn my attention now to two brief examples of how this process is applied to performances that require the actor to discover and utilize a heightened sensory awareness when enacting non-verbal scores, Samuel Beckett's *Act Without Words I* and Ota Shogo's *The Water Station* (1990).[16] Shogo's *The Water Station* requires the actor to engage the body-mind fully in communicating a nonverbal score in which "there are words, but they just can't be heard." Figure 5.4 depicts work on the first scene of the play, in which a girl (or figure) appears in a workshop setting with Gardzienice Theatre Association's Academy students.

After "watching the wind pass," the following sequence of actions takes place in the slightly adapted version I have staged:

> The delicate stream of the water ... her gaze returns toward the fine line of water, the tip of the tongue.
> [Closing her eyes] the transparent line touches the tongue.
> The touch of the water on the tip of the tongue.
> The delicate sound of the water in the gaze of the eyes.
> The tongue to the water, drinking.
> The water flowing through her body.

Figure 5.4 A group work demonstration in Lublin, Poland. Illustrated here is the principle of applying a "double" or multidirectional awareness to fill "negative" or "absent" space. Before the moment enacted here, the Girl/Figure has heard the water and descended to it. While she is sitting beside the water, Ota's text invites the Girl/Figure to "watch the wind pass." How does the actor "watch" the (invisible/absent) wind pass? The apparent problem of this paradox "fits" the approach outlined here as one must psychophysically fill absent space. One cannot literally "see" the wind pass, so one must "sense" the wind passing through the entire body-mind. In the sitting position, the actor's awareness optimally extends from the lower abdomen down through the soles of the feet and in turn along the spine up through the top of the head. As this is a workshop in which participants have not been fully trained over a long period, not surprisingly some pictured here are not as fully engaged through their body-mind as others. Note that the two women are much more engaged psychophysically along their spine line and are therefore much more able to maintain their connection to filling the negative space behind them and be ready to maintain a psychophysical connection to the breath from the lower abdomen on the action that follows.

The sky in the girl's eyes.
The girl's eyes turn to the old road.

My second example is from the conclusion of Beckett's *Act Without Words I.* In 2000–2001, I acted the role of the Protagonist as part of an evening of four short Beckett plays entitled "The Beckett Project," which also included *Ohio Impromptu, Not I,* and *Rockaby.* The play concludes with a series of five actions after the Protagonist has fallen onto the floor when the big cube is pulled out from under him. In our staging – a collaboration with director Peader Kirk – the cube was literally pulled out from under me by the onstage attendant, played by Kirk. I could never absolutely predict the precise position into which I would fall on the floor, but it was always either onto my hands and knees or onto my right side, usually with both my hands or elbows supporting my body weight so that I was not lying completely prone on the floor (Figure 5.6). This allowed me during the fall to ensure that I had adjusted the angle of my final gaze after falling to a place where my face and eyes would be visible to the audience. Beckett insists that the actor remain in the place he has fallen with "his face towards the auditorium, staring before him."

Figure 5.5 Andrea Turner playing the Girl in the opening scene in a full production at the University of Exeter. In this image, the girl fully encounters the running water with the action "the water flows through her body." In embodying this action, we worked on Andrea opening her entire awareness as she takes the water in her mouth. The action "flowing" was played by having Andrea work with following the water with her inner eye down to the deep, visceral interior, just as when learning the initial breathing exercises, where one follows the breath with the inner eye to the abdomen. She was simultaneously keeping an awareness of her back and down through the soles of her feet, so that the resonance of the action of "flowing" was literally through her thematized body.   Photograph by Jon Primrose.

Figure 5.6 Phillip Zarrilli playing the Protagonist in Samuel Beckett's *Act Without Words I*: "Does not move." Image from production videotape by Peter Hulton, Exeter Phoenix Theatre, UK.

The carafe descends from flies and comes to rest a few feet from his body.
He does not move.
The carafe descends further, dangles and plays about his face.
He does not move.
The carafe is pulled up and disappears in flies.
The bough returns to horizontal, the palms open, the shadow returns.
Whistle from above.
He does not move.
The tree is pulled up and disappears in flies.
He looks at his hands.

(Beckett 1984: 46)

The only overt physical action is the final "looks at his hands" (Figure 5.7). The previous three actions are "does not move." There is no better example than this of the requirement for the actor to "stand still while not standing still" (Scott, quoted in Benedetti 1973: 463). This means full engagement in an internal, psychophysical (not psychological) impulse and awareness on each (non)action. In playing the

Figure 5.7 Phillip Zarrilli playing the Protagonist in Samuel Beckett's *Act Without Words I*: "Looks at hands." Image from production videotape by Peter Hulton, Exeter Phoenix Theatre, UK.

Protagonist, it was my task to remain in the position into which I had fallen with no overt movement. Following my breath, and keeping my external gaze ahead through the point where my focus arrived at the end of the fall, I followed each inhalation and exhalation in turn, using my attention to my breath to maintain my exterior focus but keeping an open awareness through my entire body to the stimuli in the theatrical environment. I had to render myself into a place of "not knowing" what the next stimulus might be, even though "knowing" through rehearsal what it was. In response to each action – the carafe, the palm tree, or the whistle – my action was "does not move." Focused ahead, the carafe descends into my field of vision, but I *never* look at it. What I must internally "breath in" and register is not moving in response to its appearance. Each "does not move" was enacted with the breath through my entire body, keeping an awareness in particular of the soles of my feet, the palms supporting my body weight on the floor, and through my eyes and ears. Each action "resonated" through me, but I did not (overtly) move. My task was to psychophysically "fill" the "negative" space through my body, and thereby around me, keeping my perceiving awareness open to each stimuli so that, once the stimuli had "acted" I could embody "not moving" as my response. My final action, "looks at hands," was initiated approximately two beats after the tree had fully disappeared. It was initiated from my lower abdomen on a half-breath, out of the previous four actions of "not moving." Once initiated, the impulse riding the breath traveled through the palms of my hands and external gaze simultaneously. Shifting my body weight if/as necessary, my hands gradually began to open toward one another, and toward my gaze as it traveled on the breath, first to one hand, and then just as slowly, to the other. Keeping my gaze fixed on the second palm, I remained, riding the breath, awareness open behind me, as the spotlight directly lighting my face through my hands gradually faded to black.

CONCLUSION

In our practices as actors, actor trainers, or directors, the implications of the issues raised in this essay include the following: how an understanding of our multiple modes of embodiment and the recessive nature of each body might lead to the development of strategies for enhancing the cultivation of work on impulse, action, and a bodily based awareness in which "absent" or "negative" space is inhabited as part of the performance process. In my own training and performance work, I continue to ask, is it possible for the gestalt of the actor's body as a whole to voluntarily thematize and thereby better inhabit both the body and the space around the body, which usually "disappear?" For example, what happens when one "looks from behind" or maintains an active awareness of the soles of the feet as one part of the dialectic of the bodies in performance? These are open-ended questions of "how" about which I have provided a few examples.

APPENDIX: YASUO YUASA'S BODY SCHEME

Yasuo Yuasa proposes a body scheme comprising four interrelated experiential circuits in order to account for both how we live our bodies from within and how these experiential circuits correlate with neuro-physiological structures of the body – the object-body. The four experiential circuits are:

1. *The external sensory-motor circuit*: this is the circuit that connects the body to the external world through the sensory organs. When we receive experience through this circuit, there is an active motor response via the central nervous system.

2. *The circuit of coenesthesis*: this is the circuit of the internal sensations of the body, consisting (in Yuasa's scheme) of two subdivisions. (1) The "circuit of kinesthesis" operates in close connection with the motor nerves of the external sensory-motor circuit such as the sensory-motor nerves attached to the muscles and tendons of the limbs. These are clearly locatable motor sensations constituting an often invisible awareness that allows us to engage the external world and environment through perception and action, allowing us to engage in many physical activities "unthinkingly" – word processing at a computer, playing the piano, etc. This circuit always stands "ready to activate the body toward an action in the external world" (Nagatomo 1992: 50). (2) The second subdivision of the circuit of coenesthesis is the "circuit of somesthesis" concerned with the internal organs and the even less recognizable set of sensations experienced via the splanchnic nerves attached to these internal organs. In normal health, these sensations recede into the background of awareness. For Yuasa, these sensations form a kind of background awareness of the body. Most importantly, behind our consciousness, there is clearly what Yuasa calls an "automatic memory system" achieved through a training that does not require the conscious effort of recall, i.e., "*the body* learns and knows" (*ibid.* 1992: 51–2).

3. *The emotion – instinct circuit*: for Yuasa, this circuit accounts for our experience of emotion and instinct – those non-localized, whole-body experiences. This circuit is "correlated with the autonomic nervous system, which controls and regulates the function of the various internal organs such as the respiratory organs (lungs), the circulatory organ (heart), and the digestive organs (stomach and colon)" (*ibid.*: 52). As noted above, we do not usually have a conscious awareness of the functioning, under normal circumstances, of the internal organs; however, the "centrifugal path send out to the distal internal organs those stimuli which the brain receives from the external world *vis-à-vis* the sensory organs, converting them into an *emotional response* (i.e., pleasure or pain), which may turn into stress or a stressful response" (*ibid.* 1992: 53).

4. *The circuit of unconscious quasi-body*: this circuit corresponds to the *ki*-meridian system or network beneath the skin covering the entire body and used in acupuncture; it is roughly equivalent to the "subtle body" of yoga. This body circuit "does not conform to either the subject or object bodies," "defies our ordinary understanding," is "invisible" anatomically, and cannot be perceived via external perception. However, through the practice of various methods of self-cultivation, this "invisible" circuit can be made "visible," i.e., it is brought into awareness and utilized. The *ki*-meridian system and the *nadi* of the yogic subtle body are both understood as networks through which "energy" (*ki* in the East Asian system; *prana* and/or *kundalini sakti* in South Asia) is understood to flow. (Although yet to be fully explained biomedically, the existence and efficacy of this circuit is now fully recognized.) The experience of this "quasi-body" takes the form of sensations of "flow," "heat," and/or "vibrations," but are quite different from the experience of nerve impulses.[17]

REFERENCES

Barba, Eugenio. 1985. *The Dilated Body.* Rome: Zeami Libri.

Beckett, Samuel. 1984. *The Collected Shorter Plays of Samuel Beckett.* New York: Grove Press.

Feuerstein, Georg. 1980. *The Philosophy of Classical Yoga.* Manchester: Manchester University Press.

Filliozat, Jean. 1991. *Religion, Philosophy and Yoga.* New Delhi: Motilal.

Griffin, Susan. 1992. *A Chorus of Stones.* New York: Anchor Books.

Grotowski, Jerzy. 1997. "Towards a Poor Theatre." In *The Grotowski Sourcebook*, edited by Lisa Wolford and Richard Schechner, 26–35. London: Routledge.

Hamilton, James R. 2000. "Theatrical enactment." *The Journal of Aesthetics and Art Criticism* 58, 1: 23–35.

Johnson, Don Hanlon, ed. 1995. *Bone, Breath and Gestures: Practices of Embodiment.* Berkeley, Calif: North Atlantic Books.

Johnson, Mark. 1987. *The Body in the Mind: The Bodily Basis of Meaning, Imagination, and Reason.* Chicago: University of Chicago Press.

Lakoff, George and Mark Johnson. 1980. *Metaphors We Live By.* Chicago: University of Chicago Press.

——. 1999. *Philosophy in the Flesh.* New York: Basic Books.

Leder, Drew. 1990. *The Absent Body.* Chicago: University of Chicago Press.

Levine, David Michael. 1985. *The Body's Recollection of Being.* London: Routledge.

Loukes, Rebecca. 2003. "Psychophysical awareness in training and performance: Elsa Gindler and her legacy." Unpublished PhD dissertation. Department of Drama, University of Exeter.

Merleau-Ponty, Maurice. 1962. *Phenomenology of Perception.* London: Routledge and Kegan Paul.

——. 1964. *The Primacy of Perception*, edited by James J. Edie. Evanston, Ill: Northwestern University Press.

——. 1968. *The Visible and the Invisible*, translated by Alphonso Lingus. Evanston, Ill: Northwestern University Press.

Nagatomo, Shigenori. 1992. "An Eastern concept of the body: Yuasa's body-scheme." In *Attunement Through the Body.* Albany: SUNY Press.

Schrag, Calvin O. 1969. *Experience and Being.* Evanston, IL: Northwestern University Press.

Shogo, Ota. 1990. *The Water Station (Mizu no eki)*, translated by Mari Boyd. *Asian Theatre Journal* 7, 2: 150–83.

Varenne, Jean. 1976. *Yoga and the Hindu Tradition.* Chicago: University of Chicago Press.

Wolford, Lisa and Richard Schechner, eds. 1997. *The Grotowski Sourcebook.* London: Routledge.

Zarrilli, Phillip. 1990. "What does it mean to 'become the character?'" In *By Means of Performance,* edited by Willa Appel and Richard Schechner, 132–48. Cambridge: Cambridge University Press.

——. 1997. "Acting 'at the nerve ends': Beckett, Blau and the necessary." *Theatre Topics* 7, 2: 103–16.

——. 1998. *When the Body Becomes All Eyes: Paradigms, Practices, and Discourses of Power in Kalarippayattu, A South Indian Martial Art.* New Delhi: Oxford University Press.

——. 2002. "'On the edge of a breath, looking': cultivating the actor's bodymind through Asian martial/meditation arts." In *Acting Reconsidered*, edited by Phillip Zarrilli, 181–99. London: Routledge.

NOTES

1 Funding for the research required for this essay was provided by a grant from AHRB. The first part of this essay was originally published as "Toward a phenomenological model of the actor's embodied modes of experience" in *Theatre Journal*. It has been further revised and expanded for this publication.

2 Although the model of "contemporary acting" presented in this essay in its present form does not address the experiential bodies of actors with physical or sensory impairments, or how issues of gender or ethnicity impinge on the experiential body, the model could be elaborated in the future to account for modes of embodied experience not addressed here.

3 In this brief essay, I cannot address many of the issues raised by phenomenological approaches to embodiment and experience. Since most phenomenological accounts focus on everyday, normative experience, the second part of this essay begins to move beyond the ordinary by providing an account of one mode of embodiment and experience through which awareness is "cultivated." A fuller phenomenological account of embodiment and experience is only possible when both ordinary and non-ordinary modes are fully considered together. For a history of phenomenology from Edmund Husserl (1859–1938) to the present, and for a discussion of its limitations and possibilities, see Moran (2000).

4 As Stanton Garner explains, "Phenomenology offers to supplement the semiotic (or materialist) body with the phenomenal (and phenomenalizing) body – to counter the signifying body in its dephysicalized readability with what we might call the 'embodied' body in its material resistance. By addressing issues of embodiment, phenomenology opens up the dimension of 'livedness,' of which objectifying theory can give no account and which it must bracket in order to maintain its analytic stance. The phenomenal body resists the epistemological model of a corporeal object yielding its meanings to a decorporealized observer" (1994: 50).

5 Leder trained as a physician and received his MD before turning to philosophy. His phenomenological account is therefore informed by biomedical models of physiology, anatomy, etc. His account is also culturally sensitive, recognizing that any insight about the construction of human experience "involves an ambiguous set of possibilities and tendencies that take on definite shape only with a cultural context. ... The body's practices and self-interpretations are always already shaped by culture" (1990: 151), and I would add also by gender and ethnicity.

6 Rather than dismissing Descartes' body-mind dualism out of hand, Leder addresses his project directly, providing a phenomenologically informed account of how Descartes reached his conclusions. He argues that it is precisely our experience of the body's disappearance that is the foundation for Descartes' body-mind dualism. "Because the body is a tacit and self-concealing structure, the rational mind can come to seem disembodied" (*ibid.*: 108).

7 I focus here on the main features of Leder's account relevant to an examination of my argument in relation to actor training and performance. For an account that in many ways parallels Leder's, see Shigenori Nagatomo's version of Japanese philosopher Yasuo Yuasa's "body-scheme" (1992) and Yuasa's *The Body* (1987).

8 Leder's use of "flesh" and "ecstatic" to mark the surface body are both descriptive but also metaphorical. Similarly, "blood" and "breath" metaphorically mark the second and third bodies, respectively.

9 It is now commonly recognized that biofeedback techniques or yoga can lead to a lowering of blood pressure through operant conditioning (Leder 1990: 53).

10 On yoga, see Jean Varenne (1976), Georg Feuerstein (1980), and Jean Filliozat (1991). On *kalarippayattu* and its relationship to the yogic paradigm, see Zarrilli (1998: 123–53; and

1989). Although culturally specific, the map and paradigm of the yogic subtle body points to a type of experience of the "body" not addressed by the biomedical paradigm.

11 Since my discussion focuses on acting, I have chosen to use the term extra-daily to mark the type of non-ordinary, voluntary modes of engagement described here. The pursuit of non-ordinary modes of experience can be applied to the practice of everyday living, as is the ideal in certain forms of Buddhist engagement in the everyday world, or as evident in the legacy of Elsa Gindler and body awareness training for everyday life (see, for example, Loukes 2003).

12 Leder explains that "Such schemas are meant to have not only explanatory but phenomeno-logical power, charting experiences open to the ordinary person or to those who engage in spiritual practices. These energetic portrayals may capture the subtle and shifting quality of inner experience better than an image of fixed, massy organs" (1990: 182–3). The aesthetic inner body corresponds to Yasuo's fourth circuit, the "circuit of unconscious quasi-body," which mediates between the other experiential circuits (Nagatomo 1992: 59).

13 Whether or not the type of awareness cultivated in relation to a specific practice is transferable to other practices, or to daily life, is an interesting but complex question that cannot be fully addressed in this essay.

14 For a full elaboration of this metaphor of optimal body-mind engagement, see Zarrilli (1998).

15 Barba describes this optimal body-mind awareness as "the bridge which joins the physical and mental bank ... the river of creative process" – the actor's body and mind are "dilated" (1985: 14-15).

16 There is not space here to describe the additional process of long-term training that provides a bridge between the preliminary psychophysical training through "structured improvisations." These structures provide actors with a specific set of limited tasks to which they apply their work with attentiveness to the breath and impulse through the body discussed below. These tasks appear as performances to the observer. Another production example is *The Unseen*, my adaptation of Maurice Maeterlinck's *The Blind* for performance in a pitch-black space where the actors, denied sight, had to open and maintain the fully heightened awareness of their bodies while depending totally on their aural and tactile senses.

17 Yoshio Nagahama's experimental tests reveal that "the vibration of *ki*-energy is measured as 15–50 cm/sec. while nerve-impulses travel 5–80 m/sec." (Nagatomo 1992: 66).

6

MAKING SENSE OF FOOD IN PERFORMANCE
The table and the stage[1]

Barbara Kirshenblatt-Gimblett

What would theatre history look like if it were to be written backwards from the Futurist banquets and Dali dinners and performance art? Canonical histories of theatre take as their point of departure that which counts as theatre in the modern period – namely, theatre as an autonomous art form – and search for its "origins" in fused art forms. Central to the notion of theatre as an independent art are plays, and as an indication of the maturing of this form, a dedicated architecture or theatre (literally a place of seeing). Canonical theatre histories are written with the aim of understanding how modern theatre came to be. Understandably, the search is for corollaries in the past. Thus, Oscar G. Brockett's *History of Theatre* is a history of drama and its performance: it does not view courtly banquets, tournaments, royal entries, and street pageants as performance genres in their own right but as occasions for plays and playlets. Such histories attend not to the fusion but to the seeds of what would become an independent art form called theatre.

It has taken considerable cultural work to isolate the senses, create genres of art specific to each, insist on their autonomy, and cultivate modes of attentiveness that give some senses priority over others. To produce the separate and independent arts that we know today, it was necessary to break fused forms like the banquet apart and to disarticulate the sensory modalities associated with them. Not until the various components of such events (music, dance, drama, food, sculpture, painting) were separated and specialized did they become sense-specific art forms in dedicated spaces (theatre, auditorium, museum, gallery) with distinct protocols for structuring attention and perception. It was at this point that food disappeared from musical and theatrical performances. No food or drink is allowed in the theatre, concert hall, museum, or library. In the process, new kinds of sociality supported sensory discernment specific to gustation, the literary practice of gastronomy, and increasing culinary refinement. Food became a sense-specific art form in its own right, as Marinetti's *Futurist Cookbook* so vividly demonstrates (Kirshenblatt-Gimblett 1989).

OPERA GASTRONOMICA

Although food was removed from the theatre as the theatre became an autonomous art, the table and the stage continued to have a shared history. Indeed, the musical banquet, or *opera gastronomica*, may well have preceded the theatrical *opera in musica* by more than a century. According to Jenny Nevile, the musical banquet "had already reached a state of complete or 'operatic' composition by the late fifteenth century. The dining hall, it seems, was one of the first scenes of modern musical theatre" (Nevile 1990).[2]

A legacy of such courtly banquets, the *tish*, literally "table" in Yiddish, is a distinctive Hasidic event during which the *rebe* (charismatic leader) holds court in the community's house of study. The *tish* is a musical banquet of sorts, during which the *rebe* will bless food, deliver a discourse, lead song, and dance with his followers. It is as part of the *tish* that musical plays are performed in fulfillment of the religious obligation to gladden the heart of the *rebe* on the holiday of Purim. In what is essentially a command performance before a regal figure, the actors play to the *rebe*, who is seated directly in front of them on a throne-like chair. For those in attendance, the *rebe* and his reactions are the center of attention, not the play, and the best seats in the house are those that afford an unobstructed view of him (and secondarily of the play). The stage is literally a physical extension of the table such that the performance could be said to take place on the table itself.

The food the *rebe* blesses, while it includes the basic components of a festive meal, is present not to satisfy physical hunger but rather in the interest of commensality. People eat beforehand. The hunger they bring to the event is spiritual. Once the *rebe* has blessed the food and eaten a little of it, his leavings (*shirayim*) are eagerly grabbed by his followers, who may well number in the thousands. The *rebe*'s leavings have been transvalued by his touch.[3] While the quantities presented to him are grand and the vessels are lavish, neither he nor his followers eat out of physical hunger. Nor is the food itself spectacular, although the large braided *hallah*, a festive bread made with white flour and eggs, is beautiful. Like the courtly banquets to which it is related, the *tish* is a multi-sensory event and food is an essential component of it, even in the absence of appetite.

The European banquet is one of four types of *festa*, the others being the entry, the tournament, and the popular carnival, according to Nevile. Historians of modern operatic traditions have "detected a long series of pre-operatic experiments in musical theatre, going back mainly to the dining hall, but also the ballroom, the riding school, the courtyard, the city square, the garden and other spaces temporarily adapted as theatre before there were any such regular structures available" (Pont 1990: 117). These experiments, which were based on "the model of the sacred banquet, and its musical elaboration in the sung mass," resulted in "artistically planned and fully composed musical banquets, particularly those with music performed throughout the dining" (117).

As Nevile notes, "the official banquet had always functioned as more that [*sic*] just an elaborate meal and social occasion" (128). By combining "the skills of cooking, decoration, music, dancing, poetry, architecture (for scene construction), costume design and painting," the banquet made tangible and sensuous the power of the host and those being honored (128). However, it was not until the latter part of the fifteenth century that all the different elements that had been part of the banquet for several centuries (that is, music and dance, as well as food), were united to produce a coherent performance with a single theme – in other words, a "gastronomic opera" (128). It had become "a unified theatrical event," as can be seen in Italian examples between 1450 and 1475 (130). Such events might last as long as seven hours – the Hasidic *tish*, it should be noted, can last all night and well into the morning.

The banquet was the most "total" of Renaissance festive events, particularly in the way that it engaged the senses and the various media associated with them: "The drama of the musical banquet was finally presented as a fusion of all the arts of music, dancing, poetry, food, painting, sculpture, costume, and set design, to present a feast for all the senses, as well as the intellect, in a range of moods encompassing the tragic, the comic, and the pastoral" (134). (It could be said that the orgy is even more complete in so far as it included not only eating, singing, dancing, eating, and drinking, but also sexual activity.[4]) If the fifteenth-century French banquet was marked by abundance, the sixteenth-century banquet was characterized by rarity and refinement (Wheaton 1983: 52). Moreover, what had been a fused form became separate specialized entities, as can be seen from the transformation of the *entremets*, the between-courses divertissements. According to Barbara Santich, the *entremets*:

> were visually and theatrically spectacular, incorporating elements of surprise and trickery to amaze and impress the guests. Almost invariably, music was an integral part of the *entremets*, which were the product of the kitchen [though they were designed by professional artists], elaborated under the charge of the head cook. ... For the banquets of the sixteenth century, however, the *entremets* had undergone a transformation. The culinary and the theatrical elements separated. The *entremets* as spectacle became almost purely theatrical (music, mime, dance, and acrobatics can all be subsumed under the heading of theatre), leaving the cooks free to devote all their skills to the culinary art, the visual display.
>
> (Santich 1990: 110)

One reason for this development in France, she suggests, is the development of greater technical proficiency in the culinary arts and the movement north of Italian banquet traditions. In Santich's view, "as a total art-form, the banquet probably reached its apogee in the seventeenth century, when Louis XIV entertained at Versailles" and with Inigo Jones's Banqueting House in Whitehall, which "was more important as a theatrical setting for court masques than for feasts" (111). *Les plaisirs de l'isle enchantée*, in the spring of 1664, was the first and perhaps best remembered of Louis XIV's *grand fêtes*, thanks to the engravings by Isräel Silvestre.

According to Barbara Wheaton, the record is generally "silent on the details of banquet menus" in France, although these events were lavishly documented in engravings and accompanying text, which listed many of the foods on the table (Wheaton 1983: 42). Perhaps food was so fused with spectacle that the images and accounts that remain of the edible allegorical tableaux are the playbill and menu in one. Consistent with evidence from the Middle Ages, these commemorative documents say more about what food looked like than how it tasted. Visual effects, rarity of ingredients, opulence, and the sequence of events, Wheaton suggests, were more important than the dishes, their ingredients, preparation, or flavors. Indeed, flavor might even be compromised for the sake of appearance (15, 49). And for good reason.

These were monumental events, viewed from a distance by crowds of people over many hours. Flavor cannot be witnessed. Appearance can. Flavor is momentary. Appearance endures. The operating principle, "for show," required that appearance dominate, as did the emphasis on a legible (edible) visual language of emblems and signs. This was, one might say, a cuisine of signs, a world made edible. It was discursive food addressed to the senses. It was food to be seen, touched, inhaled, ingested, absorbed, and embodied, not only as substance but also as meaning.[5] It was made to disappear, if not down the hatch, then pillaged at the end of the meal. Wanton destruction was the height of luxury, a dramatic gesture of conspicuous consumption. A surfeit of labor, skill, and material, expressed clearly in visual excess, surpassed the limits of appetite, which is otherwise relatively quickly satiated. The fugitive nature of food is perfectly suited to such stagings.

REPAS EN AMBIGUS

Banquets were important to court life and continued into the Baroque period, a feature of which is the transferability of devices from the stage to the dining room. The *repas en ambigu* (an elaborate formal composition of dishes laid out in a room), which was fashionable in the late seventeenth century, could, "in instances of particular luxury ... transform the whole dining room into culinary theater" (el-Khoury 1997: 58). As Rodolphe el-Khoury explains:

> In the "ambigu," the temporal succession of multiple courses is thus eliminated in favor of the visual effect of a unified tableau. Such meals are composed as a spectacle for the eyes and do not necessarily involve an oral consumption of food: "the pleasure of seeing them is greater than that of touching them" states L.S.R. ... The "surtout de table," the central element of the "ambigu," is often directly transposed from the stage set of the theater and is obviously not meant for oral consumption.
>
> (*ibid.*: 58)[6]

Indeed, the *repas en ambigu* is a one-act play: "it seeks the utmost impact in the first glance; it attempts to embrace the entire range of possibilities in a single scene" (quoted in *ibid.*: 60, from Stewart 1985). Not surprisingly, the *repas en ambigu* was not only theatrical in its own right but also lent "its name to a series of plays and in 1769, to a theater specializing in the genre," according to Philip Stewart (quoted in *ibid.*: 62, from Stewart 1985: 89).

A startling contemporary example of the convergence of table and stage – with an uncanny affinity with the *tables volantes* or *tables machinées* in seventeenth-century France – occurs in *Arbeit macht frei vom Toitland Europa*, which I saw the Acco Theatre Centre perform in Haifa in 1996.[7] In this environmental performance, there is a point where the audience is ushered into a low-ceilinged room and seated on benches around its perimeter. Suddenly, an enormous table drops down from the ceiling, as if from nowhere, and we are pressed to eat delicious food, which we do, as the actors barrage us with violent language and painful "topics of conversation." Suddenly, the table is hoisted up and disappears. Compare this scene with a seventeenth-century proposal for a flying table, which could be:

> lifted all at once by a machine in such a way that the surface of the table, the frame as well as its attachments, is composed by a section of the raised floor. ... When the guests

enter the dining room, there is not the least sign of a table; all that can be seen is a uniform floor that is adorned by a rose at its center. At the slightest nod, the leaves are retracted under the floor, and a table laden with food makes its sudden ascent, flanked by four servants emerging through the four openings.

(el-Khoury 1997: 62, citing Bonnet in Grimod de la Reynière and Bonnet 1978: 64–5)

In another instance, the table disappeared into the basement and a new one descended with the next course (*ibid.*: 60). However, the spectacle was not solely for the pleasure of the diners, for their delight was a spectacle in its own right, and royal banquets might include places for spectators. By the nineteenth century, we can find the elaboration of an explicitly theatrical gastronomy: "The dining-room is a theatre wherein the kitchen serves as the wings and the table as the stage. This theatre requires equipment, this stage needs a décor, this kitchen needs a plot" (Aron 1975: 214, citing Chatillon-Plessis 1894).

CULINARY THEATRE

With the French Revolution, but already before it, such courtly practices as the banquet were supplanted by new forms of festivity, as Mona Ozouf (1988) has shown, and new forms of sociability, for which Jean Anthelme Brillat-Savarin (1971, first published in 1825) provides a manual. With the weakening of guilds, the proliferation of freelance cooks, the professionalizing of chefs, and the emergence of restaurants, food becomes part of a different mode of sociality, one that is more intimate and better suited to focused attention on the nuances of taste.[8] The restaurant emerges as the dedicated space of food theatre: "Traditionally, the menu has been a kind of playbill, varying with the theme of the drama" (Patton 1998).

About his recent design for a Houston nightclub on the theme of Shakespeare's *The Tempest*, Jordan Mozer said, "What better metaphor for a restaurateur than the magician – or the playwright – who uses his art to transform other people's lives in the span of three hours?" (quoted in Henderson 1992: 70) Mozer's circular radial plan "suggests the island upon which the play takes place" (*ibid.*: 70). The circular dance floor and skylight and the architectural twists and tilts evoke a windswept island, eye of a storm, and magic circle. Of his design for Kachina, in Los Angeles, David Kellen said, "I didn't want it to be just a specialty restaurant, but more like an abstract stage for a play set in the southwest"(quoted in Richards 1992: 76). These restaurants are overtly theatrical in their staging of another time and place. They provide a setting, an ambience, and a script for social encounters that can involve food, drink, conversation, music, and dance.

Self-consciously theatrical restaurants heighten the already staged nature of public eating places. Some clearly demarcate the front and back regions, with serene dining rooms out front and industrial kitchens in back (see Goffman 1959; MacCannell 1976). Others bring the back region of the performing kitchen forward and restage it as a back region. Artisanal techniques are specially suited to staging and are frequently visible from the street or dining room of even ordinary restaurants. The pizza maker rolls and twirls the dough in a window facing the street. The brick pizza oven may be visible from the dining room. The Indian chef slaps *naan* against the hot interior walls of a tandoori oven within a glass room looking out onto the dining room of an upscale restaurant. At Honmura An, an upscale Japanese restaurant in

Manhattan, diners can watch a chef making their soba noodles in a glass cube within an elegant dining room lined with teak. Chinese cooks wield their knives on glazed ducks and whole barbecued pigs next to the cash register. Working at a long counter, the deli man slices hot pastrami and piles it high between slices of fresh rye bread, offering tidbits to customers in hope of a tip. Sushi chefs trim the glistening fish, pat the rice into neat ovals, and artfully arrange a platter before the diners seated at the bar in front of him. Diners walk past their dinner swimming in fish tanks lining the entrance to seafood restaurants, in which case it is the food itself that might be said to perform.

Maître d's understand their dining rooms and chefs their kitchens as performances. Roger Fessaguet, former chef/owner of La Caravelle restaurant in Manhattan, which closed in 2004 after forty-three years in business, describes himself as a conductor and his kitchen as an orchestra, with sections paralleling the strings, wind instruments, and drums.[9] He is describing the experience of working in a particular type of kitchen, one that was developed by Georges Auguste Escoffier (1847–1935) to organize what were then the new large hotel restaurants. They had to produce many different meals quickly while maintaining high quality. Escoffier was inspired not by the orchestra but by the rational techniques of mass production and the divisions of labor associated with the factory. Rather than have one person make one dish from start to finish, in the manner of a traditional craftsman, Escoffier segmented the various tasks and organized a division of labor in the kitchen and interdependence between workers grouped according to type of operation rather than type of dish. Stephen Mennell compares the two approaches with respect to one dish, *oeufs à la plat Meyerbeer*: "Under the old system, it would have taken a single cook about fifteen minutes to prepare in its entirety; under the new, the eggs were cooked by the *entremettier* [department responsible for soups, vegetables, and desserts], kidney grilled by the *rôtisseur,* and truffle sauce prepared by the *saucier*, and the whole assembled in a only a few minutes" (Mennell 1985: 159). While the arrangement is efficient, it makes for a particular kind of cooking experience.

Fessaguet's characterization is meant to capture the intensity, focus, split-second timing, and extraordinary coordination required to complete innumerable dishes, each of them made of up of many components, in ever-changing combinations and sequences, so that each table in a room of many tables may be served what it has ordered for a particular course all at the same time, at the right temperature. Not only stringent quality standards but also grace under pressure must be maintained under these demanding conditions. Indeed, this consummate performance must appear effortless. Or rather, effort must be carefully staged and performed as a marker of the value of the meal and the experience. Fessaguet's orchestra metaphor – he literally "conducts" the kitchen – clearly envisions the cooking process as a performance. When everything is working, the kitchen is an ensemble performance improvising on a scenario. The diners get a three- or four-act play, each table its own performance, complete with program notes or menu. For the staff, the whole evening has a rhythm and a dramatic structure.

Timing is critical to the sensory character of food and more specifically to the interaction of the thermal, haptic, and alchemic. More than a tuning of the instruments or warming up of the performers, the kitchen runs on multiple clocks. Those clocks are set to the conditions of light, heat, cold, air, and agitation that produce wine, vinegar, pickles, olives, cheese, bread, sauces, and roasts, over years, months, days, minutes, and split seconds. Freshly picked corn must reach boiling water so quickly that should one trip on the way from the field to the pot, the corn will arrive too late, or so it is said.

Timing becomes performative in a distinctive way the closer the food comes to the diner; the more precipitous the moment twixt cup and lip, the smaller the temporal window. It is reported that Escoffier was preparing individual dessert soufflés for 100 guests at a state dinner. The after-dinner speeches went on longer than expected, and there was no clear indication of when they would end. So that the soufflés would be ready at the exact time the speeches finished, Escoffier began baking off 100 of them every three minutes until the speakers were done (Lang 1980: 93–4).[10] Only the last 100 were taken to the table. So important is timing that "as Madame de Sévigné recounted in a celebrated letter, Vatel [the *officier de bouche* of the Prince de Condé during the eighteenth century] killed himself because provisions on which he was counting did not arrive in time"(Revel 1982: 191). He had been counting on fresh fish from Boulogne for a dinner planned for the king, and "if he had not committed suicide, he would have been put to death by either the *officier de cuisine* or the master of the household" (191).

Restaurant kitchens are fascinating to watch, and some restaurants put them on display. Display kitchens, according to Lee Simon, create the perception that the cuisine is of higher quality, the preparation more careful, and the food safer, but above all they provide "an element of theater" (Simon 2004, part 1). However, not all kitchen functions are "appetizing," and washing and garbage areas are not likely to be included in the display. Simon explains that designing a display kitchen should take into account the visual impact of "layers of activity," whether in the form of equipment that is always going (rotisseries, ovens, broilers) or strategically located stations, the kinds of view afforded from the dining room, and flow (smooth rather than chaotic interaction of kitchen staff and servers) (*ibid.*, part 2).

A "display kitchen" is the centerpiece of Brentwood Bar and Grill in Los Angeles. According to an industry magazine, "culinary theater at Brentwood is packing the house"(*Foodservice Equipment and Supplies Specialist* 1990: 57). What kind of theatre is it? It is a classic example of what happens when performance, in the sense of doing, is a show. The key to this form of culinary theatre is the exhibition value of labor that has been staged in a transparent workspace. Brentwood Bar and Grill does not just have a kitchen, it has a "truly dazzling display kitchen with a Waldorf-style cooking line [that] showcases culinary talent as entertainment"(57). One kitchen consultant explicitly likens this kitchen to theatre and ballet. While this kitchen offers a work environment that is at once functional, social, and comfortable, an industry magazine says of the Waldorf-type line: "Primary, of course, is its display value"(58). Indeed, true to the etymology of theatre, from Greek terms for watching and viewing, this kind of culinary theatre converts performance, in the sense of doing, into theatre, that is, into an exhibition of itself. This restaurant, which caters to movie industry crowds, has become a place for the "beautiful people … to see and be seen, to watch and eat" (57). Thanks to the design, they can look through glass partitions from the bar and see into the dining room as well as into the open kitchen. That kitchen has been created in line with the principle of "full-exhibition design"(58). It has, in a word, been staged for viewing. As reviewers have noted, "Cooking-themed theater productions are all the rage, but nothing compares to the drama of a bustling open kitchen at a real restaurant. Plus, you get to eat the props" (Rausfeld and Patronite 2004). A prized table is the one within the restaurant kitchen itself, whether in the open or in its own glass room, with food preparation visible on all sides.

While tableside cooking has long been a feature of classic French restaurants – the waiter finishes the dish in the dining room – chefs are also moving out of the kitchen to cook in the dining room. What they call "exhibition cooking" expands the dining experience to include the sensory pleasures associated with cooking by exhibiting it. Emil Cerno Jr, the chef at Richardson-Vicks in Connecticut, prepared stir-fry in the dining room in a wok on a gas flambé range. Patrons chose their ingredients, which he prepared with aromatic "walnut or sesame oil so it smells good, and you hear the sizzle when the meat hits the oil. It looks good, smells good, sounds good and tastes good" (*Restaurants and Institutions* 1990: A-232).

However, this is cooking in the dining room, not eating in the kitchen: the meat that will go into the wok is presented in decorative cups of kale leaves, "so the presentation is nice" (A-232). Chefs become "exhibitionists." According to an industry magazine: "Customers are treated to a show in dining rooms as chefs cook a variety of food in front of them" (A-230). Note the terminology of *showing*, which suggests that doing has become demonstrating, and *exhibitionism*, which suggests a certain excess in displaying what would normally just get done. While "exhibition cooking" does produce food that patrons will eat, preparing food in the dining room before their very eyes also "gives chefs a chance to get out of the kitchen and meet their customers while giving customers opportunities to see their food freshly made" and to order (A-230). "Freshly made" is both an issue and an illusion: the omelets, for example, are made in advance and filled to order. In other words, even the idea of "freshly made" must be signified. It is not simply performed, in the sense of carrying out an action. It is show business, literally.

Exhibition cooking differs from the display kitchen. Not only does it occur outside the kitchen but also it is staged differently – from the aesthetic *mise en place* on a steam table to such specialized equipment as the butane gas burner or the enormous griddle in Mongolian barbecue restaurants. Moreover, some dishes are considered showier than others or better suited for exhibition, including the sushi bar, raw oyster bar, crepes, large roasts, stir-fry. Anything that can be completed from start to finish in a relatively short period of time is a candidate, particularly if the process involves a visible transformation. The process itself provides the dramatic structure. As one chef observed: "Tossing salads and cooking to order are show times for us, and it's good customer contact" (*Restaurants and Institutions* 1990: A-234).[11]

Entire scenes form around a particular food (pizzeria, steak house, pancake house, creperie, bagelry, crab house, lobster palace, clam bar) or beverage (coffee shop, tea house, soda fountain, juice bar, milk bar, gin palace, tap room, wine bar, cocktail lounge, beer garden). These scenes are distinguished by their architecture, décor, ambience, social style, equipage, schedule, music, fashion, and cuisine, and by the close attention paid to the details of the provisioning, preparation, presentation, and consumption of the defining food or drink.

Describing his career as a bartender since the early 1970s, Dale DeGroff had to learn finesse and showmanship. "The bar is a stage," he said. "The curtain goes up, the spotlight is on you and you perform" (Grimes 1991: C1). What does the patron see? "When shaking a cocktail, [DeGroff] counts a slow 10 times and works his silver shaker hard, alternating between a graceful over-the-shoulder flourish and a front-of-the-body maraca-style move" (*ibid.*: C1). His sense of vocation is expressed in a strong sense of pride in the history and tradition of the cocktail. The bar may be a stage, but it is also a kind of museum: DeGroff characterizes the saloons of New York as "a natural resource, like the redwoods in California … I like to think of myself as a forest ranger" (*ibid.*: C1). Wherever there are mixtures (cocktails, chili, bouillabaisse) or fermentation (wine, beer, cheese, olives) or varieties, whether by virtue of species or processing (coffee, tea), there is a wide berth for connoisseurship. Small variations form a kind of foodprint or signature by which a particular bartender or chili maker can be identified, and devotees will gather themselves around their favorite provisioner.

The cocktail, more than the other examples cited here, lends itself to fantastic elaborations. To be found at Asia de Cuba in the East Village of Manhattan, in 1998, was the Tiki Puka Puka, "a two-fisted, three-person $18 libation served in what Trader Vic's used to call a volcano bowl. Ringed with dancing hula girls, a miniature Krakatoa rising from the middle, this ceramic vessel could double as a South Seas tureen" (DeCaro 1998). The drink itself was made with rum, Cointreau, lime and tropical fruit juices, and "garnished with two umbrellas, three 16-inch straws, four cherries, six chunks of pineapple and a crushed-ice snowball doused in grenadine and 151-proof rum" (DeCaro 1998). The event – the performance, if you will – is the cocktail, fully staged in its own volcano bowl. It is a performing object and reminder, on a small scale, of the sotelties, *surtouts,* and conceits that surprised and amazed guests at the Renaissance banquets discussed earlier. Frank DeCaro relates the scene represented by this drink to the loungecore movement – "it is the latest craze among the post-neo-Rat-Pack hipsters" – and a resurgence of interest in Tiki culture. Just ten years earlier, Donald Trump closed the motherlode of Tiki culture, Trader Vic's, which had been at the Plaza in Manhattan for about twenty-five years. It had "gotten tacky," and Trump considered a health club and restaurant featuring Chinese and Japanese cuisine more in keeping with the image of the hotel (n.a. 1989).

Under the banner of the Cocktail Nation, the cocktail has also become a rallying point for a stylishly oppositional subculture of the swank and fabulous that is part retro, part queer, and part mystique.[12] According to Joseph Lanza, "The cult of the cocktail is a successful religious ceremony transformed into a secular rite. The bartender is the high priest, the drink is the sacramental cup, and the cocktail lounge is akin to a temple or cathedral that uses lights, music, and even ceiling fixtures to reinforce moods of comfort and inspiration" (Lanza 1995: 74). While DeGroff offers showmanship in the execution of his duties as a barman, Lanza is characterizing the social performance of the lounge and its intense ritualization. The language of cult and sacrament suggests not so much the Mass as the Dionysian orgy, a theme expressed more explicitly in drinks that fall under the heading "Blush on the Rocks" (Hess 1998).[13]

Both are attuned to the role of these sites as third places, which Ray Oldenburg (1989) defines as places of sociability that are neither home nor work. The founder of the Salvation Army, William Booth, recognized that "The tap-room in many cases is the poor man's only parlor. Many a man takes to beer not for the love of beer, but for the natural craving for the light, warmth, company, and comfort which is thrown in along with the beer, and which he cannot get excepting by buying beer" (Booth 1890: part 1, chapter 6). Until reformers could compete with the social attractions of the tap-room, he explained, they would not succeed in getting rid of the place and the drinking associated with it. So defining is the conviviality of the café that cybercafés have proliferated online and offline.

Even the word "cybercafé" has entered the dictionary, the 1997 *Microsoft® Bookshelf® Computer and Internet Dictionary©* to be precise. This dictionary defines cybercafé first, as a coffee shop or restaurant that provides both Internet access and food and drink, and second, as a "virtual café on the Internet, generally used for social purposes" using a chat program, newsgroup, or website (see Schumacher 1998). While the Internet allows one to enlarge the social world to which one has access from the phenomenal café, the virtual café, which is entirely online, is strictly about conviviality. And, although it borrows many of the conventions of the café, the online cybercafé cannot supply coffee. What it can supply is the kind of conversation one might expect over coffee. Not surprisingly, cafés have websites, and a cybercafé may well operate both on and offline. In a related development, the café is both the name and the model for websites and listservs associated with scenes (Café Los Negroes, NYC, is "New York's black and latino virtual hangout") and zines (Café Blue) and magazines (*Atomic Café*, now a webzine).[14]

FOOD IN THE THEATRE[15]

Commenting on the preponderance of food on the stage during the 1989 theatre season in New York, Mel Gussow remarked:

> The obsession reflects the interests of a public that is captivated by the theatricality of the dining experience, by designer restaurants where presentation is as important as the food. People demand sizzle in their fajitas – show business for the money. In the theater, it may be an attempt to win back an audience that prefers to spend its entertainment dollar (or $100) eating rather than watching. Both "Tamara" and "Tony 'n' Tina's Wedding" capture two segments of the population by serving dinner along with drama. In the other examples of theater of food, the theatergoer becomes a voyeur. Only the aroma passes his way [if that].
>
> (Gussow 1989: 5)[16]

Gussow cites the grouper tortellini in Richard Greenberg's *Eastern Standard* and the swordfish without butter in Wendy Wasserstein's *Heidi Chronicles*. Scenes are set in trendy cafés, dingy coffee shops, Chinese restaurants, and bars. Characters are waiters, diners, *maître d*'s and chefs. While cocktails are prevalent in plays about WASP society, "almost every play at the Pan Asian Repertory Theater has an obligatory eating scene, and on every opening night there is a Pan Asian banquet in the lobby"(9). Gussow even posits a "Hall of Fame for Food on Stage," to include cornflakes from Harold Pinter's "The Birthday Party"(9). He might have added the carcass from André Antoine's 1888 production of Fernand Icre's *The Butchers*. In what was a radical practice at the time, Antoine's Théâtre Libre, in Paris, was famous for using real properties, when possible, for the most realistic effect (Brockett and Findlay 1973: 91).

But what exactly are the actors on stage eating? And, under what conditions? For George Furth's "Precious Sons," Anthony Rapp had to down a mound of scrambled eggs that were really "a cold, gooey mixture of gelatin, pineapple juice and yogurt. What's more, he has to look as if he is enjoying a nice warm breakfast" (Bennetts 1986). In other words, this brand of verisimilitude demands that he really eat, but not that he really eat scrambled eggs, and that he fake the indicators of sensory response (only he knows whether the eggs are hot or cold). The act of eating – not the substance and not its sensory qualities (except for appearance) – must be convincing. The theatrical sign is indeed arbitrary. All that is required is that the food look like what it is supposed to be and that the actor be able to swallow it, a challenge in itself. Actors are asked to endure fake shrimp ("stale Wonder Bread cut to look like shrimp and painted with food coloring") and cold meat with cold, canned gravy (Bennetts 1986). They often consume what they are served under demanding conditions – at high speed, in large volume, or while doing something else. They must eat on cue whether or not they are hungry and no matter what the food is or tastes like. Is such food, which is surely more unpleasant than necessary, a test of their professional mettle?

In the case of expensive foods like shrimp and caviar, the need for substitutions are understandable, particularly when vast quantities are called for – 150 gallons of caviar for *Saturday Night Live* – and very little if any of it may be eaten. Moreover, some skits call for foods that would challenge the most intrepid of actors – eyeballs on baked potatoes or a neon-blue fish – for these are first and foremost props. Tony Ciolini, a professional restaurant chef who created food props for *Saturday Night Live* in the 1980s, made the "caviar" from forty pounds of tapioca colored with burnt caramel (twenty-two pounds of sugar) and the eyeballs (for a Halloween skit) from mozzarella and black olives (Collins 1990: 6). Food may also fill in for other substances: in response to "the request for something to accessorize the show's Flab-o-Suction machine, a liposuction device for movie stars," Ciolini and the crew thought of "using 10 pounds of custard for the suctioned flab" (6). The qualities valued here are not only the look but also the consistency of the food, for these props have to perform in their own right. Pork chops were blackened and frozen so they would respond like hockey pucks in a sketch featuring Wayne Gretzky, the ice hockey star: "he was playing a busboy who likes to clear tables with a hockey stick" (6).

Whereas these props operate outside the body, the circus, sideshow, and magic show provide a rich repertoire of stunts that challenge the body to incorporate and eject such foreign things and substances as light bulbs, swords, live animals, and fire. In juggler Penn Jillette's apple routine, "he eats 100 needles stuck into an apple; then he eats a length of thread; then he eats the apple, swallowing ostentatiously – and then pulls out of his mouth several yards of meticulously threaded needles" (Bennetts 1986). In contrast to the faux foods made as props for the stage, Jillette uses actual apples and stages the sleight of hand itself. Functions of the hand – threading a needle – are displaced to the body's interior. The body's portal, normally a barrier to "foreign" objects, is violated with impunity. There is easy, if magical, movement in and out of the mouth. Reversing the normal process of eating, what comes out of the mouth is not only intact but in better condition (the needle is threaded) than when it went in. The body's interior has the quality of chamber, the limbs retracted, where needles can be threaded, swords enter and leave, fire disappears.

Inspired by vaudeville and performance art, Blue Man Group does a send-up of art making and the art world by making a mess that becomes a painting. Their performances have been described as "an opportunity to regress," an "all-out sensory assault," and as bringing "an element of untrammeled infantile sensuality" into the theatre (Frank Rich, quoted in Hubbard 1992; Leonard 1997; Goldberg 1991). Blue Man (actually three men, heads shaved and painted cobalt blue, act in concert) is a humanoid from "inner space" that his creators picture as "having been born off a painting, being this moist gooey thing" (Leonard 1997; Hubbard 1992). Matt Goldman, Phil Stanton, and Chris Wink, who invented and often performed Blue Man, yearn for the community and communication that they identify with the salon and try to *blesh* (a science fiction term for blend and mesh) with their audience. If you sit in the first few rows, it will be under a sheet of plastic to protect you from the mess that flies in all directions. Blue Man "wades into the audience more than once, and in the ecstatic finale dances on the armrests of the spectators' seats" while the entire space of the theatre is filled with pulsating sound, throbbing strobe lights, and paper streaming down on the audience (Goldberg 1991). Blue Man also invites audience members to come up onto the stage, share the "feast," become painting tools or musical instruments, and subject themselves to the food assault.

With backgrounds in business, catering, art, and theatre, the creators of Blue Man Group draw on everything they have learned, and then some. *Tubes*, which opened at the Astor Theatre in Manhattan in 1991, is appropriately named, for they use tubes from industrial food processing, gardening hoses and their fittings, and insecticide spray cans to fling, splatter, splash, spritz, and extrude food and paint with the force and trajectory of projectile vomit. Using sixty pounds of bananas, enough jello for a seventy-pound mold, and many marshmallows and Twinkies in each performance (Goldberg 1991; Hubbard 1992), they "perform a symphony for teeth and Captain Crunch cereal, squirt snakes of banana from their chests and catch paint-filled gum balls in their mouths, among other stunts" (Hubbard 1992). This is extravenous performance. Substances are propelled through tubes that exit from the body to land where they will.

Such acts confound the boundaries of the body and the limits on what can go into and come out of it. This body's mouth is directly connected to the anus, with neither stomach nor guts in between. Indeed, the two orifices are interchangeable, for the anus is displaced to the mouth, which both ingests and excretes, as well as to other parts of the body and clothing, which exude surprising substances. This is visceral performance without viscera. This is dirt as defined by Mary Douglas as "matter out of place" in her appropriately titled essay "Secular defilement" (Douglas 1966: 36).

In contrast to food as substance, as a plastic material equivalent to paint, food becomes a character in its own right in musical revues of the 1920s that featured anthropomorphized fruits, vegetables, chickens, pastries, and every drink from Coca-Cola and sarsaparilla to Chianti and a Manhattan cocktail (for a number entitled "I'm a Great Little Mixer") (Hirsch 1987: 298).[17] Showgirls in food costumes were the dishes at lavish feasts and the ingredients for a "Follies Salad" – "Oil was slinky, draped in a very glossy one-shouldered satin gown, which fell in rivers onto the stage" (294). Erté designed the vegetable costumes for a ballet number in "Scandals" (1926) – "Potato had only small potatoes covering her breasts" (295). The "Music Box Revue" (1921) animated all the elements of the "Dining Out" scene, including the oysters, chicken, various vegetables, salt and pepper, pastry, demitasses, and "at the end of this costumed meal, a showgirl portrayed A Cigar and another The Check, and eight chorus girls were dressed as The Tip" (296). Chorus girls dressed as chocolates and peppermint sticks popped out of a big candy box in the number "Winter Garden Sweets" in "Doing Our Bit" (1917), while "Showgirls dressed as candles topped a cake formed by a single satin skirt in 'Just Sweet Sixteen' in the *Greenwich Village Follies* (1920)" (297). These edible women – the play on food and sex is fundamental to the enterprise – reverse the direction of food as a performing object. Here it is the showgirl (and the occasional male performer) that is made into an object for eating, but in the absence of actual food.[18]

Some theatre ensembles have made food an integral part of all their performances. Bread and Puppet distribute bread at their performances, while Great Small Works hold a monthly spaghetti dinner, followed by performances (see Chang 1998). They neither script the meal or bread, as the case may be, into the play nor offer a show to go with dinner. Rather, food is kept simple and elemental, abundant and cheap. The staples – homemade bread, pasta – are the basis for transforming an audience into a community, by breaking bread and eating together. As these groups establish a regular audience, a sense of community develops through shared experience over the course of many years. It is through commensality, more than cuisine, that these artists are redefining the nature and meaning of theatre.

Bread, a 1984 Bread and Puppet manifesto in the form of a recipe, opens with a long dictionary definition of "bread" from Funk & Wagnall's *New Standard Dictionary of the English Language* (1937, 1976). Bread is not only "an article of food" but also "food in general; also, the necessaries of life; as, he cannot earn *bread* for his family"(Schumann 1984: unpaginated). The meanings and usages ramify to include "to break bread," as in taking a meal or enjoying hospitality, and "to partake of the sacrament of the Lord's Supper." Peter Schumann draws on his childhood memories in Silesia for images of coarse rye bread baked in a communal oven. "Why bread?" he asks rhetorically. "In 1963 in a loft on Delancey Street in New York, as a normal frustrated city-artist and esoteric puppet show-maker, I decided to connect the bread with the puppets" (*ibid.*). This connection made the actual puppet shows more "purposeful" and less about "painterly and sculptural ambitions." It "seemed like a correct first step in the fight for the immediate elimination of all evil" (*ibid.*). Both "feed the hungry." *Bread* concludes with a list of aphorisms about bread and a "tentative recipe" for sourdough rye bread.

CONTEMPORARY *OPERA GASTRONOMICA*

In *Feeding Frenzy* (see Figure 6.1), cooking is an integral part of the musical score.[19] In precisely ninety minutes, each of four cooks prepares ten portions of ten courses. The amplified sounds of chopping, sizzling, steaming, and grinding are part of "an instructional, time delineated score" performed by four musicians on strings, reeds, pipa, and keyboard. Mr. Fast Forward's "sculptural approach to creating sound" ties the sound of the objects, substances, and processes of cooking to "the physical gesture that creates the sound" (Forward 1999). We not only see the cooks. We also hear them.

The entire room is projected onto a large screen from two video cameras that roam the space, settling for a moment on the stir-frying, the plucking of pipa strings, guests eating, or waiters rushing about. Washing over us are the slow, low-resolution, and sometimes overlapping video images, together with waves of music, noise, and chatter. I feel like a large ocean mammal, drifting in a vast dark sea of ambient sound, smells, and images. All of a sudden, a cook whacks a bell with a knife. A course is ready. Five waiters collect the servings and randomly serve them to us. We are seated at about twenty-five round tables for four. My senses are on the alert as a new course comes into view. Will the waiter choose our table for the margarita

Figure 6.1 Oui Cha, *Feeding Frenzy*. Photograph by Johannes Zappe.

rolls (frozen cylinders of margarita wrapped in Vietnamese rice sheets)? Will the mushroom matzo balls or tea-smoked bean curd skin "duck" come our way? Who will get the *crème brûlée* in individual Chinese soup spoons (the sugary surface is torched on the spot) or the Berber *seitan*, rice ball geology lesson, or poached pear in kaffir broth? Time is running out. The cooks are frantic. A large digital display at the back of the room, sometimes projected on the screen, counts down the minutes. Zero. Everything stops.

Following Escoffier, Fessaguet's kitchen must complete innumerable dishes, each made of up of many components, in ever-changing combinations and sequences, so that each table in a room of many tables may be served what it has ordered for a particular course all at the same time, at the right temperature. Forward departs from the principles of Escoffier's kitchen in two ways. First, he reverses the division of labor typical of the Escoffier kitchen. Each of Forward's cooks prepares each dish from start to finish and in an average of nine minutes. Second, he shifts the choice of what will be eaten from the diner to the waiter. What you are served is arbitrary.

Feeding Frenzy is a work that is conceived from the outset in such a way that food – its preparation, presentation, and consumption and its full range of sensory pleasures – is an integral part of the work. While very different in character, the same can be said of the edible installations of Alicia Rios, who is based in Madrid.[20]

While food in everyday life is very much about doing and behaving, the reciprocity of table and stage has a long history. One of the ways that food is made to perform is through the dissociation of food from eating and eating from nutrition, and the disarticulation of the various sensory experiences associated with food. Artists work not only with these possibilities but also with the processes associated with food as substance and food as event. And they do so at all points along the alimentary canal, from the mouth to the anus, and at all points in the food system, from foraging and cultivating to cooking, eating, and disposal. Because of the way it engages the senses, food offers particular challenges and opportunities for artists, both those interested in spectacular theatrical effects and those working on the line between art and life.[21]

REFERENCES

Aron, Jean-Paul. 1975. *The Art of Eating in France: Manners and Menus in the Nineteenth Century.* New York: Harper & Row.

Bennetts, Leslie. 1986. "On New York stages, food's the thing," *The New York Times* (19 March): C3.

Blumberg, Skip. 1985. *Flying Morning Glory (on fire).* 3.57 minutes, color, sound. Distributed by Skip Blumberg.

Booth, William. 1890. *In Darkest England, and the Way Out.* London: International Headquarters of the Salvation Army. Project Gutenberg's Etext: http://www.gutenberg. org/dirs/etext96/detwo10.txt.

Bower, Anne, ed. 2004. *Reel Food: Essays on Food and Film.* New York: Routledge.

Brillat-Savarin, Jean Anthelme. 1971. *The Physiology of Taste; or, Meditations on Transcendental Gastronomy*, translated by M.F.K. Fisher. New York: Knopf.

Brockett, Oscar G. 1968. *History of Theatre, fourth edition.* Boston: Allyn & Bacon.

Brockett, Oscar G. and Robert R. Findlay. 1973. *Century of Innovation: A History of European and American Theatre and Drama Since 1870.* Englewood Cliffs: Prentice Hall.

Chang Dong-Shin. 1998. "Building community: the spaghetti dinner," unpublished paper. New York: Department of Performance Studies, New York University.

Chatillon-Plessis. 1894. *La Vie à table à la fin du XIXe siècle théorie pratique et historique de gastronomie moderne: Physiologie, discussions, moeurs et mode pratique, service de la table et des réceptions, le boire, la cuisine, grandes recettes culinaires du siècle, la patisserie, les restaurants, nouveaux classiques de la table, mélanges et fantaisies.* Paris: Firmin-Didot.

Collins, Glenn. 1990. "There's a parody on my plate," *The New York Times* (2 May): C1, 6.

Cox, Nell. 1969. *French Lunch.* Pyramid Films.

DeCaro, Frank. 1998. "Bali hai, now on Avenue A," *The New York Times* (10 May), Section 9, p. 3.

Douglas, Mary. 1966. "Secular defilement." In *Purity and Danger: An Analysis of Concepts of Pollution and Taboo*, 29-40. London: Routledge & Kegan Paul.

el-Khoury, Rodolphe. 1997. "Delectable decoration: taste and spectacle in Jean Francois de Bastide's *La Petite Maison.*" In *Taste and Nostalgia*, edited by Allen S. Weiss, 49–62. New York: Lusitania Press.

Epstein, Shifra. 1979. "The celebration of a contemporary Purim in the Bobover Hasidic community," PhD dissertation. Austin: University of Texas.

Ferry, Jane F. 2003. *Food in Film: A Culinary Performance of Communication.* New York: Routledge.

Foodservice Equipment & Supplies Specialist. 1990. "Food as theater earns standing ovation in LA's posh Brentwood," *Foodservice Equipment & Supplies Specialist* 43, 3: 57–60.

Forward, Fast. 1999. "Feeding frenzy," New Concert Works, *MrFastForward.com.* http://www.mrfastforward.com/newconcertworks/newconcertworks.html.

Goffman, Erving. 1959. *The Performance of Self in Everyday Life.* Garden City: Doubleday.

Goldberg, Vicki. 1991. "High tech meets goo with Blue Man Group," *The New York Times* (17 November): Arts and Leisure, 26. http://www.blueman.com/newspress/theatrical.php?id=133_0_6_0_C.

Grimes, William. 1991. "A bartender who stirs and shakes but allows no new twists," *The New York Times* (27 March): C1.

Grimod de la Reynière, Alexandre-Balthazar-Laurent, and Jean-Claude Bonnet. 1978. *Écrits Gastronomiques.* 10/18 [i.e. Dix/Dix-Huit]; 1261. Paris: Union générale d'éditions.

Gussow, Mel. 1989. "The curtain rises on kelp lasagne and chopped liver," *The New York Times* (26 February): H5, 9.

[Handman, Gary]. 1996. "Food in the movies: a short bibliography of books and articles in the UC Berkeley libraries." Media Resources Center, Library, University of California, Berkeley. http://www.lib.berkeley.edu/MRC/foodbib.html.

Henderson, Justin. 1992. "Magic Muse," *Interiors* 151, 10: 70–3.

Hess, Robert. 1998. "Cocktail anxiety." http://www.drinkboy.com/Essays/CocktailAnxiety.html.

Hirsch, John E. 1987. "Glorifying the American showgirl: a history of revue costume in the United States from 1866 to the present," PhD dissertation. New York: Department of Performance Studies, New York University.

Hubbard, Kim. 1992. "Masters of splatter may turn your mood indigo: you ain't seen blue till you've seen Blue Man Group get offbeat off Broadway," *People* 37, 22 (8 June): 108–10. http://www.blueman.com/newspress/theatrical.php?id=135_0_6_0_C.

Kirshenblatt-Gimblett, Barbara. 1989. "Appetizers: Barbara Kirshenblatt-Gimblett on edible art," *Artforum International* 28 (November): 20–3.

——. 1990. "Performance of precepts/precepts of performance: Hasidic celebrations of Purim in Brooklyn." In *By Means of Performance: Intercultural Studies of Theatre and Ritual*, edited by Richard Schechner and Willa Appel, 109–17. Cambridge: Cambridge University Press.

——. 1997. "Alicia Rios, tailor of the body's interior: an interview," *TDR* 41, 2 (T154): 90–110.

——. 1999. "Playing to the senses: food as a performance medium," *Performance Research* 4, 1: 1–30.

Lang, George. 1980. *Lang's Compendium of Culinary Nonsense and Trivia*. New York: C.N. Potter.

Lanza, Joseph. 1995. *The Cocktail: The Influence of Spirits on the American Psyche*. New York: St Martin's Press.

Leonard, Roy. 1997. "Blue Man Group, feature review," *Roy Leonard's Going Out Guide*. http://www.blueman.com/newspress/theatrical.php?id=136_0_6_0_C.

MacCannell, Dean. 1976. *The Tourist: A New Theory of the Leisure Class*. New York: Schocken.

Marinetti, Fillippo Tommaso. 1989. *The Futurist Cookbook*, translated by Susan Brill. San Francisco: Bedford Arts.

McKewan, Richard. 1998. "Cocktail renaissance: the re-emergence and re-invention of the cocktail way of life," unpublished paper. New York: Department of Performance Studies, New York University. http://www.nyu.edu/classes/bkg/mckewan.htm.

Mennell, Stephen. 1985. *All Manners of Food: Eating and Taste in England and France from the Middle Ages to the Present*. Oxford: Blackwell.

n.a. 1989. "Trump to close a 'tacky' Trader Vic's," *The New York Times* (25 January): B1.

Nevile, Jenny. 1990. "The musical banquet in Italian Quattrocento festivities." In *Food in Festivity: Proceedings of the Fourth Symposium of Australian Gastronomy*, edited by Anthony Corones, Graham Pont, and Barbara Santich, 125–35. Sydney: Symposium of Australian Gastronomy.

Oldenburg, Ray. 1989. *The Great Good Place: Cafes, Coffee Shops, Community Centers, Beauty Parlors, General Stores, Bars, Hangouts, and How They Get You Through the Day*. New York: Paragon House.

Ozouf, Mona. 1988. *Festivals of the French Revolution*. Cambridge: Harvard University Press.

Patton, Phil. 1998. "Reading between the lines: deciphering the menu," *The New York Times* (4 February): F6.

Pfferman, Naomi. 2002. "A Taste for Yiddish," *The Jewish Journal of Greater Los Angeles* (4 October). http://www.jewishjournal.com/home/preview.php?id=9352.

Pont, Graham. 1990. "In search of the *opera gastronomica*." In *Food in Festivity: Proceedings of the Fourth Symposium of Australian Gastronomy*, edited by Anthony Corones, Graham Pont, and Barbara Santich, 115–24. Sydney: Symposium of Australian Gastronomy.

Poole, Gaye. 1999. *Reel Meals, Set Meals: Food in Film and Theatre*. Sydney: Currency Press.

Rausfeld, Robin and Rob Patronite. 2004. "Dinner and a show," *New York Magazine* (November 15), NewYorkmetro.com. http://newyorkmetro.com/nymetro/food/features/10313/.

Restaurants and Institutions. 1990. "Chefs as exhibitionists," *Restaurants and Institutions*, A230.

Revel, Jean-François. 1982. *Culture and Cuisine: A Journey through the History of Food*. Garden City, New York: Doubleday.

Richards, Kristen. 1992. "West by southwest: David Kellen sets a southwest stage in a new L.A. restaurant," *Interiors* 151, 10: 76–7.

Rokem, Freddie. 2000. *Performing History: Theatrical Representations of the Past in Contemporary Theatre*. Iowa City: University of Iowa Press.

Santich, Barbara. 1990. "Metamorphoses of the banquet." In *Food in Festivity: Proceedings of the Fourth Symposium of Australian Gastronomy*, edited by Anthony Corones, Graham Pont, and Barbara Santich, 108–14. Sydney: Symposium of Australian Gastronomy.

Schama, Simon. 1988. *The Embarrassment of Riches: An Interpretation of Dutch Culture in the Golden Age*. Berkeley: University of California Press.

Schumacher, Max. 1998. "The fourth place: my café is my sand-box," unpublished paper.

New York: Department of Performance Studies, New York University. http://www.nyu. edu/classes/bkg/cybercafe.fd.

Schumann, Peter. 1984. *Bread*. Glover: Bread and Puppet.

Senelick, Laurence. 2005. "Consuming passions: eating and the stage at the fin-de-siècle," *Gastronomica* 5, 2: 43–9.

Simon, Lee. 2004. "Display kitchens: a feast for the eyes." *Escoffier Online* (23 September). Part 1: http://escoffier.com/phpnuke/html/contentid-34.html; part 2: http://escoffier.com/ phpnuke/html/contentid-34.html.

Spang, Rebecca L. 2000. *The Invention of the Restaurant: Paris and Modern Gastronomic Culture*. Cambridge: Harvard University Press.

Stewart, Philip. 1985. "L'ambigu, ou la nourriture spectacle," *Littérature et Gastronomie: Huit Étude,* edited by Ronald W. Tobin. Biblio 17, 23. Paris and Seattle: Papers on French Seventeenth-Century Literature.

Toepfer, Karl Eric. 1991. *Theatre, Aristocracy and Pornocacy: Orgy Calculus*. New York: PAJ Publications.

Trubek, Amy B. 2000. *Haute Cuisine: How the French Invented the Culinary Profession*. Philadelphia: University of Pennsylvania Press.

Wheaton, Barbara. 1983. *Savoring the Past: The French Kitchen and Table from 1300–1789*. Philadelphia: University of Pennsylvania Press.

NOTES

1   This essay is a companion piece to Kirshenblatt-Gimblett (1999), which deals more fully with food in everyday life and in relation to performance art. The focus here is on the staging of food in restaurants and theatres.

2   According to Graham Pont (1990: 123–4), the term *opera gastronomica* "was first used in the title of the musical banquet, *Les goûts réunis* or *Apollo in the Antipodes: opera gastronomica in tre atti*. This was the celebration which concluded the Fourth David Nichol Smith Memorial Seminar in Eighteenth-Century Studies and the First National Conference of the Musicological Society of Australia, held at University House, Canberra, 31st August, 1976."

3   See Kirshenblatt-Gimblett (1990) for a more detailed discussion of this event. I have been attending the Purim festivities in the Bobover Hasidic community in Boro Park, Brooklyn, since 1973. See also Epstein (1979).

4   See Toepfer (1991).

5   See the chapter "Feasting, fasting, and timely atonement" in Schama (1988), for a discussion of the role of food in festivity in the Netherlands. Food in Dutch art reveals a richly iconographic language of moral discourse and visual conventions for conveying the sensory experiences of eating.

6   A particularly famous example is the *surtout* that displayed scenes from the *Opéra de Bardes,* described in 1808 by Grimod de la Reynière in *Almanach des gourmands* (el-Khoury 1997: 58).

7   For a discussion of this play, see Rokem (2000: 56–76).

8   On the history of the restaurant in France, see Spang (2000). On the professionalizing of French chefs, see Trubek (2000).

9   Roger Fessaguet, personal communication, 1989. See also the documentary film of La Caravelle Restaurant (Cox 1969). This fifteen-minute film focuses on the motion and tempo of the kitchen when it is in full swing.

10   Thanks to Mitchell Davis for alerting me to this anecdote and to Robin Leach for the citation.

11   This is in a long tradition of street food vendors and food stalls in markets, which predates the relatively recent advent of restaurants. For an excellent example of spectacular cooking

performance in an open market, see Skip Blumberg's 1985 documentary short *Flying Morning Glory (on fire)*, which celebrates the "flaming 'cuisine art' performance of a virtuoso sidewalk chef in Phitsanulok, Thailand." (Electronic Arts Intermix, http://www.eai.org/eai/tape.jsp?itemID=3079.

12 This discussion is inspired by McKewan (1998). See also Hess (1998).

13 Judging by the names of some drinks, the cult of the cocktail includes a libertine (if not adolescent) element. Hess (1998), under the heading "Blush on the Rocks," lists Orgasm, Slippery Nipple, and Blow Job. Under "Shooters," which are appreciated "for the visual effect that they impart," he includes Brain Hemorrhage, Cement Mixer, Cum in a Hot Tub, and Embryo.

14 Café Los Negroes http://www.losnegroes.com/ began in 1994 and closed in 2000; *Atomic Café* http://www.sfn.saskatoon.sk.ca/current/atomic/about.html.

15 While food in films has attracted considerable attention, much less has been written about food in theatre. On food in film, see Bower (2004), Ferry (2003), and [Handman] (1996). Poole (1999), who is both a scholar and an actor, deals with food in film and theatre.

16 Since Gussow's article, many more theatrical works have made food – cooking, eating, restaurants – their focus, to mention only *Fully Committed, Cookin',* which was developed in Korea in 1997 and playing in New York city as of this writing (http://www.cookinnewyork.com/), and *Esn: Songs from the Kitchen,* a klezmer music performance that includes cooking and features Frank London, Adrienne Cooper, and Lorin Sklamberg (see Pfferman 2001).

17 This account is based on Hirsch (1987).

18 In contrast to food on the stage, dinner theatre captures two market segments, diners and theatre-goers, by combining dinner and theatre in various ways. Eating can occur before, after, during, or as part of the performance. The two activities may be in separate spaces or both may occur in a theatre or in a restaurant. Obvious examples include dinner theatre, recreations of historic feasts, character dining, murder mystery dinners, and such theatrical restaurants as Lucky Cheng's and such environmental performances as *Tim and Tina's Wedding*. In addition, restaurants play an important role in the occupational culture of the entertainment district, as places to not only network and do business but also to celebrate. Sardi's and Elaine's in New York are but two examples. These topics are beyond the scope of the present essay.

19 I saw this performance at the Kitchen, a Manhattan performance space and laboratory for artistic experimentation, in February 2000 and first wrote about it in Kirshenblatt-Gimblett (2000).

20 On Rios, see Kirshenblatt-Gimblett (1997). For other examples, see Kirshenblatt-Gimblett (1999).

21 Warm thanks to Anurima Banerji, Sally Banes, Mitchell Davis, and Chava Weissler.

Part II

HISTORY

7

EDIBLE PERFORMANCE

Feasting and festivity in early Tudor entertainment

Denise E. Cole

The connection between food and theatrical performance is not unfamiliar to individuals of the twenty-first century. Today, audiences often attend dinner theatres, plays, operas, and other popular entertainments, which serve food during the course of the performance or at least before the show and during intermission. However, during the lavish feasts of the Middle Ages, food did not just *accompany* a performance; food *was* a performance exhibited on special occasions when wealthy nobles shared their bounty with strangers, tenants, and guests. Feasting and festivity were inextricably fused in medieval hospitality; the one did not exist without the other. Hospitality was not only an important tradition rooted in Christian tenets of charity and practiced theoretically by every stratum of society; it also gave aristocrats an opportunity for an elaborate and costly display of their power in an age that communicated not only through ocular but also through tactile and gustatory media. The early Tudors, like any European nobility of the late Middle Ages, publicized their magnificence on state occasions and holidays by inviting all classes of their citizenry – as well as foreign ambassadors – to taste, smell, touch, hear, and see wildly excessive amounts of food, drink, and revelry. All five senses were engaged: visitors were immersed in mouthwatering aromas, crammed with succulent meats, and surfeited with free-flowing drink as they were simultaneously delighted by costly disguisings, comic interludes, and soothing music. No boundaries were erected between the kitchen and the tiring house until later in the sixteenth century, when professional actors built separate structures to house their plays. In fact, as will be demonstrated, edible and human performance shared the same theatrical conventions precisely because they were both threads in the complex design of regal hospitality.

Although such aristocratic hospitality steadily declined throughout the later decades of the Renaissance, at the time of the early Tudors, it was still an obligation.[1] Part of the nobility's duty was "to entertain" or provide for the needs of guests by supplying them with food, lodging, and sometimes apparel (*OED* 1989, V).[2] The other aspect of "entertainment" was to make sure that such provisions were carried out in an agreeable manner by means of music, singing, interludes, comedies, and masks (the French spelling, "masques," was not accepted in England until the early seventeenth century). Unlike the medieval usage of this word, in the twentieth-first century the most common meaning of "entertain" is "to engage agreeably the attention of (a person); to amuse;" but this definition does not actually enter the English lexicon until 1626, when hospitality was becoming more private and random.[3] In fact, W.R. Streitberger has observed that during the early Tudor period, "'Pastime' and 'pleasure' were the two most general terms used by contemporary writers to describe court entertainments" (Streitberger 1994). These two terms were used rather than the term "entertainment" because the idea that entertainment could mean *only* a theatrical exhibition entirely separate from feasting had not yet evolved. What is regarded as two distinct events today was one all-encompassing activity during the Renaissance and Middle Ages – all part of aristocratic magnificence, or hospitality, and all sharing the same performance conventions. These shared conventions give convincing evidence that edible and human performance were considered equally theatrical. Scholars such as Allardyce Nicoll have frequently commented on the "intimate connexion between the performance of plays or of masques and the elaborate banquets which have given this age pre-eminence in the art of feasting" (Nicoll 1937), but they fail to appreciate that plays and masks/masques coexisted with feasting in one grand performance event.[4] In other words, the feast was really the catalyst for theatrical productions at court. Usually given at the end of a meal, human performance was as much a dessert as edible performances were.

Most plays of the twenty-first century engage only our eyes and ears, while the senses of touch, taste, and smell remain neglected. By disregarding three of the five senses, later audiences effectively distanced themselves from theatrical performance. This omission started to overtake the theatrical environment when guests transmogrified into patrons and paid for the revelry that had once been aristocratic largesse. In the Middle Ages, to be "entertained" meant not only hearing and seeing performance but also tasting, touching, and smelling it. Consumption was not only visual but also tactile and gastronomic. An audience member's involvement was complete and active, not fragmented and passive, because every one of his or her five senses participated in hospitality's revelry.

This sensual entertainment coexisted in the same arena – the great hall, a massive room that was the centerpiece of any noble European household of the medieval and Renaissance periods. Nothing was compartmentalized as it is today; both edible and human performance transpired simultaneously in this space. In fact, some kind of amusing pastime always accompanied even daily meals eaten here. Bridget Henisch and other scholars mention games, songs, dances, stories, and puzzles as a constant element of dinnertime enjoyment. The itinerant minstrel was certainly one of the earliest performers, singing his heroic romances around the tables of the nobility (Wright [1871] 1968). Another later and more elaborate "pleasure" was the medieval "interlude," which means "played between" (Henisch 1976). Although not completely conclusive, enough clues exist to suggest that many of these short, flexible dramatic debates were indeed "played between" courses of the meal. The title page of Henry Medwell's *Fulgens and Lucres,* written about 1497, states that the piece has been "devyded in two partyes to be played at ii. tymes," presumably between each stage of a banquet (Southern 1973). The dialogue in this script indicates that the audience had just eaten or was in the process of finishing their food (Henisch 1976). Other interludes, like John Skelton's *Magnificence*, may have been performed *during* the meal while guests were busy eating (Nuess 1980).[5]

Not only did human festivities share the same space as edible ones, they also entered from the same offstage area – the kitchen. At one end of the great hall was the dais or "high table," which was usually slightly elevated, where the great lords and ladies sat and observed the pleasurable pastimes. Interlude players, minstrels, and most masquers did not come from this area, because it was reserved for the aristocratic hosts. At the opposite end, often referred to as the "lower end," was an ornately decorated wooden screen with two or three entryways in it. Behind this screen was a corridor, beyond which were the service apartments, such as the pantry, buttery, and bakehouse, all centered on food production. Interlude actors who performed in the halls probably used the openings in this partition as exits and entrances as well as a backdrop for the action of the interlude – that is, the same doorways from which the edible performances emerged (Southern 1973).[6] The amalgamated meaning of the word "entertainment" is made manifest in the hall architecture by the dual uses of this divider, which was the backdrop to both human and edible revelry (*ibid.*; Chambers 1924, III). Essentially, this screen was used like the tiring house façade found in later Renaissance playhouses (*ibid.*). Furthermore, early scholars recognized this link when they conjectured that the layout of these screens might have served as inspiration for the back wall of the Renaissance public stages (*ibid.*). The similarity is striking when juxtaposing screens found in the great Renaissance manors with the extant evidence on the tiring house façade in the later Elizabethan public theatres. In fact, theatrical performances, whether they were affiliated with royalty or not, were always given in structures that provided hospitality, either Tudor inns or halls, linking household performances with professional ones (*ibid.*). Eventually, the amusements produced by servants of the noble householder outgrew the great hall and were appropriated by their liveried players, who transformed their "pastimes" into a separate commercial business. This action segregated theatre from its traditional coexistence with the other aspects of hospitality such as food and lodging and transformed it into an isolated commodity.

The well-documented marriage celebration of Prince Arthur, the eldest son of Henry VII, to Catherine of Aragon shows how the aristocratic disguisers stepped easily between the stage and the kitchen. One account in *The Great Chronicle of London* of the festivities surrounding this event includes this pertinent detail:

> Anoon ffrom [the] kechyn beyng behynd the Comon place, cam the fforesaid xij Gentylmen beyng styll In theyr dysguysyd apparayll, beryng everych of theym a dysch, and aftir theym as many knygthis & Esquyers as made the ful numbyr of lx, The which lx dysshys were alle servid unto the kyngys messe, and fforwyth were as many servid unto the Quene …

(Great Chronicle of London 1938)

As this description indicates, the very gentlemen who were part of a disguising also served the king food and emerged from the same area of the hall (the "Comon place" or lower end of the hall) where the servants who prepared meals worked and congregated. Who these gentlemen were is less important than the fact that they served food as well as participated in a disguising.

This tradition did not die with Henry VII but continued in the dramatizations of Henry VIII. One case in point is the May Day festival in 1515, when Queen Catherine and members of Henry's staff escorted foreign ambassadors "into the country, to meet the King" (Guistinian 1854). They rode "into a wood, where they found the

King with his guard, all clad in a livery of green, with bows in their hands, and about a hundred noblemen on horseback, all gorgeously arrayed"(*ibid.*). Henry and his cohorts were pretending to be members of Robin Hood's band of thieves who were about to partake in a sumptuous repast.

> In this wood were certain bowers filled purposely with singing birds, which carolled most sweetly, and in one of these bastions or bowers, were some triumphal cars, on which were singers and musicians, who played on an organ and lute and flutes for a good while, during a banquet which was served in this place.
>
> (*ibid.*)

Obviously, the banquet was the centerpiece for an elaborate fiction involving the legendary thief. In fact, after an impressive display of skill in archery by Henry's guards, the actors playing Robin Hood and his men, Friar Tuck and Little John, conducted the entire company into the labyrinth described above.

> Then said Robyn hood, Sir Outlawes brekefastes is venyson, and therefore you must be content with such fare as we use. Then the kyng and quene sate doune, & were served with venyson and wyne by Robyn hood and his men, to their great contentacion.
>
> (Hall [1548] 1965)

The actors, presumably professional because they spoke, pretended to be hosts to royalty and had no qualms about also acting as waiters to their guests. This example not only reiterates the fact that feasting and festivity were contained in the same system of medieval hospitality but also illustrates the spirit of hospitality – to provide for one's guests.

However, there are still further connections between edible and non-edible court performance drawn by scholars such as Enid Welsford, Bridget Ann Henisch, and others (Welsford 1962; Mead 1967; Henisch 1976; Redon *et al.* 1998; Bober 1999). They have noted the similarity between court disguisings (which is a type of allegorical dance carried into the hall by an elaborate pageant wagon) and the spectacular dish, called a *sotelty,* that often ended a feast. These gastronomic displays, which showed off a cook's artistic talents, were also carried in with the same elaborate ceremony and music as the disguisers (masked dancers), who were carried in on pageants. Another name for sotelty is *entrement* and is derived "from *intromitto,* 'to let into, introduce.' In the late Roman world the *intermissum* was an extra course or luxurious delicacy, added on grand occasions to a dinner. The term *entremet* is French, and although known in England it was not used there so frequently as *sotelty,* or subtlety"(Henisch 1976).[7] Sotelties, like disguisings and masks, were brought in towards the end of a meal. In England, sotelties ranged from stuffed peacocks complete with feathers and gilded beaks to sugar sculptures of people, animals, trees, and architecture. To add further drama, the gilded beaks of peacocks sometimes held a piece of camphor that spewed out flames, and the sugar castles sometimes contained real gunpowder (Bober 1999). One lavish feast given by Henry VIII's Lord Chancellor, Cardinal Thomas Wolsey, supplies us with an excellent example of the kinds of sotelties created at this time:

> Anon there came up the second course with so many dishes, subtleties, and curious devices, which were above an hundred in number, of so goodly proportion and costly that I suppose the Frenchmen never saw the like. The wonder was no less than it was worthy in deed. There were castles with images in the same; Paul's Church and steeple

in proportion for the quantity as well counterfeited as the painter should have painted it upon a cloth or wall. There were beasts, birds, fowls of divers kinds, and personages, most lively made and counterfeit in dishes; some fighting (as it were) with swords, some with guns and crossbows, some vaulting and leaping, some dancing with ladies, some in complete harness jousting with spears, and with many more devices than I am able with my wit to describe.

(Cavendish 1990)

Clearly, food had a function at Wolsey's feast beyond nourishment – it was presented to astound and impress his French visitors. Such theatrical edibles were sometimes given away to guests and sometimes eaten. In this case, Wolsey later gave a chess-board made of sweetmeats to one of the Frenchmen in attendance (*ibid.*).

Frequently, mottoes were carved into sugary castles or held in the mouths of sotelties such as a swan or peacock, silently declaring the virtues of their king and resembling a kind of *tableau vivant,* mirroring their living counterparts, who often rode into the hall on pageant wagons (Mead 1967).[8] Both plates of food and pageants of household disguisers were announced by the blare of trumpets and emerged from the lower end of the hall. On 13 February 1511, Henry VIII and his friends, each wearing mottoes that identified the personal qualities of the silent disguisers, rode a pageant wagon into the White Hall at Westminster:

Then was there a device or a pageaut vpo wheles brought in, out of the which pageaut issued out a getelman rychelye appareiled, that shewed, howe in a garden of pleasure there was an arber of golde. ... In which arber were, vi. ladies ... in this garde, also was the kyng and v. with him ... & euery persone had his name in like letters of massy gold. The fyrst *Cuer loyall,* The secod *Bone volure,* in the iii. *Bone espoier,* The iiii *Valyaut desyre,* The fyft *Bone foy,* The vi. *Amoure loyall.*

(Hall [1548] 1962)

Like their edible counterparts, the royal disguisers also did not speak, but they did wear mottoes just as sotelties sometimes did.

Likewise, sotelties ranged from silent displays with mottoes (like their aristocratic counterparts) to the noisier types (like the professional interlude players) such as "coffins," or stiff medieval pastries, which were consumed after the birds, rabbits, frogs, or other surprising beasts inserted between the crusts had escaped into the hall (Bober 1999).[9] Such delicious contrivances continued to become larger and more dramatic until they no longer fitted the king's board but were wheeled across the floor on their own pageants, sometimes carrying real rather than sugared people. Olivier de la Marche recorded the Feast of the Pheasant hosted by Duke Philip the Good of Burgundy in 1485. An *entremet* was fashioned of a church holding an organ and a performing choir and in another instance an orchestra of twenty-eight persons emerged from a pie (Cartellieri 1972).[10] During the reign of England's Charles I and Henrietta Maria, a cold pasty was served containing the dwarf of the Duke of Buckingham, demonstrating that not all food was silent (Mead 1967). Edible concoctions such as these so blurred the line between food, theatrical set design, and performance that it is difficult to deny the dramatic quality of consumption in the Middle Ages. Some food was more than nourishment; it was also amusing and dramatic.

In fact, guidelines for state celebrations such as coronations, weddings, and major holidays had their own set of stage directions, which were far more elaborate than interludes, moralities, or Latin comedies. Such theatrical "blocking" was printed in aristocratic household books and treatises addressed to servants of the nobility. A generic outline compiled from such writings might go like this: after the hall had been properly set out, the guests were ushered to their seats by the marshal of the hall. Each individual was then seated according to a strictly prescribed system of ranking (Furnivall 1868).[11] After each had found their seat, the monarch and family came from their chambers into the hall, but before anyone sat down, each diner washed their hands, beginning with the highest-ranking official – the noble host. After washing, each guest was seated and processions of succulent dishes began to emerge from behind the hall screen and placed before the host and guests. When dishes were emptied, they were removed and replaced with more food. Maskings, disguisings, dancing, and gambling could occur during or after each course. The hours of eating were finally brought to a close when the spice plate and wine were served. A final washing of the hands took place, followed by everyone's departure (Coulton 1956).[12]

All of this activity occurred while minstrels moved about the hall or stood in galleries built above the entryways while people feasted. Trumpeters served an additional function by marking the high points of the dining ritual. They blared a signal for guests to wash their hands, which began the meal; they announced the entrance of each new dish from the kitchen into the hall; and they introduced the entrance of both the royal maskers and interlude actors (Henisch 1976). Both kinds of performance had the same conventional entrance.

An Italian ambassador gives an idea not only of the sumptuous environment that enveloped the princely hospitality of Henry VIII but also the tasty productions present at one of his banquets. A letter written by Francesco Chieregato, Apostolic Nuncio in England to Isabella d'Este, Marchioness of Manuta (918) on 10 July 1517 mentions:

> The guests remained at table for seven hours by the clock. All the viands placed before the King were borne by an elephant, or by lions, or panthers, or other animals, marvellously designed and fresh representations were made constantly with music and instruments of divers sorts. The removal and replacing of dishes the whole time was incessant, the hall in every direction being full of fresh viands on their way to table. Every imaginable sort of meat known in the kingdom was served, and fish in like manner, even down to prawn pastie (*fino alli gambari de pastelli*); but the jellies (*zeladie*), of some 20 sorts perhaps, surpassed everything; they were made in the shape of castles and of animals of various descriptions, as beautiful and as admirable as can be imagined.
>
> (*Calendar of State Papers Italy* 1867–74, II)

This description indicates not only the many types of soteltie found at Henry's court but also one of many theatrical methods for conveying them. The elephants and panthers that brought in the food were probably either household officers in animal costumes or pageants made to look like animals. In any case, food had a theatrical set designed especially for it.

Another aspect of these succulent court productions that allied them with the nobility's masks and disguisings is the medieval fondness for disguising food – disguise that probably affected taste. Although sotelties were designed to create wonder in the minds of guests, some foods were disguised merely as practical jokes (Adamson 1995). Chefs knew how to make a cooked chicken jump and cause a mouthwatering roast appear to be covered in worms. These jokes were known by all classes of people and could be found on the dinner tables of any household. Furthermore, many foods were dyed unnatural colors such as saffron yellow, a color used repeatedly in recipes (Mead 1967).[13] "Saunders" or sandalwood made foods red, while parsley produced a green color (Bober 1999). Blood could render food black or red, depending on the quantity of blood used or natural dyes added. More often, foods were given more than one color. When preparing a "capon in Salome," the cook is instructed to "take a little saunders and a little saffron and make it a marble colour" (*Two Fifteenth Century Cookery Books* [1430, 1450] 1888). Pomegranates, so named because of their similarity to the fruit's shape, were a kind of meatball, which recipes advised should be covered with two sorts of batter, one green and one yellow (*ibid.*). Such disguise is perhaps most obvious in the directions for assembling a cockatrice: "Cokyntryce, – Take a capon and scald him, and draw him clean and chop him in two across in the waist: take a pig, and scald him, and draw him in the same manner, and chop him also in the waist. Take a needle and a thread and sew the fore part of the capon to the after part of the pig, and the fore part of the pig to the hinder part of the capon, and then stuff them as thou stuffest a pig. Put him on a spit and roast him. And when he is done, glaze him with yolks of eggs and powdered ginger and saffron, then with the juice of parsley without," that is, color it a fantastical yellow and green (*EETS* 1888). Another frequent recipe was the hedgehog (this simple soteltie could also be found in the homes of both the high-and low-born). There are a number of different versions of this dish, but an English version was a "giant sausage surrounded by a group of slightly smaller ones, apparently representing a mother hedgehog and her litter. The sausages are to be filled ... and decorated with fried pastry slivers representing the hedgehogs' spines" (Hieatt *et al.* 2000).

This love of disguise repeats itself in the court mask, disguising or mummings performed at the court of Henry VIII. Dancers participating in these pastimes literally wore masks that concealed their identities. Cavendish reports a famous incident when Henry VIII and his cronies, pretending to be French shepherds, invaded a feast given by Cardinal Wolsey. He and his friends were masked and insisted on speaking French. Wolsey guessed that Henry was somewhere among this jovial group of gamblers, but when he said that he believed he could pick out the king, he was wrong. He chose Sir Edward Neville, who most resembled Henry VIII (Cavendish 1990). Although this might have been staged for the benefit of his guests, it still demonstrates an important goal of a court mask – disguise.

But dyeing foods for an elaborate feast or turning them into jokes was not the only means of camouflage. So far, this discussion has emphasized the shared conventions between food and revelry. This mostly appealed to the visual and aural senses, but in the case of disguise another of the senses enters. Although disguise is usually accomplished visually, it can also apply to taste. A royal chef aimed to transform food into what it was not; he sometimes masked the taste of food with exotic spices and sauces. He (this occupation was dominated by men at this time) was a creative artist who wanted to advertise his master's wealth by his excessive use of expensive spices, which were certainly not readily available to everyone. This inordinate use of spices in cooking not only covered tainted food but also allowed guests to taste the bounty of princely magnificence (Bober 1999; Mead 1967). Another argument suggests that humorial medical theories that were thought to aid digestion encouraged this love of spices (Bober 1999). The practice of loading any kind of food with numerous and sometimes even irreconcilable flavorings may have erased any distinctive taste.[14] Some typical spices and flavorings were ginger, mace, saffron, sugar, cinnamon, nutmeg, pepper, cloves, ground almonds (all sorts), honey, milk or cream, wine, vinegars, raisins, currants, and prunes, the majority characterizing quite a love of sweets. Nor was this all. Despite the heavily flavored dishes that made up a meal's numerous main courses, the evening was brought to a close by partaking of even more spices. The silver and gold spice plate, often richly gilt, divided into compartments and filled with various seasonings, sugar plums, and other sweetmeats, was accompanied by sweetened wine or *hippocras,* which finalized the eating experience.[15]

The main focus of this highly flavored cuisine was meat, central to all English feasts even today. The entrance of platters of beef, mutton, pork, chicken, pheasants, peacocks, hares, swans and many other kinds of bird would have each been announced by trumpeters and placed on boards in front of ravenous guests (Mead 1967; Bober 1999). However, even more exotic was the medieval taste for fish – including eels, porpoises, frogs, seals, oysters, shrimps, and whales. Because so many of these animals were really too large to be served whole, they were more often "hewn" or cut into bits, boiled, and buried in sauces, stews, and gravies – all heavily seasoned. Fowl was one type of meat that frequently made it to the table *in toto*, and it was the job of the skilled carver to slice up portions for his famished guests to grab (Furnivall 1868).

This brings us to those who grabbed the meats, breads, beer, wine, and ale offered them – the audience or guests of the monarch, whose complete participation in the monarch's hospitality meant not only seeing and hearing the edible revelry presented before them but also tasting, touching, and smelling it. Henry's guests savored highly spiced sauces and the exquisite sweetness of exotically stewed fruits and colored jellies as well as fondling these delicacies in their hands and between their fingers. Because the fork was not yet popular in England at this time, only the knife and spoon were common tableware, but even these two implements were not used as much as the fingers. Although food was seized from communal platters and bowls with knives and spoons, it was the fingers that usually brought it to individual lips.

However, there was a fourth alternative to using fingers, spoons, or knives. Individuals could slice off a portion of something called a "trencher" to sop up any delectable liquids. A trencher, a kind of plate, could be hewn out of coarse bread, pewter, or even wood, the latter two materials probably reserved for the aristocrats. When trenchers were made of stale bread, which was frequent, they not only served as optional silverware but also as a kind of towel to wipe an individual's knife clean (Mead 1967; Henisch 1976). If a guest was still hungry, he or she, along with servants and the poor, sometimes even ate trenchers of bread after they were thoroughly soaked with juices and could no longer hold any more food.

Furthermore, individuals sitting next to each other always ate from the same trencher, along with the same glass or drinking cup. Except for knives, spoons, and napkins, a diner always shared everything on the table. In England, the dishes seem to have been set out on the table and then passed around. Consequently, eating was a very cooperative experience surrounded by the sounds of music, the smells of numerous incoming dishes, and the touch of greasy meats and plump puddings.

Such extremely sensual activities required a few rules of etiquette. Courtesy literature, a genre of literature that described aristocratic behavior, sometimes included advice on managing such an intimate encounter (Furnivall 1868; Della Casa 1632).

For example, banquet guests were instructed by these writers not to blow their nose on the tablecloth or to wipe their hands on it. Instead, a napkin was to be used. Guests were forbidden to touch their food after putting their hands in their hair or to put chewed food back on the communal plate. Then, as today, people were advised not to stuff their cheeks with more than they could hold or to speak with their mouths full. If a guest blew their nose with their hand, they were advised to wipe it on their shirt. If their dogs had accompanied them, it was recommended that guests not grab for food after they had given their pets an affectionate pat (Henisch 1976).

In fact, hounds often wandered about freely during a banquet, and favorite hawks flew from beam to beam in the high hall ceiling (Mead 1967). Rushes were strewn on the floor of English manors and new ones added until the mass became so loathsome that it was removed (*ibid.*). An ancient biographer of Eramus reports on the sage's opinion of England's sanitary habits at this time:

> Eramus ascribes the plagues (from which England was hardly ever free) and the sweating-sickness, partly to the incommodious form and bad exposition of the houses, to the filthiness of the streets, and to the sluttishness within doors. The floors, says he, are commonly of clay, strewed with rushes, under which lies unmolested an ancient collection of beer, grease (?), fragments, bones, spittle, excrements, [t.i. urine] of dogs and cats [t.i. men] and every thing that is nasty, &C.
>
> (Jortin 1808)[16]

If this is no exaggeration, then we might understand why Cardinal Wolsey held in "his hand a very fair orange whereof the meat or substance within was taken out and filled up again with the part of a sponge wherein was vinegar and other confections against the pestilent airs: to the which he most commonly smelt unto, passing among the press [crowds]" (Cavendish 1990).

However, devouring these edible productions was not the only type of consumption going on. Guests also consumed the theatrical productions as well. When the pageants that bore the disguisers into the hall were no longer needed, they were taken to the lower end of the hall, and those in the audience stole the valuable tokens decorating them. Observers also grabbed any loose ornaments falling from either costumes or pageant, thereby eating away or devouring the human performance as well.

Edward Hall, whose history of Henry VIII provides some of our best evidence of royal pastimes, chronicles one of the most famous examples (mentioned earlier) of consumption on 13 February 1511. At this feast, celebrating the birth of Henry's short-lived son, the crowds literally tore off the gold from Henry VIII's costume as well as broke the pageant wagon that had brought Henry and his friends into the hall:

> In the meane season the pagiaunt was conueyed to the ende of the place, there to tary till the daunces were finished, and so to have receyued the lordes and ladies againe, but sodanly the rude people ranne to the pagent, and rent, tare, and spoyled the pagent, so that the lord Stuard nor the head officers could not cause them to abstaine, excepte they shoulde have foughten and drawen bloude, and so was this pagent broken.
>
> (Hall [1548] 1965)

The pageant that had been "conueyed to the ende of the place," or the other end of the hall, close to the screens that cloaked the corridor to the many service apartments, was suddenly attacked by members of the audience, who "spoyled" it. But the crowd did not stop with the pageant; the people also assaulted the king "and stripped hym into his hosen and dublet, and all his compaignions in likewise. Syr Thomas Knevet stode on a stage [graded seating], and for all his defence he lost his apparell. The ladies likewyse were spoyled, wherfore the kynges garde came sodenly, and put the people backe, or els as it was supposed more inconuenience had ensued" (*ibid.*).[17] Although the guards pushed these eager guests back, Henry did not punish or imprison them, because as with the food they consumed, grabbing, pulling, and touching the costumes and pageant wagons were all part of the complete sensory experience of medieval hospitality. The paraphernalia of human performance was dismantled, devoured, and digested just as the edible productions were. Nor did this custom die out with the Tudor monarchs. Ben Jonson mentions that devastation (or breaking) of later masque setpieces continued into the Stuart period.[18] However, as medieval hospitality diminished so did the entire sensual experience of theatrical celebration, which eventually died out in the eighteenth century – the Age of Enlightenment or Reason, when the delights of the five senses were segregated from each other and replaced by logic.

Although the theatricalization of medieval and early Renaissance feasts is widely known, the presentation of food that made up these feasts was more than a mere accompaniment to human performance. Food *was* performance – all part of the aristocratic display of princely magnificence, advertised through noble hospitality. Furthermore, because edible and human theatrics were both part of hospitality's complicated system, they both followed the same kind of performance conventions. Because of this, food was not only a meal; it was also a marvel.

REFERENCES

Adamson, Melitta Weiss. 1995. "The games cooks play: non-sense recipes and practical jokes in medieval literature." In *Food in the Middle Ages*, edited by Melitta Weiss Adamson. New York & London: Garland Publishing.

Anglicus, Bartholomew. 1956 [thirteenth century]. *De Proprietatibus Rerum*. Reprinted in G.G. Coulton, *Social Life in Britain from the Conquest to the Reformation*. Cambridge: Cambridge University Press.

Bober, Phyllis Pray. 1999. *Art, Culture, and Cuisine, Ancient and Medieval Gastronomy*. Chicago and London: University of Chicago Press.

Calendar of State Papers and Manuscripts Relating to English Affairs Existing in the Archives and Collections of Venice and other Libraries in Northern Italy, vol. II 1867–73. Edited by R. Brown *et al.* London: Longmans, Green, Reader and Dyer.

Cartellieri, Otto. 1972 [1929]. *The Court of Burgundy: Studies in the History of Civilization*, translated by Malcolm Letts. New York: Barnes & Noble.

Cavendish, George. 1990 [1962]. *The Life and Death of Cardinal Wolsey and the Life of Sir Thomas More by William Roper*, edited by Richard S. Sylvester and David P. Harding. New Haven and London: Yale University Press.

Chambers, E.K. 1924. *The Elizabethan Stage*, Vol. III. Oxford: Clarendon Press.

Della Casa, Giovanni. 1632. *Galateo of Maister John Della Casa, Archebishop of Beneuenta*, translated by Robert Peterson. London: Raufe Newbery dwelling in Fleetstreate a litle above the Conduit.

Furnivall, Frederick, ed. 1868. *Early English Meals and Manners*. Early English Text Society: Oxford University Press.

Great Chronicle of London, The. 1938. Edited by A.H. Thomas and I.D. Thornley. London: printed by George W. Jones at the Sign of the Dolphin.

Guistinian, Sebastian. 1854. *Four Years at the Court of Henry VIII*, Vol. I, translated by Rawdon Brown. London: Smith, Elder & Co.

Hall, Edward. [1548] 1965. *The Union of the Two Noble and Illustre Famelies of Lancastre and York*. Reprint, New York: AMS Press.

Heal, Felicity. 1990. *Hospitality in Early Modern England*. Oxford: Clarendon Press.

Henisch, Bridget Ann. 1976. *Fast and Feast, Food in Medieval Society*. University Park and London: Pennsylvania State University Press.

Hieatt, Constance B., Brenda Hosington, and Sharon Butler. 2000 [1996]. *Pleyn Delit, Medieval Cookery for Modern Cooks*, second edition. Toronto, Buffalo, London: University of Toronto Press.

Jonson, Ben. [1605] 1995. The Masque of Blackness. *Court Masques: Jacobean and Caroline Entertainments 1605–1640*, edited with an introduction by David Lindley. Oxford and New York: Oxford University Press: 1–9.

Jortin, John. 1808. *Life of Eramus*, Vol. I. Printed by R. Taylor and Co. for J. White. Referred to by Sir Henry Ellis in *Original Letters*, Vol. I, 328, note. Cited in Frederick Furnivall, ed., *Early English Meals and Manners*. (Early English Text Society: Oxford University Press, 1868).

Lancashire, Ian. [1515] 1988. "Orders for Twelfth Day and Night circa 1515 in the Second Northumberland Household Book." *English Literary Renaissance* 10: 3–45.

Mead, William. 1967 [1931]. *The English Medieval Feast*. London: George Allen & Unwin.

Nicoll, Allardyce. 1937. *Stuart Masques and the Renaissance Stage*. London, Toronto, Bombay, Sydney: George G. Harrap & Co.

Neuss, Paula. 1980. Introduction to John Skelton's *Magnificence*. Manchester and Baltimore: Manchester University Press and Johns Hopkins University Press.

Oxford English Dictionary, second edition, Vol. V. 1989. Edited by J.A. Simpson and E.S.C. Weiner. Oxford: Clarendon Press.

Redon, Odile, Françoise Sabban, and Silvano Serventi. 1998. *The Medieval Kitchen, Recipes from France and Italy*, translated by Edward Schneider. Chicago, London: University of Chicago Press.

Southern, Richard. 1973. *The Staging of Plays before Shakespeare*. London: Faber and Faber.

Streitberger, W.R. 1994. *Court Revels, 1485–1559*. Toronto, Buffalo, London: University of Toronto Press.

Two Fifteenth Century Cookery Books. [1430, 1450] 1888. Edited by Thomas Austin. Reprinted by Early English Text Society, No. 152. EETS: London. Cited in William Mead, *The English Medieval Feast* (London: George Allen & Unwin, 1967).

Welsford, Enid. 1962 [1927]. *The Court Masque*. New York: Russell & Russell.

Wright, Thomas. [1871] 1968. *The Homes of Other Days: A History of Domestic Manners and Sentiments in England*. New York and London: D. Appleton & Co. and Trubner and Co.

NOTES

1   Felicity Heal's book, *Hospitality in Early Modern England,* defines and maps the decline of English hospitality in both the aristocratic and church settings.

2   In fact, the earliest meaning of the verb "to entertain" actually has to do with hospitality and not with merrymaking. See William Caxton's text *Eneydos* (xx, 74), written in 1490, which reads, "I haue them not onely receyued but entreteyned [entertained], furnyshed and susteyned, etc.," which means, "to receive as a guest; to show hospitality to."

3   Francis Bacon writes in *Sylva*, "All this to entertain the Imagination that it waver less," which is the first time the word entertain means "to amuse," well over a hundred years after it entered the English language and only after hospitality was on the decline (*OED* 1989, V).

4   Although Nicoll recognizes the intimate relationship between feast and festivities, particularly

the chapter "The banqueting house" (28–32), he does not see that theatrical performance at court would not exist at this time without feasting.

5 Paula Neuss, in her discussion of John Skelton's *Magnificence*, makes an excellent case for this interlude being played during a meal in a Tudor hall. She writes, "References to 'this night' (ll.365, 670) suggest that the play takes place during the evening, and some sort of banquet may be going on, for Fancy refers to the audience as 'this press/ Even a whole mess' (ll.994–5)" (Neuss 1980). "Mess" means a serving, usually for more than one person. See her section under "Staging" for further points in her argument.

6 Southern describes the set-up for theatrical performance in great detail in the chapter "The great Tudor hall." Southern's whole book deals with various ways of staging productions in a hall (Southern 1973); E.K. Chambers also discusses how the great hall was used to stage court theatrics, specifically interludes (Chambers 1924, III).

7 In addition to Henisch, Bober (1999) and Mead (1967) make similar statements.

8 Mead gives a number of examples of mottoes and ballads.

9 Bober explains how these marvels were accomplished: "This is not difficult to accomplish on a modest scale. Birds or any other creatures that will create a sensation by jumping about (frogs, rabbits) or flying are not, of course, baked. A large pie shell of requisite depth is baked blind with a hole in the bottom stopped by a regular pie (a reward to guests after the surprise if you do not make it of the shortening-less medieval dough) through which the birds are introduced just before the 'unveiling'" (Bober 1999).

10 "In culinary treatises emanating from royal households, notably Maitre Chiquart's *Du Fait de Cuisine*, culinary and artistic feats are described in the greatest detail: the *Chateau d'amour* ("Castle of Love") had crenelated walls and four towers defended by little soldiers, who were repelling a naval assault on a fish-filled sea painted on fabric. At the foot of the towers, guests were tempted by an enormous pike cooked in three ways, a bear's head, a roast swan covered in its own plumage and positioned to appear poised for flight, and a glazed suckling pig – all these creatures breathing fire. In the middle of the castle's courtyard, a Fountain of Love flowed with unlimited quantities of rose water and spiced wine; and a multitude of perfectly roasted birds tumbled from the galleries of a dovecote. And so forth" (Redon *et al.* 1998).

11 Frederick J. Furnivall in *Early English Meals and Manners* provides a number of medieval texts that outline the proper ranking at the hall tables.

12 This order is based upon the order given by Bartholomew Anglicus, *De Proprietatibus Rerum*, as printed in G.G. Coulton. Also see Lancashire (1988: 10) for the specific ordering of Twelfth Night ceremonies. Also see *Collection of Ordinances and Regulations for the Government of the Royal Household, Made in Divers Reigns, from King Edward III to King William and Queen Mary.* Also *Receipts in Ancient Cookery* MDCCXC for further references to court ceremonies; and Furnivall (1868) for specific instructions on ranking and other household rules.

13 See also Redon *et al.* (1998): "To achieve these colors [black, tan, white, blue, yellow, pink, or green], our treatises used natural products as base ingredients, such as the leaves used in herb and green vegetable pies (chard, spinach, and so forth) or the herbs used in green sauces (such as parsley and basil). They also pressed spices into service ... cinnamon for a camel's hair tan (in combination with golden raisins) and saffron for yellow ... Pink garlic sauce ... was colored by red grape-juice, sky-blue sauces by blueberry pulp, and black by dark raisins, prunes, chicken livers, and darkly toasted bread."

14 Hieatt *et al.* argue that medieval cooking used spices sparingly. However, I share Bober's view. She argues that because no standard measurements were employed at this time, it is very difficult to know exactly how much of anything was added to any given dish. She writes: "This [argument] is not fully convincing in the light of documents like the *Menagier* in which the

Goodman of Paris recommends the amount of spices to purchase for a dinner offered to forty guests: 'One lb. powdered columbine ginger; Half a lb. of ground cinnameon; 2 lb. lump sugar; One oz. saffron; A quarter lb. of cloves and Grain of Paradise [melegueta pepper] mixed; Half a quarter lb. of long pepper; Half a quarter lb. of galingale [galangan, or laos powder]; Half a quarter lb. of mace; half a quarter lb. of green bay leaves'; Eileen Power, *The Goodman of Paris,* 241, quoted by Bridget Ann Henisch, *Fast and Feast: Food in Medieval Society* (University Park, PA, 1976) 106. For the same occasion, the after dinner *boutehors* [or English reresupper] required 'candied orange peel, 1 lb.; Citron, 1 lb.; Red anise, 1 lb.; Rose-sugar, 1 lb.; white confits, 3 lbs.,' and he noted that little remained of the spices afterward. It should be noted that, had he been of the aristocracy rather than a rich bourgeois, the Goodman would have had a kitchen boy whose sole task would have been to grind the spices to powder in a mortar" (Bober 1999).

15 Although recipes vary slightly, *hippocras* was red wine that "was always simmered with cinnamon, ginger, and sugar, to which pepper and grains of Paradise were usually added, and perhaps red coloring from sandalwood" (Bober 1999).

16 In Erasmus' own words, "Tum sola fere sunt argilla, tum scirpis palustribus, qui subinde sic renovantur, ut fundamentum maneat aliquoties annos viginti, sub se fovens sputa, vomitus, mictum canum et hominum, projectam cervisiam, et pixcium reliquias, aliasque sordes non nominandas. Hinc mutato coelo vapor quidam exhalatur, mea sententia minime salubris humano corpori" (Furnivall 1868).

17 Nor was this an isolated example. On 17 March 1510, Hall refers to another instance when Henry distributed the golden ornaments on his jousting costume to his Spanish guests and "commaunded Every of them to take therof what it pleased them, who in effect toke all or the more parte: for in the beginning they thought that they had bene counterfait, and not of golde" (Hall 1965).

18 Ben Jonson writes in his opening commentary in *The Masque of Blackness*: "with the rage of the people, who, as a part of greatness, are priviledged by custom to deface their carcasses [pageants]" (Lindley 1995).

8

INCENSE & DECADENTS
Symbolist theatre's use of scent

Mary Fleischer

At the turn of the last century, the sense of smell became a new topic of investigation in many fields, including psychology, sexuality, anthropology, and the arts. Hans Rindisbacher has shown that the discourse about the sense of smell underwent an important paradigm shift:

> In the time from about 1880 to the 1910s, significant shifts take place in olfactory perception. ... [Smells] are no longer mere object smells, but they enter into an interactive perceptual relation with that vibratory organism the modern human has become, breaking down borders of subject and object, transgressing present and past, linking immediacy and memory.
>
> (Rindisbacher 1992: 147)

Smell might well have been the Symbolist sense *par excellence*. While the naturalists and realists used detailed descriptions of smell as a literary device to imbue the environment with a moral atmosphere or to enrich the verisimilitude of their works, the Symbolists used smell in suggestive, mysterious, and expansive ways to dissolve barriers between subject and object, individual and environment. The idea that art should be an evocation of a hidden reality through symbolic means was a central belief of the Symbolists. In Mallarmé's formulation,

> To *name* an object is to suppress three-quarters of the enjoyment of the poem, which derives from the pleasure of step-by-step discovery; to *suggest*, that is the dream. It is the perfect use of this mystery that constitutes the symbol: to evoke an object little by little, so as to bring to light a state of the soul or, inversely, to choose an object and bring out of it a state of the soul through a series of unravelings.
>
> (Mallarmé 1995: 141)

The aesthetics of suggestion and mystery demanded that artists seek ways to reawaken and reconceptualize the senses. Huysmans' hero Des Esseintes of *A Rebours* (*Against the Grain*, 1884) gives his highest praise to one of Mallarmé's works, because it lulled the senses, like some mournful incantation, some intoxicating melody, with thoughts of an irresistible seductiveness, stirring the soul of the sensitive reader whose quivering nerves vibrate with an acuteness that rises to ravishment, to pain itself.

(Huysmans 1969: 185–6)

Responding to the fragmented, dehumanized, and materialistic qualities of modern life, the Symbolists strove to regain a lost wholeness through unearthing links to myth and ancient rituals. In Paul Claudel's dialogue "Le Poète et le Vase d'encens," the Poet longs to inhale the lamp's perfumes so as to recapture the inspired breath of past poets, although its smoke also dissolves boundaries and subsumes identities (Claudel 1965: 836–47). The Symbolists were drawn to border states of consciousness, where divisions between body and soul blur, and they experimented with sensory correspondences or synesthesia. Charles Baudelaire's poems and essays were influential in promoting the idea of "correspondences," as this often-cited stanza indicates:

Like prolonged echoes mingling far away
in a unity tenebrous and profound,
vast as the night and as the limpid day,
perfumes, sounds, and colors correspond.

(Baudelaire 1958: 13)

That Baudelaire included the "secondary" sense of smell indicates the Symbolists' fascination with the more "primitive" and intangible senses of taste, touch, and smell, and their interest in discovering new "languages" of sensation. Alain Corbin charts the rise of the "perfume-artist" through the early nineteenth century (Corbin 1986: 198), but Huysmans' Des Esseintes is a self-proclaimed perfume poet:

Seated now in his study at this working table, he was ordering the creation of a new *bouquet,* and had reached that moment of hesitation so familiar to authors who, after months of idleness, are preparing to start upon a fresh piece of work ... he would use effects analogous to those of the poets, would adopt, in a measure, the admirable metrical scheme characterizing certain pieces of Baudelaire's. ... He wandered, lost in the dreams these aromatic stanzas called up in his brain, till suddenly recalled to his starting point, to the original *motif* of his meditations, by the recurrence of the initial theme, re-appearing at studied intervals in the fragrant orchestration of the poem.

(Huysmans 1969: 109–10)

Oscar Wilde's *The Picture of Dorian Gray* (1891) is also redolent with scent, and although perfumes create a generalized atmosphere of decadence and imminent sensuality, the use of smell, especially as it permeates interior monologue, becomes a means to point to deeper levels of experience:

The worship of the senses has often, and with much justice, been decried, men feeling a natural instinct of terror about passions and sensations that seem stronger than themselves. ... But it appeared to Dorian Gray that the true nature of the senses had never been understood, and that they had remained savage and animal merely because the world had sought to starve them into submission or to kill them by pain, instead of aiming at making them elements of a new spirituality. ... And so he would now study perfumes. ... He saw that there was no mood of the mind that had not its counterpart in

the sensuous life, and set himself to discover their true relations, wondering what there
was in frankincense that made one mystical and in ambergris that stirred one's passions.

(Wilde 1988: 101, 103–4)

As Constance Classen points out, the quest to sanitize modern life made the artistic
evocation of all kinds of smells, foul or fragrant, a means of rebellion against sterile
bourgeois conventions (Classen 1994: 87). And the inherent formlessness of smell, its
transgressive ability to permeate the atmosphere and dissolve boundaries, made it a
suggestive medium and metaphor for overrunning conventional concepts of subject
matter and form.

The interest in scent seemed to be everywhere at the turn of the century, and it even
permeated the experimental Symbolist theatre of the day. As a theatrical and dramaturgical element, smell is intriguing and problematical. The theatre has traditionally
focused on engaging an audience through its eyes and ears, and the production of a
smell onstage can be a conceptual as well as a technical challenge. Yet the Symbolist
theatre, in its quest to explore subjective experience, liberated ideas of time, space,
character, and sensory experience in the theatre. Symbolist poets and novelists rarely
wrote their texts or plays for any existing theatre, and many of their pieces remain
unperformed or, as some critics would insist, unperformable. These works frequently
employ scent as visual and/or verbal images, and occasionally as an actual smell as
part of the *mise en scène*.

Andrei Bely's *The Jaws of Night* (1907) is set in an indeterminate time during
the reign of the Antichrist. The sun has been extinguished, and a small group of
Christians wait atop a mountain plateau, close to the sky and its kaleidoscopic effects
of strange glows and auras. The landscape is a spiritual one, with a deep abyss to one
side of a mountain, and the faithful endure in a state of half-sleep. Sounds, colors,
lights, and movement all combine to create this highly sensory atmosphere. At several
intervals during the first half of this "Fragment of a Planned Mystery," a Prophetess
picks up a silver censer and blows on grains of incense, a ritual gesture that invites
the sacred presence of God:

PROPHETESS: (*Lifting the censer to her trembling mouth, she blows upon it through
parched lips. The grains of incense begin to smoulder. A ghostly little puff of flame trails
off into smoke. The smoke rings, floating past the sleeping elder, acquire a bright glow of
their own.*) There … There … What is the use of moans and groans? When there was
light, we rejoiced. Now that the light is gone, we shall manage without it somehow.
We shall endure everything. (*She stands erect and begins to go up and down the rows of
Christian women swinging the censer. The women bow down, like white lilies swayed by a
gentle breeze. She moves off behind the rocks. The faint clang of the censer continues to
resound.*)

(Bely 1985: 172)

Here, actual scent could be used onstage, but more importantly, the qualities of
its smoke are abstracted and intermingle with the play of light and movement; the
sound of the censer echoes, perhaps suggesting church bells, an alarm, or the vastness
of the empty space.

Although incense and perfumes have been used in several Symbolist productions,
it is not always evident whether the scent was simply dispersed for a general atmospheric effect or whether the scent was somehow orchestrated into a synesthetic kind

of experience. In 1893, Joséphin Péladan staged his play *Babylone* at the Central Dome of Champs de Mars, a very large space. Frantisek Deak reports that

> At the beginning of the production a lot of incense was burned, creating a veil of smoke which lingered for a while. This was to create an exotic, ritualistic, and religious atmosphere. The incense had an olfactory effect and also heightened the visual one by decreasing visibility even more.
>
> (Deak 1993: 126)

In Wilde's *Salomé*, the air is heavy, and there are many references to perfumes and flowers, but no stage directions call for actual scent. However, for an unrealized production planned to star Sarah Bernhardt in 1892, Wilde elaborated on the use of incense, according to his designer, W. Graham Robertson:

> "A violet sky," repeated Oscar Wilde slowly. "Yes – I never thought of that. Certainly a violet sky and then, in place of an orchestra, braziers of perfume. Think – the scented clouds rising and partly veiling the stage from time to time – a new perfume for each new emotion!"
>
> (Robertson 1945: 125–6)

For the first production of Maeterlinck's *The Blind* at the Théâtre d'Art in 1891, it has been cited that the theatre was "sprayed with perfume to make it more atmospheric" (see Slater 1997: xiv). Although it is impossible to substantiate the reference, Maeterlinck's play does make use of the sense of smell, as well as touch, in rather startling ways. The play is structured around the waiting of the blind for a priest who has left them stranded in a forest. Maeterlinck strips the play of all extraneous detail so that we focus on their predicament as felt through the senses other than sight. In his stage directions, Maeterlinck requests that the audience first see the blind symmetrically arranged in the space, which is strewn with obstacles; the sighted audience is therefore initially put into a position of knowledge and assumes that it will merely be a matter of time until the characters are aware of their situation. However, as we watch the blind rely on sound, touch, and smell to orient themselves, we also experience the landscape with a heightened sensitivity to its sensory qualities. Since breathing and inhaling smell makes us aware of our own bodies, the use of actual scents (asphodels, rotting leaves, sea air) in *The Blind* might have drawn the audience into a more intimate experience of waiting and underscored the corporeality of these figures and the particular sensorium that they endure.

In Gabriele D'Annunzio's novels *The Child of Pleasure* (1889) and *The Flame of Life* (1900), the observation of everyday detail is transposed into the "language of flowers and silent things." In each, the central character is a master artist who feels his relationship to things with extraordinary acuteness and takes great pleasure in savoring the correspondences between inner sensibilities and the physical world. "Minds that have the habit of imaginative contemplation and poetic dreaming," reflects D'Annunzio's protagonist, "attribute to inanimate objects a soul, sensitive and variable as their own, and recognise in all things – be it form or colour, sound or perfume – a transparent symbol, an emblem of some emotion or thought" (D'Annunzio 1991: 192). The setting of D'Annunzio's play *The Dead City* (1899) is "everywhere ... crowded with statues, bas-reliefs, inscriptions, sculptural fragments: evidences of a remote life, vestiges of a vanished beauty" (D'Annunzio 1923: 1). Anna, the blind and statuesque protagonist, has a highly tactile and olfactory sensitivity to the physical world and the inner truth of the other characters. As her brother Leonardo exhumes the jeweled and masked bodies of the House of Atreus, ancient sorrows visit new victims. The power of fate is captured in this play through many references to smell. While night-time sea breezes are "perfumed with myrtle and mint," the sunlit, drought-stuck earth is "malignant, it seems that exhalations of monstrous crimes still arise from it" (*ibid.*: 18).

La Pisanelle, ou La Mort parfumée, D'Annunzio's play written for Ida Rubenstein, choreographed by Michel Fokine, and staged by Meyerhold (at the Théâtre du Châtelet in 1913), centers on an Italian courtesan who is brought to medieval Cyprus for sale. Over the course of a complicated plot, Pisanelle transmutes from prostitute to nun to princess-bride until at the end, a drunken and dancing Pisanelle is killed by her slaves, who suffocate her with poisoned roses. From his study of Bakst's designs for the production, Charles Mayer describes the final effect:

> She appeared in a tight tunic of Parma violet, glittering with gold threads, worn over long Turkish trousers of vermilion satin richly embroidered in gold. Her long train of black velvet lined with white satin and weighted down with gold and silver embroidery was discarded as she began the "Dance of Perfumed Death." Then, in an unforgettable sado-erotic *coup d'oeil* she was gradually smothered in blood-red roses by slaves dressed in robes of clinging Indian red silks.
>
> (Mayer 1989: 39)

Although actual scent was not used, the vivid colors of the costumes and décor emphasized the many verbal images of flowers and perfumes to create the atmosphere of erotic intoxication.

The "secondary" senses of taste, touch, and smell are usually gendered as female, and the Symbolists's desire to forge new unities led them to blur lines between femininity and masculinity and to create androgynous characters. While Symbolist aesthetes might well become "feminized" through their interests and pleasures, female characters were usually typed as primitive and bestial, saintly or satanic. Of the few women Symbolists, Madame Rachilde (Marguerite Eymery Valette), dubbed Mademoiselle Baudelaire by her admirers, was notorious. Rachilde is best known for her novel *Monsieur Venus* (1884), which, as its title indicates, subverts gender codes, but it also provocatively uses scents, mostly of flowers, to explore transgressive sexuality. In her play *Volupté* (produced at the Athénée-Comique in 1896), two unnamed adolescent lovers find themselves in a forest and play a flirting game of expressing painful pleasures. "The pain of smelling hyacinths!" she confesses to him,

> Oh, that one, my dear, you cannot imagine how much pleasure it gives me! I go lie down on the ground up against a big pink hyacinth which sticks up at the back of the garden, near a hedge. It's in the shade, like we are here. I pull my skirt up over my head and I put my arms around the flower so that all the perfume is mine, and I breathe ... I breathe ... It's like eating honey while the bees fly by and brush my eyelids with their sugary wings! (*She is almost swooning.*) But it is so delicious that it makes me forget you...!
>
> (Rachilde 1998: 87)

In *L'Araignée de Cristal* (1894), the sweet, intoxicating scent of honeysuckle is identified with a sexually predatory mother who forces her "terror-stricken" son to confront his fear of women and mirrors with disastrous consequences; the innocence of this particular fragrance masks her hidden and dangerous desires.

Scent was used most ambitiously and schematically in Paul Napoléon Roinard's production of *The Song of Songs* at the Théâtre d'Art in 1891. Founded by eighteen-year-old Paul Fort the previous year, the Théâtre d'Art encouraged interdisciplinary collaboration between poets, actors, and artists within a Symbolist aesthetic. When Fort began, there was no established style of "Symbolist staging" or a genre of "Symbolist drama" to draw upon, and the theatre, initially calling itself "Théâtre Mixte," was eclectic in its methods and materials.

Initially, the Théâtre d'Art staged readings of poetry, in a "performance" where costumed actors intoned poetry against music and backgrounds painted by artists from the emerging "Nabis" school. The reciter of poetry is freer than the actor in a play to experiment with the music and inflection of speech for aesthetic rather than discursive effects. Here voice, music, and décor were employed in a new kind of synthesis where the visual did not predominate. In his memoirs, Fort emphasizes that if there was one principle that guided the theatre, it was the concept that

> "La parole crée le décor comme le reste." [Fort is quoting poet Pierre Quillard]. Retenez bien cette phrase. Elle eut les plus extrêmes conséquences sur tout le théâtre contemporain, aussi bien en France qu'à l'étranger. Le décor doit être une simple fiction ornementale qui complète l'illusion par des analogies de couleur et de lignes avec le drame.
>
> (Fort 1944: 31)

The Nabis painters who worked with the Théâtre d'Art (Paul Sérusier, Pierre Bonnard, Maurice Denis and others) created backgrounds that were two-dimensional and stylized, that explored color and form in an abstract and decorative fashion. The acting style that evolved at the Théâtre d'Art was stylized and statuesque, movement was slow and hieratic, and the use of scrim and evocative lighting on a mostly bare stage helped to integrate the actor into the whole décor. The poet or theatre artist could now use color, light and shape to evoke an inner reality rather than illustrate an objective one. In 1891, Fort announced that performances at the theatre would henceforth

> conclude with the mise-en-scène of a painting of a new school which has not yet been exhibited publicly or which is still in progress. The curtain will be raised for three minutes to show the tableau vivant. Actors and models will represent the immobile and silent figures. ... The combination of scenic music and perfumed scents relevant to the subject of the painting will prepare and subsequently perfect the artistic impact of the work. ... As Baudelaire stated, the perfumes, colors, and sounds are in reciprocal correspondence.
>
> (Deak 1993: 142)

Although the staging of these Symbolist tableaux did not occur in the way that Fort had planned, it is significant that Fort includes "perfumed scents" as equal components engaged in "reciprocal correspondence." By including scent, Fort implies that the Théâtre d'Art was not merely staging Symbolist texts in a new artistic style but was creating a synesthetic experience that pushed beyond the boundaries of current artistic practice and thought.

Ronaird's *The Song of Songs* disrupted several ideas about theatre and art. As Kirsten Shepherd-Barr has pointed out, Roinard's choice of Solomon's *Song of Songs* from the Old Testament, a non-dramatic text, challenged assumptions about genre and added a mythic and ritualistic dimension:

the enactment of scenes from biblical sources (themselves shrouded in myth and mystery), the use of incense-like scents, the involvement of the audience, the incantatory nature of the dialogue … would also have worked on the performative level of enacting an entire set of assumptions about art shared by a small community of the indoctrinated.

(Shepherd-Barr 1999: 154)

The biblical text is a collection of love lyrics attributed to Solomon in the tradition of Egyptian and Syrian wedding festivities. The eight poems are structured as a dialogue between a "Beloved" and her "Lover" with commentary from a Poet and a Chorus. The imagery is erotic, and the text contains many references to perfumes, scents, and incense. In the fourth poem, for example, the Lover exclaims:

How fragrant your perfumes,
more fragrant than all spices!
Your lips, my promised bride,
distil wild honey,
Honey and milk
are under your tongue;
and the scent of your garments
is like the scent of Lebanon.

(*Song of Songs* 1990: 778)

Deak writes that Roinard left the biblical text unchanged and considered himself only a "translator" (Deak 1993: 153). While Roinard's complete text has not survived, we do have the scenario that he provided the audience at the Théâtre d'Art. This is a conceptual scenario that implies not only how Roinard adapted the source material but also how he orchestrated speech, sound, sight, and scent into a kind of synesthetic score.

From a dramatic view, Roinard allegorizes the original poems and delineates its figures as "actual" characters of "Pastoral King" and "Pastoral Queen"; the first "symbolizes the divine spirit" and the second "the human spirit" (Roinard 1976: 129–35). Where the source poems told a love story of intense physical and emotional attraction, Roinard's story strangely mutes the physicality and emphasizes the intellectual and moral aspects of the King testing the Queen's loyalty and love. Roinard provides two more categories of character: "expletive characters" or presences that enhance the overall allegory (the "Spirit of Solomon" and the "Spirit of God") and "supernumeraries" (a chorus each for King and Queen).

Roinard's subtitle, a "Symphony of spiritual love in eight mystic devices and three paraphrases," along with the layout of the scenario, gives some idea of the structure of the performance as it proceeds through eight sections of the story with eight corresponding sensory experiences. For each poem or "mystic device," Roinard provides elaboration under three headings: "real meaning," "mystical meaning," and "musical meaning," and he proscribes the exact fusion of speech inflection, music, color, and scent. For the First Device, Roinard sets out:

Orchestration: speech: in i–e, illuminated with o (white)
music: in C
color: pale purple
scent: frankincense

(Roinard 1976: 130)

Deak explains that the speech setting means that the vowels "i" and "o" were stressed when the verse of this First Device was spoken. The music (by Flamen de Labrély) was in the key of C, the color of the stage was light purple, and the scent that was vaporized within the auditorium was frankincense (Deak 1993: 154).

Roinard designed and directed the production, and it was common practice at the theatre for poets to direct their own work. In the program, Roinard explained his intent of "synthesizing the atmosphere of the dream which envelops the *Song of Songs*" (Roinard 1976: 129). Deak describes the setting as consisting of three painted drops (with aspects of the iconography as described above) and a scrim. The costumes were simple white draped cloths, and the lights were not dimmed; the overall brightness probably allowed for better changing and mixing of colors. Thus each Device would express a dominant tonality of color, light, voice, music and scent.

Nine scents in all were used over the course of the performance – frankincense, white violets, hyacinth, lilies, acadia, lily of the valley, syringa, orange blossom, and jasmine – and were released from the proscenium, from hand-held vaporizers from various positions in the house and, as Roinard calls for in his scenario, the onstage lilies were to have given off fumes of incense (*ibid.*: 130–5). How much scent was used, how quickly it dissipated, and how it intermingled was unclear. The experience of the scent would be compromised by the relative distance a spectator was from the source of the perfume and the ambient scents already present in the audience.

The Song of Songs had two performances, a matinée dress rehearsal for the press and an evening performance, at the Théâtre Moderne on 10 December 1891. The audience reaction was mixed. Kirsten Shepherd-Barr relates that Julien Leclercq, the reviewer for the *Mercure de France* (a publication supportive of the Symbolists), noted with regret that the audience could not be silent because it was sneezing so much in reaction to the perfumes, yet he praised the music, scenery, and Roinard's ability as a director, while blaming the audience for a lack of refinement (Shepherd-Barr 1999: 155). Deak explains that "some found the whole thing preposterous and could not suppress their laughter, especially when seeing the young symbolist poets as stagehands vaporizing the perfumes; others found it, even while recognizing certain problems, a sublime experience" (Deak 1993: 155–6). But Henri Fouquier in *Le Figaro* was not so understanding and worried that the performance was dangerous: "There are those who laugh at the vaporizers of the Théâtre d'Art, but can one be sure that the perfumes they exhale are not seriously turning our heads? I am inclined to think they are and I am starting to wonder if we are not losing the genius of our race: our reason" (Whitton 1987: 31). One is reminded of Arkadina's response to Treplev's use of scent during his daring, Symbolist-inspired theatre performance in Act One of Chekhov's *The Sea Gull* (1896): "It reeks of sulfur. Is that really necessary?" she admonishes her son upon being affronted with fumes intended to evoke the power of evil (Chekhov 1977: 14).

Similar to other Théâtre d'Art programs, *The Song of Songs* had little rehearsal, was cast with several inexperienced actors, and was part of a long bill of pieces so that the audience found it difficult to maintain its attention, as Roinard describes:

> The curtain went up at one o'clock in the morning with few people present. The choruses sang out of tune, the music got too loud, the colored lights came out badly and the scents even worse. The declamation seemed long – nothing astonishing at that hour

of sleep. Only the decor got applause, from which its author could derive only internal satisfaction because nobody else knew that he had designed it.

(Deak 1993: 156)

Perhaps the audience was distracted from entering into this sensory experience by the rather programmatic scenario. Perhaps Fort did not have sufficient funds to purchase enough perfume to adequately fill the theatre, as Gertrude Japser indicates (Jasper 1947: 63). Or perhaps audience members were affronted by the engulfing, transgressive nature of scent in the theatre. While it had its failings in performance, *The Song of Songs* stands as perhaps the only example of the period where scent was utilized in such a formal and conceptual fashion.

REFERENCES

Baudelaire, Charles. 1958. "Correspondences." In *French Symbolist Poetry*. Translated by C.F. MacIntyre. Berkeley: University of California Press.

Bely, Andrei. 1985. *The Jaws of Night*. In *Doubles, Demons, and Dreamers: An International Collection of Symbolist Drama*, translated and edited by Daniel Gerould. New York: Performing Arts Journal Publications.

Chekhov, Anton. 1977. *The Sea Gull*. In *Anton Chekhov's Plays,* translated and edited by Eugene K. Bristow. New York: W.W. Norton.

Classen, Constance. 1994. *Aroma: The Cultural History of Smell*. London: Routledge.

Claudel, Paul. 1965. "Le Poète et le Vase d'encens." In *Oeuvres en Prose*. Paris: Éditions Gallimard.

Corbin, Alain. 1986. *The Foul and the Fragrant: Odor and the French Social Imagination*. Cambridge, Mass.: Harvard University Press.

D'Annunzio, Gabriele. 1923. *The Dead City*. In *The Eleonora Duse Series of Plays*, translated by G. Mantellini, edited by Oliver Sayler. New York: Brentano's.

——. 1991. *The Child of Pleasure*, translated by Georgina Harding. St Ives: Dedalus.

Deak, Frantisek. 1993. *Symbolist Theater: The Formation of an Avant-Garde*. Baltimore: Johns Hopkins University Press.

Fort, Paul. 1944. *Mes Mémoirs*. Paris: Flammarion.

Huysmans, J.K. 1969. *Against the Grain*. New York: Dover Publications.

Jasper, Gertrude R. 1947. *Adventure in the Theatre: Lugné-Poe and the Théâtre de l'Oeuvre to 1899*. New Brunswick, NJ: Rutgers University Press.

Mallarmé, Stéphane. 1995. "Interview with Stéphane Mallarmé (1891)." In *Symbolist Art Theories: A Critical Anthology*, translated and edited by Henri Dorra. Berkeley: University of California Press.

Mayer, Charles S. 1989. "Ida Rubinstein: a twentieth-century Cleopatra." *Dance Research Journal* 20 2: 33–51.

Rachilde. 1998. *Pleasure [Volupté]*. In *Madame La Mort and Other Plays*, translated and edited by Kiki Gounaridou and Frazer Lively. Baltimore: Johns Hopkins University Press.

Rindisbacher, Hans. 1992. *The Smell of Books: A Cultural Study of Olfactory Perception in Literature*. Ann Arbor: University of Michigan Press.

Robertson, W. Graham. 1945. *Time Was: The Reminiscences of W. Graham Robertson*. London: Hamilton.

Roinard, Paul Napoleon. 1976. *The Song of Songs of Solomon,* scenario translated by Lenora Champagne and Norma Jean Deak. *The Drama Review* 20, 3: 129–35.

Shepherd-Barr, Kirsten. 1999. "'Mise en scent': the Théâtre d'Art's *Cantique des cantiques* and the use of smell as a theatrical device." *Theatre Research International* 24 2: 152–9.

Slater, Maya. 1997. "Introduction" to *Three Pre-Surrealist Plays*, translated by Maya Slater. Oxford: Oxford University Press.

Wansbrough, Henry, ed. 1990. *Song of Songs.* In *The New Jerusalem Bible.* New York: Doubleday.

Whitton, David. 1987. *Stage Directors in Modern France.* Manchester: Manchester University Press.

Wilde, Oscar. 1988. *The Picture of Dorian Gray*, edited by Donald L. Lawler. New York: W.W. Norton.

9

SENSING REALISM
Illusionism, actuality, and the theatrical sensorium

Stanton B. Garner Jr

In the fall of 1991, the New York Theatre Workshop presented the American premiere of *Mad Forest*, Caryl Churchill's 1990 play about the Romanian Revolution, at the Greenwich Village Perry Street Theatre. The production, directed by Mark Wing-Davey, was provocative in its strategies of audience address. Denied the comfort and invisibility of conventional modern spectatorship, the audience was made to share the physical demands to which the play's characters are subject. Wing-Davey and his set designer made resourceful use of the intimate seating of the Perry Street Theatre: uncomfortable chairs and benches comprised the front row, and these were extended into the rubble that surrounded the edge of the stage (by the end of the play, several spectators were sitting on the floor amid this rubble). The radio music in the first scene was turned up to a painfully high decibel level, and the continual lighting of cheap cigarettes subjected the audience to a cloud of acrid smoke. As Wing-Davey explained in a discussion following the performance, *Mad Forest* deals with the physical and cognitive discomforts involved in encountering a society as removed as that of Romania. These strategies for physicalizing reception paralleled the text's concern with the linguistic barriers to this kind of intercultural contact: Churchill specifies that each scene in Acts 1 and 3 opens with a subtitle spoken in Romanian, then English, then Romanian again, as if even the drama itself must contend with the cumbersome mediation of language texts and phrase books.

The accentuation of Churchill's audience address in terms of the sights, sounds, smells, and environmental tactility of performance reflects the modern theatre's expanding preoccupation with the theatrical sensorium and its multiple experiential channels. One thinks of Marinetti's Futurist theatre, which sought to transform the theatrical auditorium into a space of sensory dynamism and exchange. Seeking the precursors of this theatre, Marinetti celebrated the Variety Theatre for its reliance on "swift actuality" (Marinetti 1971: 116) and for its generation of what he termed the "Futurist marvelous" (117). The marvelous is characterized by sensory invasion, the subversion of intellect by "body-madness" (120). Marinetti proclaimed "the new significations of light, sound, noise, and language, with their mysterious and inexplicable extensions into the least-explored part of our sensibility" (117). At every turn, in other words, the Futurist theatre should activate the spectator's sensory reflexes. In words that anticipate the expanded *mise en scène* of Wing-Davey's *Mad Forest*, Marinetti writes:

> The Variety Theatre uses the smoke of cigars and cigarettes to join the atmosphere of the theatre to that of the stage. And because the audience cooperates in this way with the actors' fantasy, the action develops simultaneously on the stage, in the boxes, and in the orchestra.
>
> (Marinetti 1971: 118)

Among his more playful suggestions, he proposes sprinkling the seats with dust "to make people itch and sneeze, etc." (121).

Marinetti's manifestoes (and the Futurist evenings that sought to realize theory in performance practice) exemplify the sensory transgression of the stage–audience barrier that would characterize early twentieth-century *avant-garde* theatre: the *bruitisme* of Dada performance; Antonin Artaud's "cruel" theatre; Bertolt Brecht's presentational theatre, where stage and audience confront each other across a space of mutually sensory self-presence (here, once again, cigar and cigarette smoke play an important role in joining stage and audience). Futurist Luigi Russolo's 1913 treatise *The Art of Noises* proposed a theatre in which the noises of trams, motors, and shouting crowds would replicate the sonic landscape of urban modernism.[1] In each case, it is the realist theatre against which these sensory theatres defined their transgressive operations. For Marinetti, the Variety Theatre's "body madness" opposed itself to the conventional theatre, which "exalts the inner life" (120) against the life of the senses, with its "profound analogies between humanity, the animal, vegetable, and mechanical worlds" (117). Implicit in Artaud's attacks on conventional "psychological theatre" is his repudiation of a mimetic realism in which – far from participating in the direct contact between organisms – "the public is no longer shown anything but the mirror of itself" (Artaud 1958: 76).

It is this repudiation, this belief that realism as a theatrical practice forecloses the theatre's sensory channels of address, that I would like to address here. For it is my contention that the development of modern realism is crucial to the emergence and articulation of the theatrical sensorium as this has manifested itself in the theatre and drama of the past 125 years. Exploring this connection allows us a broader insight into the theatre as experiential medium. The varied, often conflicting, deployments of sensory experience within realism illuminate the boundaries, activations, and displacements through which theatre's play of actuality takes place. It illuminates, as well, the complexities attendant upon the body's sensory openings, and its modes of disclosure, within the mutually inherent fields of spectatorship and performance. Finally, attention to sensory address in the theatre can help to illuminate the internal dynamics and representational volatility of realism itself, still one of the most misunderstood and undervalued of theatrical aesthetics.

The central issue is one of repression – or bracketing, to employ a more formally neutral term. Through the strategies of illusionism, realist stagecraft and dramaturgy seek to enforce a separation between the dramatic stage world and that of the audience, to relegate each to different ontological and experiential spheres. The dynamic is familiar: the dramatic world is constituted as autonomous field to the extent that the worlds of audience and performance are bracketed out, deactivated as fields of attention in their own right. The technological developments that enabled and accompanied the realist revolution in the nineteenth century worked both to heighten the verisimilitude of the represented world and further to enclose this world in representational self-sufficiency. The institution of gas lighting, for instance, allowed light on stage to assume greater perceptual realism, but it could do so only through the eclipsing, the putting out of play, of the actual lighting (or non-lighting) of the theatrical auditorium as a whole. Light, in this sense, is fictionalized and at the same time detheatricalized, in that its technological origins in the performance moment are placed "out of attention."

But what actually strikes the retina in such a production: an actual or a fictional light? The former, as it always does inside and outside the theatre. Fictional or illusionistic light inhabits, and is inhabited by, an actual light that conveys its fictional phenomenality (the rising sun at the opening of *The Cherry Orchard* (1904), for example) through the operation of real photons striking real eyes. There is an instability in this, born of the paradox of the actual in theatrical realism: that the stage produces the illusion of the real through its actual materiality and the simultaneous suppression of this. As its own paradoxical name suggests, illusionism carries within itself the means by which the real is constructed and an instability with which its fictional autonomy is continually threatened.

I have written elsewhere about this bifurcated mode of presence characteristic of the theatrical field, whereby theatrical objects oscillate between the illusionistic (fictional, virtual) and the actual (Garner 1994: 39–45). This perceptual instability characterizes all forms of theatre, no matter how strident their claims to radical actuality, but it reveals itself with particular complexity in the theatres of realism and naturalism. The documents of these movements betray the movements' competing claims. August Strindberg's famous preface to *Miss Julie* (1888) urges the enclosure of the stage and a bracketing of the auditorium's actual spatial relationships. Setting, mime, monologue, costume, make-up, acting – all are naturalized within a guiding scenic illusionism. Strindberg recognizes the sleight of hand that this involves and the difficulty of surmounting the actual on behalf of scenic verisimilitude (or true-seeming): nothing is more difficult, he writes, than to get a room on stage to look like a room (Strindberg 1981: 73). That this consolidation depends on the effacement of the audience–stage relationship and its sensory and other modes of presence is emblematized in Strindberg's wish that the actor might deliver important scenes with his or her back to the audience, thereby reinforcing the discontinuity between the dramatic world and the environmental actuality that serves as its perceptual ground.

And yet there are equally powerful currents in realist theory and practice that undermine illusionistic autonomy. Émile Zola's writings on naturalism in the theatre, which profoundly interested Strindberg, in fact advance a different relationship between stage and audience. Like Strindberg, Zola calls for the overthrow of artificial conventions and the theatrical installation of the real. Unlike Strindberg, though, Zola envisions a stage reformed to the point where it becomes continuous with the auditorium, not further separated from it. Such a stage finds its realism in an actuality drawn from the world beyond the lights and outside the theatre. Drama should be set in factories, the interior of a mine, a railway station, a race track, and the reality of such representations is legitimized by the importation of extra-theatrical materials: the actual clothes of tradespeople, for instance. Strindberg's naturalism, disciplined by an aesthetic of enclosure and removal, anticipates the hermetic art of high modernism, its achievement commensurate with the attainment of autonomy. Zola's, by contrast, draws upon the tradition of actuality staging that characterized much earlier nineteenth-century theatre, and it prepares the theoretical ground for the theatrical importation of real objects on the naturalist stages of André Antoine and David Belasco (it also stands as a little-acknowledged precursor to twentieth-century environmental theatre). As the argument between Chekhov and Stanislavsky over the latter's plan to use real frogs, dragonflies, and dogs making sounds onstage in the Moscow Art Theatre's production of *The Sea Gull* (1896) illustrates, this contradiction between the competing demands of illusionism and actuality lies at the heart of realist stagecraft.[2]

According to Zola, one of the key transformations effected by "the great naturalistic evolution" has to do with "the gradual substitution of physiological man for metaphysical man" (Zola 1968: 367).[3] This emphasis is consistent with the turn toward environment in realism and naturalism; a concern with the body in its material surroundings entails an interest in the body as sensory agent. Realism, in this sense, opens the theatrical body to the fact of its embodiment, and it foregrounds the sensory exchanges between bodies and between body and setting. Actuality staging intensifies this foregrounding: the use of actual water on stage, for instance, makes possible heightened effects of tactility and sound. Actors/characters can dip their hands in water, get wet, while the sound of water running over stones creates immediate, almost visceral sonic effects. At the same time, illusionism requires that this sensory field be disciplined, its channels of address contained within the boundaries of representation. Illusionism constitutes itself, in part, through the materials of the actual world – "ingests" them, in Bert States' resonant phrasing (States 1985: 37) – but the autonomy of its representation hinges on the containment of the performance sensorium as this involves actor, stage, and audience in an actual, not fictional, field of sensory exchange.

The audience poses special risks here. If illusionism requires that the spectator become invisible in relation to the dramatic world, then his or her sensory participation in the field of performance must be carefully delimited. Touch, taste, and smell – the senses that most undermine the distinctions between subject and object, here and there – are strictly contained, or bracketed entirely. Sight and hearing are subordinated within the directed operations of watching and listening; the participants in a potentially open field of visual and auditory stimuli (to which they themselves contribute) are disciplined as "spectators" and "audience." Eye and ear are dematerialized as sensory agents, denied their own location, so that they may serve as receptors of theatrical and dramatic information. Paradoxically, then, the discovery of "physiological man" that realism and naturalism achieve is accompanied – in theory, at least – by a perceptual deactivation of the audience's own physiological presence, and the sensory performance field that realism inaugurates is bound within specific structures of perception and attention. From the audience's point of view, the realist theatre attempts not only an "imprisonment of the eye" (to quote States again [69]) but a wider restriction of the sensory apparatus as a whole.

The major texts of late nineteenth-century realist drama regularly play out this dialectic of sensory activation and repression. The dramatic worlds of Ibsen's plays, for instance, contain a powerful sensory stratum; their recourse to speech, which Shaw so admired, is accompanied and counterpointed by a nonverbal language of sight, sound, smell, taste, and feel. In *The Wild Duck* (1884), attention is drawn to the delicate flavor of Tokay wine, the chilly air of the Ekdal studio, the acrid smell left by Gregers' misadventures with the stove in his room, and the pain of bright light on Hedvig's eyes. A similar sensory subtext establishes itself in *Hedda Gabler* (1890) from the play's opening moments. Even before characters enter in Act 1, Ibsen's stage directions have established the perceptual contours of Hedda's world. The drawing room is decorated in dark colors, cluttered with furniture and objects clearly moved from a larger household into this one; the floor is covered in "thick carpet," and this sense of heaviness and enclosure is reinforced by curtains. In one of the most interesting of Ibsen's stage effects, the stage is covered with flowers, bouquets of which "are placed about the drawing room in vases and glasses" (Ibsen 1965: 695). This crowded room is one of thick textures and hyper-sweet smells, and its density of sensory stimulation underlies the play's atmosphere of oppressiveness and claustrophobia. And yet, as even this characterization suggests, the sensory stimuli of this stage-world are subject to strategies of containment, subordinated to the diegetic demands of the play's realist representation. In *The Wild Duck*, the audience does not share the taste of Tokay, except vicariously; it does not smell the smoke from Gregers' room or feel the cold of Ekdal's loft. One discerns in *The Wild Duck* and *Hedda Gabler*, as in all of Ibsen's later plays, a sensual field held in check, pressing up against the restrictions of the play's realist aesthetic, longing (like the play's protagonists) to break through the repression of the conventions to which it subscribes.

In truth, it does. While the polemical attacks of those advocating a non-realist stage practice in the early twentieth century presented realism in terms of its most illusionistic pretensions, the movement's twin allegiances (to illusionism and actuality) destabilize its strategies of sensory containment at every turn. As the earlier example of light demonstrates, the actuality that bodies forth representation also presents its own claims to attention. The notorious carcasses of beef in Antoine's 1888 production of Ferdinand Icre's *The Butchers* are objects within the play's dramatic action and real objects in their own right, with their own textures and smells. This sensory stratum, like the stage as a whole, works to counter the positioning of those in the auditorium as detached spectators/audience. There are directorial opportunities here as well. The phenomenality of the realist stage subverts the boundaries of illusionism: Hedda's gunshot is both an event in the play's dramatic narrative and an acoustic event whose sharpness startles the ear even as it is not entirely unexpected. Paradoxically, the greater the drive toward actuality, the more precarious the sensory discipline of realist performance becomes. Indeed, the more realist stage practice works to incorporate the world outside the theatre within the sphere of illusion, the more it risks theatricalizing the actual in performance, bodying it forth in a kind of hyper-actuality. What drives this process is the alienation of the object within illusionism itself.

By approaching realism through the phenomena of theatrical sensation, I am proposing a different, more complicated picture of this aesthetic than is generally offered. Despite its own claims, realism is not solely a system of disciplines that fixes the relationship between stage and audience; rather, it is leaky, marked by representational instabilities, animated by contradictory ontologies of the real and the actual that lie at the heart of theatre as a representational medium. Its referentiality is multiple, perceptually dialectic. Even as it installs the body as the experiential center of a "real-ized" scenographic field, it works to discipline the sensory channels of this field under the aegis of mimetic referentiality. At the same time, even as realism attempts severely to limit the spectator's sensory participation, the actuality of its material field threatens to reclaim the spectator as physiological/sensory agent. Realism sets into play a game of concealment and revelation, and it is not unusual for even canonical realists to play with the shifting boundary between the illusionistic and the actual. The well-known effect in Act 2 of *The Cherry Orchard* when the silence of the open air is broken by a distant sound – "as if from the sky, like the sound of a snapped string mournfully dying away" (Chekhov 1964: 348) – could be seen as one such moment when realism explores its perceptual seams. Characters wonder at the sound, try to account for it, but the various explanations they come up with – a bucket breaking loose in a mine shaft, a heron, an owl – fail to incorporate its sudden appearance within the dramatic fiction. Instead, when the sound is first heard it reverberates onstage and off, disturbing the dramatic illusion; unsubordinated by the otherness of Chekhov's world, the sound exists within a sensorium that underlies and exceeds the illusion to which the stage pretends. The echoes of this troubling actuality hover over the scene, at least until the characters succeed in talking it back down.

The history of realist stage practice in the modern and contemporary theatre has been marked by a deepening interest in the representational and phenomenological instabilities particular to this aesthetic. As a corollary of this, it has shown an interest in realism's sensory opportunities. The extension of one of realism's central projects – the incorporation of materials from the extra-theatrical world – has allowed contemporary realism to deepen its exploration of its latent sensory registers. The use of metallic materials in the 1998 National Theatre production of Tennessee William's *Not About Nightingales*, for example, established an almost visceral acoustic field: the clanging of prison doors and the rattling of bars operated both in the play's narrative realm and in the spatialized encounter of materials, bodies, and nerves. And while the steam of the play's climactic scene was not actual, it spread beyond the stage and into the audience with stifling effect. The production's material and tactile density owes debts to Brecht's theatre and (even more) to the Living Theatre's 1963 production *The Brig*. But its inheritance reaches much further back, to the transgressive actuality of the realist tradition itself.

Contemporary playwrights have likewise been fascinated by realism's contra-dictory manipulation of the theatre's sensory fields. Probably no postwar dramatist has shown more interest in realism's sensory possibilities than Sam Shepard. Moving into realism from his more openly experimental plays of the 1960s and early–mid 1970s, Shepard approaches its conventions deconstructively, pressing the sensory actuality of the realist stage to the point where, like the Old Man's rocker in *Fool for Love* (1983) it violates illusionism's frames. Throughout his career, Shepard has been fascinated by the senses: the experiential textures they make available; their different modes of spatializing the environment; the ways they negotiate and subvert the boundaries between self and other, inside and outside. Shepard's early plays are direct in their sensory investigations: the feel of bath water on the human body, the way biscuits feel when swallowed – "a hunk of dough that goes down and makes a gooey ball in your stomach" (Shepard 1986: 49) – the snap, crackle, and pop of Rice Crispies when milk is poured on them, the smell of farts. At times in these early plays the audience is directly involved in the theatre as sensory realm: a steaming turkey is carved onstage in *Action* (1975), the audience is instructed in the technique and sensations of breathing in *Chicago* (1965), and the auditorium is completely filled with smoke in *Forensic & the Navigators* (1967).

When Shepard moved into realism with *Curse of the Starving Class* (1978), *Buried Child* (1978), and his other plays of the late 1970s and early 1980s, he shifted his attention to the repressed yet volatile sensuality that has characterized this tradition from the start. Employing materials not usually found in the theatre, while accentuating those that are to the point where they assume a kind of hyper-actuality, Shepard's "realist" plays achieve sensory effects that violate the boundary between audience and play. To focus on one of the senses that Shepard calls into play, Shepard's family play reveals a heightened awareness of theatre as olfactory space. Given that its signals involve actual molecules permeating an unlocalizeable space, smell is one of the most transgressive senses as far as illusionism is concerned. As Louis observes to Joe in *Perestroika* (1992), the second part of Tony Kushner's *Angels in America* (1991–92):

> Smell is ... an incredibly complex and underappreciated physical phenomenon. ... We have only five senses, but only two that go beyond the boundaries of ourselves. When you look at someone, it's just bouncing light, or when you hear them, it's just sound waves, vibrating air, or touch is just nerve endings tingling. ... [Smell is] made up of the molecules of what you're smelling.
>
> (Kushner 1992: 30)

In Scene 8 of *True West* (1980), Shepard avails himself of these transgressive possibilities. The scene opens with the set covered with toasters that Austin has stolen from his neighbors to prove his manhood to his brother Lee. The setting at this point is already marked by Shepard's deconstructive hand. One chrome toaster is realism; fourteen chrome toasters, on the other hand, are something else, a form of hyper-realism. The functional materiality of the appliance – the gleaming tactility of its chrome surface – is defamiliarized through multiplication. When Austin proceeds to place slices of bread in each toaster (all are plugged in) and pushes down the handles, the sensory reach of these objects is extended. The bread cooks in the toasters, individual slices pop into view, and the theatre is filled with the smell. As with the artichokes cooking onstage in *Curse of the Starving Class*, Shepard's stagecraft here re-embodies his spectators by challenging the perceptual bracketing with which realism seeks to erase their sensory presence to play and stage. In so doing, Shepard implicates his audience in questions of hunger – actual and literal – that are attendant upon an embodied life in contact with its material and human environments.

It is easy to think of Shepard's as a kind of resistant realism, in which the conventions of realist theatre are inflected by the disruptive techniques of 1960s experimental theatre. It is likewise common to think of *Mad Forest* in the context of presentational anti-realism, Brechtian and otherwise. Yet despite their debt to a range of theatrical practices, this drama also represents the playing out of a representational logic within realism itself. Realism both disguises and foregrounds the sensory channels of theatrical address, and in the slippages and instabilities between these operations it lays a foundation not only for the mimetically sealed theatre that Brecht imagined it to be but for excursions into the sensory field of theatre and its modes of audience, actor, and character experience. Cooking toast, the painful decibels of a radio turned up loud, smoke filling a room (or the eating of bread at the end of Bread and Puppet performances and the physical involvement of the audience in contemporary environmental performance): these emerge from the heart of the realist project as the other side of its strategies of containment and as an inevitable consequence of the conflict between illusionism and actuality staging. Rather than positing realism as a conservative point against which the many "anti-realistic" practices of the twentieth century are marked, it is more useful, in the end, to recognize that these concurrent and later movements are often in dialogue with realism, extending its reach, playing out its contradictory modes of disclosure, exploring the implications of the physiological/sensory body that realism brings to theatre.

REFERENCES

Artaud, Antonin. 1958. *The Theatre and Its Double*, translated by Mary Caroline Richards. New York: Grove Press.

Chekhov, Anton. 1964. *Major Plays*, translated by Ann Dunnigan. New York: New American Library.

Garner, Stanton B., Jr. 1994. *Bodied Spaces: Phenomenology and Performance in Contemporary Drama*. Ithaca, NJ: Cornell University Press.

———. 2000. "Physiologies of the modern: Zola, experimental medicine, and the naturalist stage." *Modern Drama* 4: 529–42.

Ibsen, Henrik. 1965. *The Complete Major Prose Plays*, translated by Rolf Fjelde. New York: New American Library.

Kushner, Tony. 1992. *Angels in America: Perestroika*. New York: Theatre Communications Group.

Marinetti, F.T. 1971. "The Variety Theatre." *Selected Writings*, edited by R.W. Flint, translated by Arthur A. Coppotelli. New York: Farrar, Straus and Giroux.

Russolo, Luigi. 1986. *The Art of Noises*, translated by Barclay Brown. New York: Pendragon Press.

Shepard, Sam. 1986. *Chicago*. In *The Unseen Hand and Other Plays*. Toronto: Bantam.

Simmons, Ernest J. 1962. *Chekhov: A Biography*. Chicago: University of Chicago Press.

States, Bert O. 1985. *Great Reckonings in Little Rooms: On the Phenomenology of Theatre*. Berkeley: University of California Press.

Strindberg, August. 1981. Preface to *Miss Julie*. *Five Plays*, translated by Harry G. Carlson. Berkeley: University of California Press.

Wilson, Eric. 1995. "Plagues, fairs, and street cries: sounding out society and space in early modern London." *Modern Language Studies* 25, 3: 1–42.

Zola, Emile. 1968 [1881]. *Naturalism in the Theatre*. Excerpts translated by Albert Bermel. In *The Theory of the Modern Stage*, edited by Eric Bentley. Harmondsworth: Penguin.

NOTES

1 For more on the notion of acoustic landscape, see Wilson (1995).

2 "The stage is art. There is a canvas of Kramskoi in which he wonderfully depicts human faces. Suppose he eliminated the nose of one of these faces and substituted a real one. The nose will be 'realistic,' but the picture will be spoiled" (Anton Chekhov, quoted in Simmons 1962: 430).

3 For a discussion of Zola's concern with the organic body, see Garner (2000).

Part III

CONTEMPORARY PERFORMANCE

10

GUIDING SOMATIC RESPONSES WITHIN PERFORMATIVE STRUCTURES
Contemporary live art and sensorial perception

Stephen Di Benedetto

Blackness. Damp earth. Must. Rumbling from the trains above. I taste dry grit on my tongue, maybe iron. My arms go straight out in front swishing back and forth checking for obstacles, and I use my foot to test if the ground is secure and flat in front of me. Maybe it is just that I am in a crumbling tunnel beneath south London, but I wonder how I will ever find my way to the faint light and see what objects Robert Wilson has laid out as part of his *H.G.* installation.[1] On a bright sunny day a few years later, across the world on the third floor of the DIA Centre for the Arts in New York city, I stumble through a maze of gauze walls, set up by Robert Irwin, making my way by the diffuse light that penetrates them.[2] I begin to watch the shadows of others wandering through the space; the roar of the city seems faint, my breathing slows down, and I just watch. In Ireland yet a few more years later, I enter a flat on the north side of Dublin.[3] There is the smell of coffee and stale sweat as I walk across the creaking floorboards, through the back hall and out into the bright sun of the back garden. People are milling about, and some dirty garden furniture is offered up for us to sit on and wait for the event to start. Are the residents acting, or are we just sitting around? I have only my perceptions of the experience moving through the environments, monitoring my sensations of the smells, sounds, sights, and occasional tastes of the environment. To understand each of these artistically mediated events, I must activate my awareness of the performance sensorium. I must adjust my expectations of what a performative event is so that I may take an active role in the way in which I am attendant to the event.

As human beings, our biological composition dictates that our knowledge and exploration of the world take place through the senses. Rudolf Arnheim explains:

> If perception were nothing better than the passive reception of information, one would expect the mind would not be disturbed by being left without such input for a while and might indeed welcome the repose. The experiments on sensory deprivation have shown, however, that this is not so. When the visual, auditory, tactile and kinaesthetic senses are reduced to unpatterned stimulation – nothing but diffuse light for the eyes and a steady buzz for the ears – the entire mental functioning of the person is upset. ...

The continuous response to the environment is the foundation for the working of the nervous system.[4]

We are genetically programmed to respond to the visual, aural, tactile, and aromatic. Our senses guide us and confirm for us our perceptual awareness – unsure of my footing I tentatively reach my foot out and test the ground in front. As Tuan Yi-Fu describes:

The sense, under the aegis and direction of the mind, give us a world. Some are "proximate," others "distant." The proximate senses yield the world closest to us, including our own bodies. The position and movements of our bodies produce proprioception or kinaesthesia, somatic awareness of the basic dimensions of space. The other proximate senses are touch, sensitivity to changes in temperature, taste and smell. Hearing and sight are considered the senses that make the world "out there" truly accessible.[5]

As Tuan observes, hearing and sight are the most accessible of the senses and have been relied upon in our interpretation and understanding of artistic mediation. It is only by exploring the role of sensorial perception and stimulation that we can broaden our understanding of the capabilities and possibilities of nonverbal expression in the performing arts.

As sentient beings, we seek out stimuli to inform us about the world. If artists harness words, line color, and movement, are not smell, taste, and touch just as viable and malleable stimuli? Tuan's description of the senses suggests the potential for the arts:

Smell, compared with sight and hearing, affects our emotions at a more deeply buried level. The olfactory sense is linked to a primitive part of the brain that controls emotions and mood and the involuntary movements of life, including breathing, heartbeat, pupil size, and genital erection.[6]

If our senses, like smell, affect our involuntary and primitive receptors, is this not a potent expressive tool where artists can trigger an involuntary reaction and thereby guide the visceral experience of an event? The perception of taste, smell, sound, touch, and vision will serve as a framework with which to understand the ways in which artistically mediated environments influence a spectator's perception of an event. Using methodologies drawn from phenomenological perspectives, I will examine the way in which several live art events triggered a sensorial journey for their attendants. The experiences of these events by the attendant bodies worked to expand the way in which the body is aware of the ways it perceives the world. In other words, can we begin to think of the sensual stimulation generated by events as asking those present to be attendant to, or actively participate in, the event?

Applying an awareness of phenomenology to the study of contemporary art and performance allows a range of questions to be asked about the role of the five senses in artistic expression. What are the ways in which spectators can become aware of the full range of sensations offered from performance or live art events? To what extent do artists consciously use sight, sound, smell, touch, and taste as expressive forms? What are the possible ways in which the senses influence one's experience of artwork? What means do we, as bodies attendant to these events, have to chart and describe these experiences?

FINDING A LANGUAGE

Part of the problem of trying to consider the operations of the senses in performance is the role of language as the limiting function in our description of, or even perception of, artistic experience. Language or words exist to provide the conscious filtering of experience into communication. Right away we have a problem – filtering. The mere use of language already filters the broad range of stimuli into a cognitive and linguistic framework – a framework that subscribes to the rules of semiotics and cultural socialization – a world that is different from the realm of the senses in which bodily perception rules. So how can we talk about the senses, whose filtering into language limits us to centuries of intellectual discourse that devalues and distrusts the sensuous world?

The acknowledgment of the realm of the senses demands a different style of presentation – academic language is not always the best way to describe the subjective experience of perception. By trying to broaden our understanding of the way in which the nonverbal operates in performative acts, we must loosen our conception of the grammar of our criticism, which inevitably leads us down well-worn paths that privilege linguistic cognition. After all, as Rudolf Arnheim has shown, language is not our only means of thinking; the visual is another nonverbal or intuitive means of thinking. Our sensorial language is extremely limited; can the word "sweet" help us to distinguish between the sugary taste of a fresh strawberry and that of a fresh pecan pie? Immediately, language becomes a potential limitation in describing the full range of the sensation. Likewise, the expression of emotion in the arts has been thought of pejoratively since the Greeks because of its unpredictability. As Arnheim charts the course of anti-sensorial discourse, it is important to acknowledge the primacy of physiological experience.[7] We perceive the world through our senses, and what is beyond our senses is beyond our knowledge. To describe precisely the subjective impressions of sensations, a more poetic or sensual language is necessary. Joanna Frueh suggests that an erotic language is more appropriate to describe bodily engagement because it loosens scholarly language and is sloppy and intimate like sex. She explains: "A critical erotic puts an end to the scholarly tradition of disembodiment. The erotic scholar's lust for the written intimacy of body and mind exceeds personalisation of style and any statement of standpoint."[8] She calls for a subjective, image-driven language to capture the transient sensations of phenomenological experience.

By relating artistic experience to physiological experiences, Frueh is able to speak succinctly and specifically about mediated artistic experience. Not only must discourse about our visceral responses to the smells, tastes, sights, sounds, and touches describe our emotions, it must also break from accepted academic constraints. We must take a step back from the logic and order of the academic discourses to be able to use words to describe a barrage of momentary experience. At the root of talking about theatrical experience is the terminology to describe those present at the performance, such as "audience" or "spectator." These words contain preconceived notions of the manner in which a perception occurs; you are there either to listen or to watch. Perhaps a more neutral term ought to be used that is without the denotative baggage. A word like Boal's "spect-actor," which captures the notion of watching and active participation, is clumsy. Rather, the word "attendant" suggests presence and even can be thought of in the Catholic sense of being "attendant to mass," implying presence and participation.

What follows is a range of experiences of theatrical expression that depend on stimulation of one or more of the senses that are often neglected in the analysis of performance. The best medium with which to draw out the techniques and to call attention to the analytical possibilities of the performance sensorium is the realm of live art. "Live art" is a British term used to describe inter-medial performance – that is, performance that uses aesthetic concepts drawn from painting, sculpture, dance, music, theatre, and performative acts that do not subscribe to traditional definitions of medium and genre.

Theatre and the visual arts share many compositional and aesthetic approaches to expression. The bridge between the visual arts and theatre can be seen through the genre of live art. During the 1990s, many visual artists used performative techniques to create live events where the live proximity between the attendants and the artists highlighted the attendants' role as participants; one could click on a mouse and deliver a shock of pleasure or pain to Epizoo, or have a flashlight shine up into Annie Sprinkle's vagina. These types of event, typical of experiences across the world, take place in small venues such as London's Institute of Contemporary Arts, or Riverside Studios, usually to an audience of less than 100 made up of artists, students, and scholars. The presentation of this work points to a growing preoccupation with articulating the place of the body and bodily functions in contemporary society. Kristine Stiles explains the significance:

> Performance artists insisted that the exigencies of the body exceeded mere represen-
> tation and, moreover, that Enlightenment notions of aesthetic distance, indifference,
> and autonomy were dangerous fictions that had little to do with the actual conditions
> upon and in which real human beings live and artists produce art.[9]

Attendants have had to remove that distance to understand the operations of where art is experienced and produced. Grounded in ideas of space, time, and action, live art is a contemporary manifestation of the cross-disciplinary experimentation of movements such as Bauhaus, which tried to tear down the barriers between the visual arts, crafts, and performing arts. Live art has evolved into an area of practice that ranges from conventional theatre techniques, dance, and music, at one extreme, to video, film, and time-based installation work at the other.

Homo sapiens is naturally inclined to be interested in others of the species, and our experiences are grounded in our bodies. James Elkins describes the significance of this for the visual arts:

> Every picture is a picture of the body. Every work of visual art is a representation of
> the body. To say this is to say that we see bodies, even when there are none, and that the
> creation of a form is to some degree also the creation of a body.[10]

Elkins believes that we perceive bodies in the abstract images of Jackson Pollock and in the natural landscapes of a Japanese garden. But because theatre, performance art, and live art use bodies as primary expressive forms, we must consider how perceiving art objects can inform our perception of theatre. Human proximity adds to our perception of the odours we smell and the objects we touch. Live art is concerned with living, breathing organisms and their by-products.

Contemporary culture is obsessed with bodies; with advertisers using bodies to sell, or by creating an obsession to mask smells or blemishes with various products. Stiles points out:

> Never was "the body" a more contested or beleaguered site than at the end of the twentieth century. The very prevalence of a nomenclature of "the body" signalled a dramatic shift away from the consideration of human beings as complex, sensate, psychophysical, soul-embodied beings with consciousness to figuring us simply as "bodies."[11]

The mass proliferation of somatically obsessed images has denigrated the body to a consumer object to be bought and sold, rather than embraced and touched. However, the visual arts harness the body as object to resist current cultural trends and try to reactivate our sensorial awareness through strategies, asking spectators to challenge their perceptive habits.

Contemporary artists exploit these concepts to create rich sensory experience. One strategy is to take the event out of the traditional stage/auditorium configuration of the proscenium theatre and to work in galleries or in site-specific locations to encourage a different relationship between spectator and actor. Spectators have set expectations of what a performance will be like when they walk into a Shubert theatre; they will sit in the dark quietly and passively absorb the spectacle. Meanwhile, if the same people should walk into the Museum of Modern Art, they would expect to move about and actively engage with the artwork. Taking performative acts outside the theatre encourages a more active participation, where one must be attendant to the performance. The performer, La Ribot explains, "Out of a theatre, the relationship with the audience changes, because in the gallery they are much closer. I feel they can smell me. The work is much more in the skin – sensitive, sensorial, soft."[12] The proximity to the performers and their bodily exertions adds to the level of information that the attendant picks up about the performance. Franko B describes the same sort of tactic in the formation of his live compositions. He activates the attendant's awareness. He explains:

> When I go to a museum and I see a beautiful painting, that's the nearest to this I can think of to what I want my work to be able to do: to create that, but in real life. So I mean creating a very beautiful image with the difference [that] people can smell it, and also they can touch it.[13]

Franko B employs a range of media, such as blood and bodily effluvia, to insure that his spectators will have a range of sensorial experiences. Perhaps his images will fade from memory, but a semblance of the experience will remain within the sense memory. That memory is embodied thinking, and only through an active awareness of sensorial stimuli can the experience begin to be spoken about, using language and cultural models of interpretation. By trying to touch our senses, he asks us to embrace being human and to recover our contact with other humans.

Our sense perceptions are manifestations of our consciousness of the world. By becoming more aware of this consciousness and noting what stimuli trigger the sensations of mediated experience, we can understand the mutable layers of expression. As artists make conscious use of triggering our sensations, analysts must be bold and break from passive modes of critical inquiry. If we embrace the subjective personal sensations generated by an event and tie them to the form of the artwork, then we can make tangible the sensorial experience of the arts. For Stelarc, this process will be complete only when we adapt the instrument of perception – that is, when our bodies mutate into a new form:

> It may seem a rather mechanistic view of the body, but to me the ultimate parameters of the body are the physiological ones, and without altering the sensory input one cannot have a significant new cerebral direction.[14]

There is no split between mind and body, so to change one's thinking, one must change one's body. Stelarc resorts to machinery. His third arm is an attempt to change his experience and awareness of the world. However, most other live artists are satisfied with human physiology and would rather emphasize a reawakening of the senses through artistic mediation and by training attendants of art to become more active in the experience.

THE PROBLEM OF UNINTENTIONAL STIMULATION

One evening while watching a production of August Wilson's *Jitney* at the Alley Theatre, my companion leaned over and asked who was smoking a pipe on stage. The aroma of pipe tobacco filled the house long before we could determine from where and from whom it was emanating. Eventually, an actor gestured with his pipe, and all was revealed. However, the question lingered of why they used real pipe smoke, when they did not use car exhaust or other smells to fill in the smell of the environment. Can smell ever be more than mere artifice used to make authentic a bit of naturalistic mimesis? Whether generated consciously or created as a by-product of the actions of a piece, use of other modes of sensorial stimulation adds another dimension to information transmission. How do we talk about sensory perception in theatre, where many of the smells are mere accidents? How do these experiences break free from the production into a deliberate enrichment of the experience and shape of the event?

If smell guides us in everyday life by giving us key information (pheromones for sexual attraction; disease with the smell of a sore throat or a festering wound; smells related to the menstrual cycle, lactation cycles), then why not shape it to manipulate experience? We also outwardly manipulate scent in our day-to-day routine with perfume and fragrance designed to allure and attract: for example, the smells of aromatherapy designed to give us a sense of well-being, or a room freshener or candles used to neutralize household odours. Smell can tell us where we are, create a mood, trigger behaviour, mask, entice, and repel. It can denote social status: does the person smell of expensive perfume or stale urine? There are natural smells (roses), biological smells (sweat), and manufactured or industrial smells (iron ore); the town of Gary, Indiana, is still identifiable by the smell of burning iron.

In the exertions and activities of everyday life we generate scent. Regardless of whether it is by design or by accident, these smells fill our world. Theatre makes use of natural material and in so doing produces scent. An example will serve to show the consequence if the way in which even in a large auditorium, these fragrances drift their way to the nostrils of the attendants. *Fragile* is a movement piece by Fabulous Beast Dance Theatre Company that transforms a theatre studio into a dirt promontory. To stage right is a giant aquarium sealed with tarnished brass, large enough for bodies to fight underwater. Downstage of that is a giant rope. Upstage left is a giant wooden structure that looks rather like a lifeguard chair. To the left of that is an outdoor shower, and downstage from that is a bathtub filled with chalk. There are a few props, some bottles of milk, many cans of Guinness, oranges, a saw, and a ladder. The program describes the action:

> When cutting an umbilical cord requires a large saw and taking a shower turns into a physical impossibility, life can be a continual heartache. In the world of *Fragile* owning a piece of fruit can be a killing matter. And who does the fat blue Buddha think he is? God.[15]

Onstage movement guides the attendant through a series of episodes whose actions, movements, corporeal shapes, and interrelationship create an abstract narrative. A woman emerges from the tank, and a male and a female creature fight over teaching and taking care of her, while a large blue male sits above, drinks beer, and watches. No definitive story can be told, but the attendant's reactions to the smells generated during performance, such as perspiration mixed with make-up, can lead to a deeply personal narrative.

Company members were fascinated by the range of descriptions of smells that attendants commented upon after the performance. People wanted to know how, for instance, the smell of crushed oranges was supposed to inform their interpretation of the dance. However, the choreographer explained that the smells were accidental. Although the smells that were generated during the course of a performance, including orange, wet soil, hops from Guinness, milk, and chalk, were such a pivotal part of my perception and experience, nevertheless they were unintentional. Michael Keegan-Dolan explains:

> The smells in *Fragile* just happened as a by-product of the imagery. I see an image, it develops in my mind, we try and realise it, and the smells attached come gratis. I could lie and say it was an enormous part of the concept, but it honestly was not. Besides, I have a broken nose and a damaged olfactory nerve, and I cannot smell shit, literally.[16]

The smells generated provided body and substance to the abstract moving images – the smells of milk on flesh streaming down the naked body of a principal female dancer brought home the seminal and amniotic qualities of the movement. We saw slimy, sticky bodies, but with the smells these images became visceral. They became real to my sense memory, and no longer were they image, movement, texture, and color but an experience that called upon memories of playing down by the river as a child, digging in the mud, concocting bombs out of baby powder, toothpaste, and water. The sight of writhing bodies dripping mud is visually arousing, but the mingled smells of the different elemental objects such as milk, dirt, and hops accentuate memories of playful experimentations with love in the forests, where bodily fluids mingle with dirt and river water. Sensory memory makes the abstract images of birth and sex come together in the experience of the composite sensation received over the duration of the event. These actions by the dancers trigger sense receptors, which in turn activate memory.

SENTIENT BODIES

Epizoo is a performance/installation by Marcel.Li Antunez Roca. It is an interactive media event in which Roca submits himself to the whims of the attendants. In it, he hooks his mouth, nose, ears, glutei, and pectorals up to a pneumatically movable machine. This machine is connected to a computer with a touch pad. The attendants use the pad to click points on an image. This sets in motion animation movies, sound, and compression relays. These relays trigger the machine to contort his body.

To understand the experience, it is useful to think of Nicolas De Olivera, Nicola Oxley and Michael Petry's definition of installation art: it is a term "to describe a kind of art-making which rejects concentration on one object in favour of the relationships between a number of elements or of the interaction between things and their contexts."[17] This definition can be expanded to include the presence of the attendant within the context, experiencing the sensation of those relationships. As they move through the space, the attendant experiences a composite sequence of sensorial data in the form of their knowledge of spatial and aesthetic relationships.

In the case of *Epizoo*, the attendant enters a dark, open space. Loud music blares. There is a machine with a stainless steel cap; it has wires and a flame-thrower on it. The machine is set up in the centre of a bank of screens on which are projected animation films and the screen of a computer desktop. A video camera records the attendants' entrance; we see ourselves milling about the space on the projection screen. There is a message telling the attendants that we are part of an interactive performance and that we should stand near the machine if we want to play. The computer hardware is on a raised platform, or control station, in the space directly in front of the machine. A few of us are really excited to play, and we do not have to wait long before Roca enters wearing a red loincloth. He puts on the parts of the machine – the helmet, a waist belt, and tongs in his cheek.

The attendant is invited to send shocks of pleasure or pain to Roca. Using the computer one can manipulate the machine, spinning him around or contorting his body: touch the buttock image, and without mercy an electronic knife hacks into it. Press the pectorals, and a virtual dog's tongue caresses his flesh. At the head, a touch will cause his mouth, ears, and nose to be pulled in various directions. When the attendant/controller steps away for the next person to manipulate his body, the lights go down on him and burning gasses spout from his head. It is like watching a cartoon with a real person getting all of the abuse, except that Roca has a release button if he becomes over-stimulated.

As the attendants enjoy the sociality of the club, we jockey for our turn to get our hands on the controls to manipulate the morphing screen images and, well, to torture Roca. What fun, mediated sadism, where the attendant's actions and indirect touches inflict pain on another body. Part of the allure of this experience is in its danger to the performer and to the spectators. What would happen if the machine went haywire? What responsibility do I have to consider the body on which I am inflicting pain and pleasure? What are the implications of watching this and participating in this activity? Are we, as attendants in proximity to this action, voyeurs or sadists? What are the ethical considerations of participating in an event like this? How does our relationship with technology inadvertently affect others? Are we really inflicting pain? It is only a click of a mouse, and we do not actually touch flesh upon flesh. How much we get out of the experience has to do with how much we think about our relationships to the event and how much we are aware of our reactions to the presented stimuli. Sensations trigger thought processes, which in turn begin the interpretative process.

Our bodies are wired to respond to certain types of stimulus – in Roca's case, literally. Arnheim explains why these sensations are critical to human thought:

> To interpret the functioning of the senses properly, one needs to keep in mind that they did not come about as instruments of cognition for cognition's sake, but evolved as biological aids for survival.[18]

When artists use these types of system, they are tapping into our pre-linguistic models of experience. Roca literalizes these stimuli in his body to highlight our lack of sensorial awareness in our own bodies during the event. We are cut off from our experiences with those around us and need to reach out and touch flesh against flesh in pursuit of social activity.

ACTIVATING THE WEB OF SENSORIAL PERCEPTION

La Baraque was part of *Le Campement*, a group of performances in spaces situated together outside the Industrial Palace in Prague, consisting of *La Baraque* (the hut), *La Tente* (the tent), and *Le Tonneau* (the barrel).[19] *Le Campement* can be described as a meeting place where circus, café, pub, and cabaret come together. The program for the event describes it as returning

> To those times when nomadic actors travelled to meet their audiences allowing themselves to be influenced by them. The individual performances are built on a desire to search for a common space shared by both spectator and performers. It is an atmosphere and a feeling that make the performance continuously unrepeatable and completely unique every evening.[20]

Crowds gathered at the encampment and were directed to one of the three performance spaces. If we consider the encampment as an installation, we can begin to consider each component as an element designed by the artists as part of their larger project to create a meeting between the attendant and the artists in a given space. Every aspect of one's experience, from entrance and seating to the trips to the bathroom, became part of the event.

As attendants, we did not know what to expect. We were led into the hut and told we could sit anywhere at any of the long, wooden communal tables. Strangers were squeezed together. In the center of the hut to one end was a large wood-burning stove with a large black cauldron of soup simmering. Bottles of wine could be bought, and bread was passed out to each of the tables. We sat, ate, and chatted with those around us. When was the event going to start? Little by little, we began to realize that this was the event and that there were actors moving through the room, leading each table in small actions; an actor might play a word game, or do a sleight-of-hand magic trick. Someone might peek in through a window and shout. A bird may run free through the crowd with someone chasing, a puppet may peek in and swing across the ceiling, or a woman might sing a ballad. The performers were creating a mood, a rhythm, and a tempo for the evening, which required that the each person should be attendant to the world around them. It lulled us into paying attention to the small details and actions of the crowd around us.

The troupe of artists aimed to heighten the spectators' awareness and interaction with the world around them. They describe the aims of the experience in the hut as

> [A] conscious demolition of the barrier between the audience and the stage liberates both spectators and actors and offers a possibility of a joint experience. The hut has long wooden tables where as many as 150 people can be seated, walls of Canadian cedar, a ceiling of sail cloth, an old dance floor, music, wine and soup. All of this in the company of actors, musicians and the large marabou bird Charles will create a nomadic and even Gypsy atmosphere which will draw the spectator into a secluded world where everything is possible.[21]

Everyone in the space of the hut was forced to engage in social activity. We were all piled in on top of one another on long benches; if one person were to move or get up, five others would have to shift. If you wanted some bread, others would have to pass it down the table; you might have to collaborate with others at the table to interact with the performers. One had to be sensitive to the needs of others: smoke in the eyes from cigarettes; being too loud so others could not pay attention to what might be going around them. Imagine, theatre where you were forced to chit-chat with those around you. The troupe created an artistically mediated experience that called upon the attendants to monitor the sounds, smells, and bodies of others and to imagine what might be chance and what might be staged. As the hours rolled on, and the crowd grew restless, drunk or bored, the performers surprised us with the smallest things, such as an engine revving outside and headlights streaming through the window, or shouting. Toward midnight, the simmering soup was ladled out of the cauldron and each table was invited to break bread and to share soup. The performance had a flavor and smell, and it encouraged us to be human and social.

If one were to ignore the small sounds, little acts, or to shut out the atmosphere, there would be nothing left to distinguish it from a boring night out in a strange place. There was little text spoken, little spectacle, and no conventional structure. All one had to comprehend the event were one's wits and perceptions of the changes in atmosphere, tone, and temperature. The heat of the stove, the stinging of the cigarette smoke in one's eyes, and the sounds of the crowd chatting away were all the stimuli one had to experience. Its structure encouraged the use of the senses to explore its mediated world; the installation activated taste, touch, smell, sound, and sight.

WHERE DO THE SENSES LEAD US?

Many of the sensory performances that I have mentioned encourage conversation and social exposure. Rather than sitting passively in the dark, we are required to participate and explore. You may be invited to share food, cut open clothing, or inhale the fragrance of simmering food, thus forcing you to become social animals and break free from the constraints of social decorum. Ultimately, due to the stimulation of a multi-sensory experience, the participants in any event are forced to use their bodies to explore and seek out input that will lead them to consider the way in which we interact with others, situate ourselves in an environment, and survive. If we are encouraged to use the full range of our sense perception, we become active participants rather than passive, isolated viewers detached from the artistic experience.

What are called for are different methodologies for understanding the way in which we monitor sensorial stimulation. Two things are necessary. (1) A phenomenological approach that looks at and responds to the art object – pre-linguistic and pre-cognitive. This would provide the data for the academic traditions of theatrical analysis to apply their models. (2) A revised sensual language – a language that tries to address image and sensation, much like the jargon that wine connoisseurs use to describe the palate of a vintage. This might be a poetic language, or language tied to the body. We need to break down the set ways of thinking to open up the potential of seeing and understanding from a different viewpoint.

Our senses are the tool that our body uses to negotiate and move through the world; by their very nature, they orchestrate our interaction with others and our environment. Thus we do not only attend the event, we are also attendant to the event and participate in it. We become actors responding within the constraints of an artistically mediated structure designed to trigger behavior or sensorial memory. By activating all senses or senses that are beyond words or sight, we can break through the constraints and patterns offered by conventional theatrical invitations. Artists who harness more than our eyes and ears encourage us to wake up, to be alert to the world around us, and to interact actively with the objects and creatures around us. It is an invitation to live, to feel, and to be a part of a larger community.

NOTES

1 Robert Wilson, *H.G.*, a site-specific installation in the Clink, London, April 1995. For a description of the ways in which the installation serves as an exemplar of how the senses can be employed theatrically, see Stephen Di Benedetto "Stumbling in the dark: facets of sensory perception and Robert Wilson's 'H.G.' installation." *New Theatre Quarterly* 17.3 (August 2001): 273–84.

2 Robert Irwin, *Prologue: x 18'*, an installation for Dia's faculty on 548 West 22nd Street, New York, 11 June 1998.

3 Read Co. production of *Living Space*, performed at the Dublin Youth Theatre, 30 June 2001.

4 See Arneheim, Rudolf. 1969. *Visual Thinking*. Berkeley: University of California Press, 19.

5 See Tuan, Yi-Fu. *Passing Strange and Wonderful: Aesthetics, Nature and Culture*. Tokyo: Kodansha International, 1993. 35.

6 *Ibid.*, 56.

7 See Arnheim, Rudolf. 1969. *Visual Thinking*. Berkeley: University of California Press, v.

8 See Frueh, Joanna. 1996. *Erotic Faculties*. Berkeley: University of California Press, 9.

9 See Stiles, Kristine in *Performance Artists Talking in the Eighties*, compiled by Linda M. Montano, Berkeley: University of California Press, 2000.

10 See Elkins, James. 1999. *Pictures of the Body: Pain and Metamorphosis*. Stanford, Calif.: Stanford University Press.

11 See Stiles, Kristine in *Performance Artists Talking in the Eighties*, compiled by Linda M. Montano, Berkeley: University of California Press, 2000.

12 See Palmer, Judith. "La Ribot: how to stay distinguished when you're dancing in the nude." *The Independent*, January 2001, 7.

13 Franko B. "Interview by Gray Watson 13 June 2000", http://www.ainexus.com/franko/interview.htm.

14 See Bennett, Marc. 1999. "Stellarc interview." In *Body Probe*, David Wood, ed. London: Creation Books, 44.

15 Program for *Fragile* by Fabulous Beast Dance Theatre, performed at the Project, Dublin, Ireland, 26 June 2001.

16 Michael Keegan-Dolan, email correspondence.

17 Nicolas de Olivera, Nicola Oxley, and Michael Petry. 1996. *Installation Art*. London: Thames and Hudson, 8.

18 Arnheim, Rudolf. 1969. *Visual Thinking*. Berkeley: University of California Press, 19.

19 Program for *Le Campement* performed by a consortium of companies in front of the Industrial Palace in Prague, Czech Republic, 27 June 1999.

20 *Ibid.*, 3.

21 *Ibid.*, 4.

11

CONTAINMENT + CONTAMINATION
A performance landscape for the senses at PQ03

Dorita Hannah

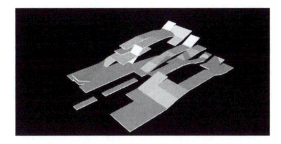

Figure 11.1 Computer-generated image of the performance landscape. SCAPE @ Massey.

This project began with a feverish body unleashing itself in space; a contaminated body, and body as contaminant, threatening to erupt through the borders of its own skin and refusing to be contained within established forms for housing performance. It was prompted in Germany (March 2001) during Nigel Charnock's performance piece *Fever*, staged in the sedate surroundings of Mainz's Kleines Haus theatre. The agitated body of this extremely physical dancer seemed to seek a more vertiginous experience as it hurled itself around the stage, burst through the proscenium arch and landed convulsing in the arms of the neatly arranged audience. Witnessing this visceral and futile battle with the prescribed passivity of the playhouse highlighted the inherent resistance of the architecture and its lack of porosity. In contaminating his surroundings, Charnock's feverish body dis-eased the onlooker and unsettled the role played by theatre architecture, a role that was fundamentally rejected by the twentieth century theatrical *avant-garde* but rarely explored by architects themselves.

The playhouse itself seems an irrelevant architectural typology in this age of liquescence, where nothing is stable, where fiction constantly folds into reality, and where sedentary structures can no longer house the mediatized spectacle of daily life. The boundaries of performance have become blurred, and the built form appears a redundant means for housing the artform. Although theatre buildings continue to be constructed, they remain passive receptacles for performance, maintaining (instead of challenging)

Figure 11.2 View of the Hall. SCAPE @ Massey.

the artform and disciplining the collective body into well-behaved citizens rather than creative participants. While the embodied nature of live performance endures in theatre, its inherent viscerality is seldom utilized to shape a spatial materiality. This gap between body and building prompted the event staged in the 2003 *Prague Quadrennial* as the "Heart of PQ," where notions of spatial containment and contamination were explored as a means of manipulating theatrical space. If we unhouse theatre from the confines of its dark and disciplined interiors, what can we find?

Every four years since 1967, the city of Prague has hosted its international exposition on contemporary theatre architecture and stage design, gathering together those committed to visually shaping the performance event. The numerous displays from over fifty countries highlight the quandary of how to exhibit theatrical events, which through their temporality are disappearing acts. The "Heart of PQ," was a departure

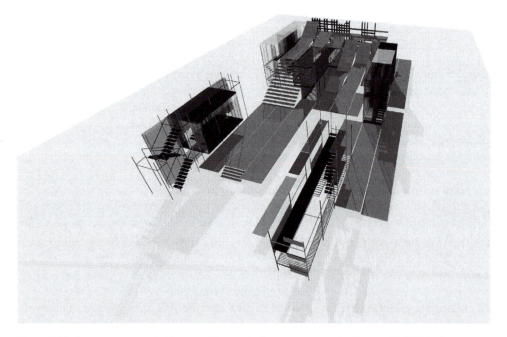

Figure 11.3 Computer-generated image of towers in the performance landscape. SCAPE @ Massey.

from the traditional exhibitions, which represent theatre and its architecture via the archival remains of models, artifacts, and images. It presented space and performance as a "lived experience" via a temporary architecture offering a range of dynamic spatial conditions for performance exploration over a two-week period.

Erected within the spectacular confines of Prague's Industrial Palace and combining the arts of exhibition, theatre, and architecture, the project provided an experimental site for interaction and encounter for performers and public alike. Its design emerged in collaboration with a number of international artists from Russia, Kazakhstan, Japan, Britain, Canada, Samoa, South Africa, and the Netherlands and was spearheaded by the Czech Theatre Institute and the New Zealand design team SCAPE @ Massey. This global, interdisciplinary alliance resulted in a site-specific installation that sought to challenge, disrupt, and eliminate the borders that traditionally exist in theatre, so new relationships could be explored between the body and the built, between the viewer and the viewed, and between the designer and the director. It was predicated on the uncontainability of performance and the utilization of the sensory body as a performative contaminant.

The elements of this architectural sensorium came together to form a performance landscape within which five towers were embedded, each assigned one of the classic senses (smell, hearing, taste, touch, and sight) and organized around a long table, where all these faculties cohered. Bound within a platform of undulating timber planks, each scaffolding tower was developed with an allocated artist, or group of artists, to be occupied by performers and/or public. These vertiginous structures (2.5 metres wide, 12 metres long and 7–11 metres high) formed containers for the (uncontainable) senses, which were then fleshed out with performance, opening out to or exclosing the surroundings.

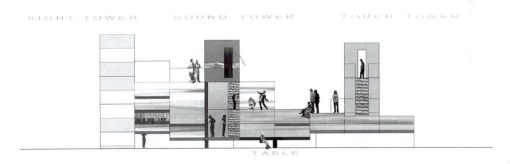

Figure 11.4 Elevation/section of the performance landscape. SCAPE @ Massey.

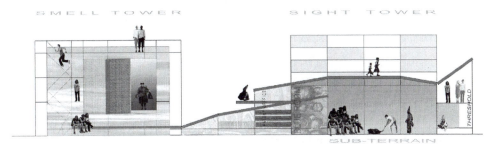

Figure 11.5

Figure 11.6 Visual artists and curators of the Tower of Taste. Photos by Rastislav Juhas.

Figure 11.7

Figure 11.8

Each tower vacillated between the notions of containment and contamination, controlling and corrupting space in turn. The "tower of smell," occupied by South African company Monkey's Wedding Theatre, conjured up the "exotic" of unknown Africa as a complex package spilling its contents into a wooden crate where stories and rituals were shared. Within this pungent space, foreign objects (such as animal skins, horns, bones, and herbs) leaked, drifted, and permeated from above and below. A more contained sound-box in the "tower of hearing" was perched high above the platform, inside which Japanese sound artist Sachiyo Takahashi invited guests to mix sounds from the other towers in a low-tech sound ceremony. Canadian multi-media group Recto-Verso occupied their blind-box, blurring vision as performers slid up and down a smoke-filled vitrine of sound, light, and moving images viewed from platforms on either side.

The sealed tower of "sight" contrasted with the more open anarchic kitchen of "taste" occupied by Russian visual artists Akhe Group, whose structure steamed, smoked, clanged, and swayed as they laid siege to it and their surroundings. The work, like the tower itself, was expansive and physical. They interacted with other performers and other spaces, leaving culinary traces behind that contributed, over two weeks, to the creation of a pungent and pervasive odour. Although "taste" was their allocated sense, they engaged the other senses with gusto. Their music leaked through the space, used to effect when they played a tango to protest against and disrupt the ritual killing of a chicken by South African and Samoan performers, and they used fire in their evening performance despite the ban on open flames by the authorities. Over two weeks, their theatrical appetite continued to dress the skeletal structure of the tower with the remains of its spectacles, cladding it with food, utensils, and curious objects that rusted, rotted, and decayed. This anarchic kitchen was contagious in more ways than one.

Figure 11.9 Carol Brown (UK). Dancers on the landscape. Photo by Rastislav Juhas.

Figure 11.10 Carol Brown (UK). Promenade evening performance. Photo by Rastislav Juhas.

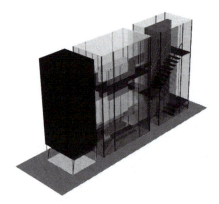

Figure 11.11 Computer-generated image of the Tower of Touch. SCAPE @ Massey.

Akhe's gastronomic chaos was counteracted by the controlled minimalism of their neighboring "tower of touch," curated by British-based choreographer Carol Brown. Through her proposal that contemporary touch is more visual and technological than physical, an anatomical theatre was created that brought the visitors so close to the body that many wanted to avert their eyes. The dancer lay on a stainless steel table/slab/bed within the structure encased in an opaque plastic shroud. She was viewed from above through a vertical slot that fragmented the view of the performer's vulnerable body (narrating stories in fragments) moving in and out of the narrow frame. Distance and fragmentation were further emphasized when the spectator also lay horizontal under the adjoining black projection silo, gazing up at live video images of the performer, separated by the skin of the shroud.

Figure 11.12 Carol Brown (UK). Tower of Touch. Photos by Rastislav Juhas.

The lightness of touch in Carol Brown's work was often threatened and sometimes sabotaged by the cacophony of the hall. Its minimalism highlighted subtle interplays and required a more defined framing of the event. Playing with notions of voyeurism, her tower proved both calming and confronting.

While the artists in each tower focused on their own specified domains, they also played with the places in between as well as the hall's peripheral zones. These

Figure 11.13

Figure 11.14 Looking towards the Tower of Touch. SCAPE @ Massey.

surrounding spaces could be claimed and reclaimed by audience and performers. The undulating landscape, generally accessible to the visitors, challenged their bodies in balance and athleticism with its various surfaces, textures, and heights. It was at once stage and auditorium, uniting the body of the performer with that of the crowd.

Like all performances, the "Heart of PQ" was a series of vanishing events. Two and a half years in development, two weeks under construction and a fortnight in action, it took less than twenty-four hours to dismantle. The performers were contracted to inhabit the space for fourteen days with a constantly shifting program of scheduled and spontaneous events. Visitors drifted into the hall via a number of entrances and exits, happening upon the installation, described by Carol Brown as "a polyphonic mapping of performance and a contestatory site for strong energies and competing passions." All who entered the site became in some way implicated in its dramatic environs, the dynamics of which ranged from a visceral onslaught on its occupants to offering a

Figure 11.15 Projection silo: Tower of Touch. SCAPE @ Massey.

place of calm and rest. Visiting performers negotiated the site, children enjoyed the physical challenges of the landform and more cautious bodies avoided its vertiginous qualities. This carnivalesque marketplace, with its hit-and-miss events bathed in daylight and summer heat, contrasted with the evening program, which allowed each group, focusing on their specific sense, to present their artistry with a greater control of light, movement, sound, taste, touch, image, and smell. They either placed the audience in seating zones or moved them through the installation's labyrinth.

The notion of gathering performers from a number of continents and placing them in a shared space to explore the limits of built form and their own bodies is, on one hand, a utopian idea fated to fail and, on the other hand, a dystopian experiment where failure is productive. Like the mythical city of Babel, this project was an unsustainable dream, resulting in confusion, tension, and the pervasive threat of collapse. Differing languages, cultural practices, and spatial conventions led to misinterpretations during the design process and the production. Yet in the theatre conflict is a generative force, and out of the confusion emerged moments of great beauty, insight, and communality.

Figure 11.16 View of the Hall. SCAPE @ Massey.

In unhousing theatre and dis-easing the body, the "Heart of PQ" offered risky ground for those who dared to test it. As an international research project in real space and real time it has left us with traces to be savoured, scrutinized, recalled and revised in future projects and collaborations.

CREDITS

Produced by the Czech Theatre Institute
Supported by Massey University and Creative NZ
Dramaturgical concept: Tomas Zizka
Architectural concept: Dorita Hannah
Design Team: (SCAPE @ Massey) Dorita Hannah, Sven Mehzoud, Lee Gibson
Initial concepts developed with Josh Dachs of FDA and Rodrigo Tisi in 2001, were further inspired by the work of third-year interior design students at Massey University in 2002.
Web Design (http://pq.scape.org.nz) by Liz Cretney.

Invited artists/curators:
Touch: Carol Brown Dances (Great Britain)
Taste: Kyzyl Traktor (Kazakhstan)
         Akhe Group (Russia)
Smell: Mau Dance Company (NZ/Samoa)
         Monkey's Wedding Theatre (South Africa)
Sound: Sachiyo Takahashi (Belgium/Japan)
         Ryuzo Fukuhara (France/Japan)
Sight: Recto-Verso (Canada)

Figure 11.17 Mau Dance Theatre (New Zealand). Photos by Rastislav Juhas.

Figure 11.18

Figure 11.19

12

SEEING NOTHING
Now hear this...

Martin Welton

THEATRE IN THE DARK

In "On Acting and Not-Acting," Michael Kirby states that "In most cases, acting and not-acting are relatively easy to recognize and identify" (Kirby 1995:43). In the dark, however, deprived of vision, how are we to do so? The etymological root of the word "theatre" is the Greek *theatron*, or "place of seeing." The 1998–2000 production of *War Music* by Sound and Fury Theatre Company, performed entirely in darkness with an utter lack of any visual reference in its proceedings, undermined one of the central means by which "theatre" is most often defined.

War Music was adapted from the poet Christopher Logue's "account" of books 16 to 19 of Homer's *Iliad*. The cast (including one actor blind from birth) moved around and through the audience, each variously taking up the narration, as well as the characters that people the epic. A quadraphonic system allowed recorded sound to move in all directions throughout the performance space.

The space at Multi-A in Bristol, which I attended in October 1998 following a premier at BAC in London as part of a "theatre in the dark" season, was effectively just a large room. By completely enclosing a space within this room with blacking cloths, *War Music* brought some of the atmosphere of a more conventional theatre production to bear upon it, since this blacking is commonly found in modern theatres. Any familiarity brought by this was soon ruptured by the seating arrangement, two banks facing one another that dominated the space, creating the impression that although there was a degree of familiarity in the surroundings and proceedings, something different was about to happen.

A special licence had been obtained to extinguish even the emergency safety lighting, and the resulting effect was quite unsettling. The darkness also meant that the familiar visual cues, which would have allowed an audience to remind themselves that they were attending theatre, were withdrawn. Above and around the seating, a figure eight of guide ropes was suspended with which the actors found their way around the space in the dark. To one side, behind a blackout curtain, the production team cued music and special effects live. Having taken their seats and received a short list of instructions on safety procedures from the stage manager, the audience was gradually submerged in darkness.

WAR MUSIC

I'm sat in the far right-hand corner, at the back. The stage manager gives instructions about what to do if you need to get out: call the nearest stage assistant's name, and they come over with a torch. The lights go out, then the safety signs at the exits too. The actors are holding candles. Each speaks an individual line, setting the scene of what had happened up to this point in the Trojan War. As each comes to the end of his or her line, they blow their candle out. Christopher Logue's adaptation of Homer's *Iliad*, *War Music*, begins:

Now hear this:

and we are plunged into darkness, A great clap, a rumble of thunder, and Patroclus comes crying to Achilles' tent.

There is no light, none at all. I wave my hand in front of my face just to check, but there is nothing. Only my sensation of my own movement confirms it is there. Soon the darkness seems very thick, tangible almost. After a while I have given up keeping my eyes closed, it seems pointless with all the sound going on, and all the voices.

The story unfolds: Patroclus persuades sulking Achilles to lend him his armour and his army of Myrmidons to rout the Trojans attacking the Greek ships.

Cut to the fleet.

The narrative makes jump cuts; moves from close-up to long shots, transports us to a bird's-eye view of the battle plain. Vengeful gods confuse the mêlée further: flesh rips, bones snap; Akafact's death brings gasps from the darkened room:

God blew the javelin straight; and thus
Mid-air, the cold bronze apex sank
Between his teeth and tongue, parted his brain,
Pressed on, and stapled him against the upturned hull.
His dead jaw gaped. His soul
Crawled off his tongue and vanished into sunlight.

(Logue 1984: 22)

As a voice somewhere to my left describes the spear's flight and grisly arrival, a sound of speed and purpose begins on the other side of the room and rushes through the space towards me, and over my head, to finish with a ugly "thock" somewhere in the corner behind me. The stapling of Akafact. In the darkness the sound seems "solid" somehow. And yet this "solidity" is ambiguous; it is as if in the absence of sight, hearing has rushed in to take over this function. Certainly "seeing" is "believing" to some extent, but now, as hearing replaces sight as the primary sense there's a struggle to endow what I hear with the same concreteness as the seen. Words and sound are more "concrete" than is ordinarily the case, but this concreteness also retains a certain ambiguity. A flight of arrows that whizzes overhead has the individual hiss of each shaft but is hyper-real; it leaves room for the imagination. It could be a volley of twenty, each pointed barb and feathered flight clear to the mind's eye, or a blur of a hundred thousand performing a perfect parabola from bow to target. This is contrasted by other sounds in the room, which remind us of the very realness of flesh and heighten the horrors of battle. There is the sound of one's own breathing, the gentle rustling of clothes, confirming that you are still here even in the darkness; and there are performed sounds, matching the actions of the story. As Achilles washes his hands and prepares to pray there is the sound of water being poured into a bowl, and gentle splashing. There is the sound of the actors moving around us, reaffirming that this is a play (of sorts), that Sarpedon, Achilles, and Agamemnon all require their human transports who share our space and time.

The actors' voices, four male and one female, each pick up the narrative, interchange characters. The voices move about the room; now behind me, now beside me, now down low, now raised up somehow on the far side of the room. The voices move us from Achilles' tent to the walls of Troy and back, offering aerial descriptions, flashbacks, interludes. At times I stop following the story; although I know it, it is not for that reason. It is for the cadences of sound, the subtle shifts of pitch and rhythm. There is "meaning" here, but not in a lexical matching of words to memory. The spoken words become "things" in their own right, no longer yoked to but defined by that which they describe. "APOLLO"; the word describes the god, of course, but in the dark it takes on a musculature all its own; it exists in the space.

The actors move about us. At some point I feel someone brush my shoulder, and the effect is chilling. Far from feeling safe, cocooned in the darkness, I suddenly feel afraid. I am now conscious not just of the soundscape, or the unfolding story, but also of the extent to which we are surrounded by the action. I know that the actors are moving around us; I can hear and feel them but can only speculate as to what they do as they move.

My senses are thrown; I am not used to hearing on its own. It's not like lying in bed, eyes closed, listening to the radio. I am aware of my clothes on my skin, of my bum on my seat. Although I can't see or feel them, I'm also intensely aware of the woman to my left and the couple sat in front of us. The blackness is so strange, so unpredictable, that at times I almost want to touch them, to gain through feeling some kind of recognition that others are here, that I haven't hallucinated the whole thing.

> Saying these things Patroclus died.
> And as his soul went through the sand
> Hector withdrew his spear and said:
> "Perhaps."

> (*ibid.*: 39)

When the lights come up, its over, and we are applauding, I feel a strange relief, and a pleasure in having shared all this with strangers, knowing that we will leave as strangers, but knowing that we take a little something in common away with us.

What I have just described is my experience of "theatre in the dark." Following this, the questions that I now wish to ask are: can theatre really be best described as a "place of seeing?" And is *seeing* believing?

More than any other sense, it is through vision that we are mostly aware of the materiality of the world around us and the objects in it. Certainly, touch offers the ultimate confirmation of material quality (hard–soft, hot–cold, rough–smooth, etc.), but the sheer range of the visual field at any given moment, and a general confidence that what we see conforms to a materially knowable (i.e. touchable) world, means that we can rely on vision to offer a fairly dependable idea of the objects and activities around us. However, this dependable idea is not by any means perfect; indeed, as Peggy Phelan has put it:

> When Newton discovered the prismatic properties of light the human eye became a poor creature, an organ whose limitations define its properties more precisely than its powers. (Aristotelian philosophy is undone by Newton. Vision cannot be the guarantee of knowing once one knows that vision is never complete.) Unable to perceive the full range of color inherent in light, the human eye is physiologically falsifying.
>
> (Phelan 1993: 14)

In the total blackness of *War Music*, one was left with a sensual experience as disturbing as it was exhilarating. Under such circumstances, how is one to bring into play those casual conventions by which we so often judge performance? Unsighted, off-balance, surrounded by very real actors and sound effects, how does one construct meaning, make sense of what is going on?

Before exploring *War Music* itself, it is perhaps necessary to consider vision, since it would seem that it is through this sense that theatre is apparent to us. The optic nerves contains more than half the afferent nerve fibres that serve the brain; the cerebral cortex itself is, in large part, dominated by the visual system. These are the brute neurological facts of "seeing" as we currently understand them. The brain seems to be irreducible from knowledge – never more so than in contemporary neuroscience – and, in so far as the senses are connected to this, knowledge seems to be dominated by vision. Given the contemporary vogue for suggesting evolutionary answers to everything, this has led to many interesting hypotheses, extending from vision's importance to our survival as a species to our development of language, art, and so on. Quite apart from vision seeming to dominate the means by which we understand on a neurological level, it also remains the dominant sense culturally.

Phelan suggests that the certainty of vision was crippled by Newton's optical experiments. While this may or may not be the case, the desire for visual (and more generally perceptual) certainty does not quite seem to have gone away. Thus, even if it is accepted that vision has apparent deficiencies, the ongoing attempts at *explanation* suggest a desire that they will somehow lead to a new clarity; somehow we will be able to *see through* these quirks. It is almost as if we need to restore to vision the certainty of the *camera obscura* model that Newton's discoveries so undermined:

> A model of vision in terms of a geometric optics, that is, a model of an incorporeal relationship between the perceiver and the object of perception, a process undertaken by a free, sovereign, but isolated individual with clear boundaries between inside and outside, observer and observed, existing within a stable space and continuous time.
>
> (Lury 1998: 158)

Once vision had been shown to be uncertain, the grounds of knowledge itself appeared to be equally shaky. Indeed, the more vision was revealed to be a bodily process, the more unreliable it seemed. The body is all too mortal, and knowledge – "the truth" – has long been presumed to be lasting, constant.

As Constance Classen notes, sight is '*the* sense of science" (Classen 1993: 6). That scientists are so concerned to attempt to explain sight (in spite of its faulty optics) should hardly be surprising therefore, since, as she goes on to suggest: "the detachment of sight, distancing spectator from spectacle, makes the cherished objectivity of the scientist possible" (*ibid.*: 6). If it were possible, through sophisticated understanding of its "defects," to return to vision the unmediated characteristics of the *camera obscura*, then "seeing is believing" could once again be a reasonable truth claim. Indeed, the very language of understanding itself is at stake.

Vision seems to need light. Without light, "seeing" becomes irrelevant; or does it? This is certainly true if we characterize it only in terms of an inner *representation* of the world out there and confine ourselves to the means by which "out there" gets "in here." Contemporary cognitive science uses the word "representation" to cover an extraordinary number of concepts and categories, which, as Susana Millar notes, are "particularly open to misinterpretation when they are assumed to imply each other" (Millar 2000: 105). Generally speaking, however, a representational view holds that there is an inner system that corresponds to the external things being thought about. This suggests some process of ongoing translation between the external world and the inner system. Issues concerning representation inevitably remain tied to questions of its *interpretation*, which considerably problematizes a discussion of artistic practice. Many working in the field of cognitive science would have us believe that (in cognitive terms at least), *a representation is its own interpretation*; but this does not seem to move the debate very much further from the *camera obscura* model.

Performed almost entirely in the dark (with the exception of the opening moments of candlelight), *War Music* is perhaps the closest most of its sighted participants (spectators and actors alike) will ever get to the experience of blindness. Closing your eyes or wearing a blindfold cannot offer the same queering of vision as that of opening one's eyes in total darkness and seeing *nothing*. It is tempting to describe this in negative terms, but it is my suggestion that seeing *nothing* is still to some extent *seeing*, albeit seeing that is not characterized by light. Similarly, blindness need not be thought of simply as a "lack" of vision; and, indeed, given the absence of a firm definition of blindness, it is difficult to state what that lack might actually entail.

Blindness is frequently characterized by the sighted as a "lack" or as a "disability" – a dysfunction – and thus a source of pity. However, as both Ron Michalko and Constance Classen point out in their studies of the senses, for many blind individuals, the other sensory means by which they engage with the world, while different, are nonetheless full and rich. Indeed, the exclusion of these other sensory experiences in a hyper-visual culture is lamented by both authors.

That we live in a visually dominated culture is attested to not only by the profusion of visual metaphors in language but also by the proliferation of the symbol. Indeed, much of the visual wealth surrounding us, on which we have come to rely so heavily, passes almost unnoticed, so it should hardly be surprising that the dominance of the visual passes with little question in everyday life:

> Consider a driver on a typical North American highway. The progress of the vehicle is dependent on a series of visual judgements made by the driver concerning the relative speed of other vehicles, and any maneuvers necessary to complete the journey. At the same time, he or she is bombarded with other information: traffic lights, road signs, turn signals, advertising hoardings, petrol prices, shop signs, local time and temperature and so on. Yet most people consider the process so routine that they play music to keep from getting bored.
>
> (Mirzoeff 1999: 5)

The dominance of vision, its range over a given situation, has long been linked to characterizations of male power and agency, to the power of the male gaze to see at a distance and command, and hence to be "objective." While there have been concerted efforts to unpick the narratives of links between masculinity, power, dominance, and sight, the visual remains as the chief mode of explanation, as Classen notes:

> In many contemporary academic works sight is so endlessly analyzed, and the other senses so consistently ignored, that the five senses would seem to consist of the colonial/patriarchal gaze, the scientific gaze, the erotic gaze, the capitalist gaze, and the subversive glance.
>
> (Classen 1998: 143)

Such is the pervasiveness of the visual that to recast a deconstructed world in its terms seems irresistible. However, *War Music* restricted the tendency toward the visualization of experience; it had to be approached in its own way. The visualization of experience extends into the conception of the imagination as a "picture/film in the head." I do not intend to propose that this is a wholly false account; rather, I hope to suggest not only that can imagination employ and draw on the full range of human sensation, on our sensory relationships with the world, but also that the realm of imagination is as much one of immediate experience as it is of the distanced contemplation suggested by a picture-in-the-head model.

In *War Music*, in pitch blackness, and unattached to any perceivable symbol, gesture, motif or facial expression, the words of Logue's text were afforded no permanence. In the darkness, they could come into being only in the actors' mouths, in the spectators' ears, and disappear. Not only was the occurent nature of performance underlined but also its transience, since there were no remaining traces to seize upon, nothing to backloop, to reread. Doubtless, many spectators (and indeed the actors themselves) made concerted efforts to construct a picture/film in the head; maybe they actually managed to do so. Even if this were the case, is it legitimate to describe their experience as an attempt to reconstruct the visual as if it might be something we could understand if taken out of their heads?

In an interview, the blind *War Music* actor Ryan Kelly made striking use of the metaphor "I see" (i.e. "I understand"), although he has never actually seen anything. Although he also referred to the audience "listening" to the performance, he was quick to qualify this, saying that "I'm not too fussy about words, because I use them anyway" (personal interview, May 2000). Ron Michalko, himself blind, notes that many phrases connected to sightedness are employed by the blind, partially to facilitate "fitting in" (what he terms "passing") and partially because they are the most direct and descriptive terms available in the language. To say "I hear" or "I feel" does not always offer the same direct communication of understanding as "I see." He (Michalko) is critical of the tendency to attempt to restrict language use to those situations relating to one's own direct experience. That the blind in some sense "see" is not the point that both he and Kelly are making. First, he is suggesting that the blind not be denied the use of language that is descriptive of acts and events beyond their direct experience; after all, we are each at the very least able to *imagine* that which we have not actually done. Additionally, he is suggesting that they are capable of experience that is "like" sight – that passes for it – in that vision is able to provide a rapid and relatively consistent evaluation of the world around us in a way that other sensory modalities are not, and which may be extended metaphorically.

Was the experience of *War Music* like blindness then? Given the sheer diversity of descriptions of blindness, this is difficult to assert definitively. Perhaps forms of blindness where there is absolutely no retinal sensitivity to light come close. However, the shock of the new undergone by spectators and actors alike when confronted with the darkness, and the temporary duration of this condition, suggest that it was partial at best.

Discussing rehearsals for *War Music*, Ryan Kelly described difficulties in preparing the other cast members for the experience of being unable to see:

> I was trying to get them to do stuff like "walk across this room totally confidently with your eyes shut, or blindfolded," or whatever, and they lost their tempers with one another, and all sorts; they didn't understand what they were handling. Because it's something I handle all the time, I learned not to [impose the experience on others]. They had to deal with it in their own way. If people go blind through life, then they've got to deal with it, it's as simple as that.
>
> (personal interview, May 2000)

His desire to allow them to come to cope on their own terms suggests that it is important to consider blindness and the absence of sight in the performance on a personal level. Kelly's experience of attempting to prepare his fellow actors suggests that this is in no sense easy. However, it is not because blindness is a *dis*ability that it is pertinent here but because the removal of a sense most of us take for granted causes us to consider the means by which all of our senses cooperate (and as Thorne Shipley (1995) suggests *conflict*) in order to constitute our particular experiences of our environments and allow us to act upon and within them. What do we learn of *ability* in the absence of sight?

Sitting in the dark, the eyes cast about for some – any – source of light. The eyeballs roll in their fleshy cavities, muscles squeeze and pull, the pupils expand to their limits. It is not only that the darkness makes you *feel* something. To be looking out at this apparent nothing has a sensation all its own; one's awareness of sight as engagement is piqued. This awareness also is there in the "lit" world, albeit subdued. In downplaying this engagement, we either take the visual for granted or we enter into a discourse of power and reason that vision has not, of itself, created. *War Music* allows us to consider vision in terms of an altered sense ratio from within a visual culture. This offers an opportunity to "make sense" of theatrical vision afresh, to reclaim the visual in the theatre for the realm of the senses. The importance of representation, interpretation, the symbol and the text will doubtless remain, but with their place within the theatrical sense ratio altered.

How we see has important implications for how we hear, touch, and so on. This complex interplay is crucially important to consideration of *War Music*. While the performance was played in total darkness, the visual cortex of spectator and actor alike was still operative. As suggested earlier, seeing *nothing* is still to some extent seeing. Equally, the interplay of the other senses with this "blinded" visual cortex must be regarded as being as important to the experience as any other individual modality.

Unlike vision, the senses of touch and hearing do not offer continuity. Things and events have little duration ontologically; they come into being as sounds or feelings and disappear just as quickly. There is little stability of scene; instead, the world is grasped only in a state of constant engagement. Seated in the darkness, although the memory of the seating arrangement must have been in the spectators' minds to some extent, their inability to see it denied them easy reference to it. The memory of this collective physical reality must have been brought home particularly during the passages of battle in which the Trojans and Greeks approach one another from either side of the field of battle. Whether Patroclus, Hector, Panotis, or Ajax, the actors began these passages from behind either section of the audience, so that they were placed directly opposite one another literally as well as figuratively. Their being slightly behind the audience was also important; by enclosing them in an auditory manner the performance situated them *within* the action.

When asked about his approach to acting in the dark, the *War Music* actor Rob Vesty told me that:

> You kind of assume "well it's in the dark, no-one sees what we're doing." I think the physicality of the piece took us all by surprise. ... It was a physical piece; you really used space. You couldn't be seen, but it just proves that you need the physical expression to give way to the vocal expression ... I almost felt like a conductor at times, the weight of the language, the poetry, and the rhythm of the thing ... What I really loved was the alliteration or the rhythm of the speech, and I was really moving with it, really finding the weight of it, and that really manifested itself in me.
>
> (personal interview, 2000)

"Manifested itself in me" is a key statement in this interview, which took place eighteen months after the original 1998 performance. It articulates a feeling that although *War Music* seemed for the spectator (theatrically speaking) to have existed as words in space, it nevertheless required a very physical involvement on the part of the actors for this to take place. The cast of *War Music*'s first experience of full darkness was not until the dress rehearsal, which makes Rob's expression of surprise at the physicality this drew out of them all the more interesting and offers an insight into the process of embodiment involved. His surprise suggests a challenge to a belief that, first, the physical has meaning only if it can be seen and, second, that the relationship between this physicality and the actor is not necessarily a mutual one, that this physicality is somehow an effect rather than a process.

How then did the process of acting involved in *War Music* challenge such beliefs? Since there was nothing to see, all attention had to be given to speech. Can the spoken word be more than a medium, a transmission of meaning from one consciousness to another? Can its resonation in the body of the speaker, in the air, and in the ear of the listener provide it further layers of meaning that escape the lexical confines of the enunciation as text? To consider the spoken word simply as a carrier of meaning, rather than also as a creator of it, not only reduces its complexity but also represents human communication, and indeed humans themselves, in systematic terms. The spoken word is rich with possibilities for meaning, but far from existing *a priori*, it is in the acts of speaking and of hearing that they are born.

By shifting its participants' focus from interpretation to the immediacy of sensation, *War Music* emphasized not only the means by which sensory stimulation offers information and *affirmation* about the environment but also the importance of sensory interplay in the creation of meaning. This means extending a conception of the senses beyond the conventional five. "Touch," for example, is not only a passive response to external stimuli; it also has active elements. "Haptics" (from the Greek *haptein*, to touch) is often used to describe this active or movement-reliant sense of touch. Given the complexity of the range of sensation (proprioception and extero-ception, skin tactility, skin pressure, and so on) that characterizes this active state, "haptics" can be thought of as an umbrella term for a variety of related sensory perceptions.

Haptics are the building blocks of a sense of self. In the apparent absence of anything to *see*, the haptic senses are piqued: not necessarily any more sensitive, but forming a more important part of awareness. Concurrent with this, one's awareness of what is close to the body (especially that which is touching it directly) is also raised. What constitutes the world in this situation takes on a far more temporary nature: move away from a stimulus so that it is no longer apparent to touch and it no longer exists for you outside of memory.

For the sighted spectator, the constant sensation of being seated occurred in relation to the memory of having *seen* where one was seated and where one was in relation to whom and to what; each person must have carried the visual memory of the appearance of the space with him/her throughout the performance. In most sighted experience, as suggested, touch is subjugated by sight. However, was touch really subjugated by visual memory during the performance? I suggest not. This has serious implications for the consideration of memory and imagination as being recourse to visual or visual-like experience.

The haptic senses tell us both *how* we are being and *where* we are being, to the extent that the two are irreducible. Haptic sense provides an experiential base for a wider sense of *being*. In Shakespeare's *The Merchant of Venice*, it is on the basis of a shared sensory world of feeling/touch that Shylock pleads for clemency from the Venetian gentiles: "If you prick us, do we not bleed? If you tickle us, do we not laugh?" [III, i]. The haptic senses can perceive only that which is immediate to (e.g. skin tactility) or within the body (e.g. proprioception), and as such they are a means by which the environment directly impacts upon our sense of self.

As Blau (1990) suggests, theatrical performance is delineated from other forms of experience on account of a fundamental breach between actors and spectators. Generally speaking, this breach is marked visually – by a proscenium arch, the actors' spectacular costumes, lighting, seating arrangements, and so on. In *War Music*, however, the spectator seemed actually to be located within this breach on account of the enveloping sensations of sound, touch, and darkness. This, I suggest, prevented any easy sense of spatial location and so resisted attempts to characterize the experience in terms of representation.

What then, sensually speaking, was present during the performance? Suppose for a moment that we assume that the senses were working on the basis of correspondence with one another, either by affirming the knowledge offered by a dominant one or by creating some sort of general agreement. What if we also say that it was charac-terized by darkness, by *nothing*? While there is, unquestionably, a certain veracity to this claim, did the senses other than vision simply confirm this nothingness?

In opening one's eyes and seeing "nothing," the usual distance associated with seen objects was collapsed. However, since distance is characteristic of the visual experience, there was an inevitable struggle to create or account for this, which was involved in a further conflict with the ways in which the performance constantly directed one's attention "inwards" via the auditory and haptic senses. Rather than existing in terms of representation and interpretation, *War Music* can be considered as an embodied event played out sensorially rather than conceptually.

This has important ramifications for a wider theory of theatrical performance: it suggests on the one hand that representation, if not an overemphasized concern in both critical and practical approaches, too often obscures the necessity of experience, which is always grounded in the sensual. On the other hand, since even in conventional performance actors (and therefore spectators) rarely see themselves directly, performing surely has more to do with negotiating a process of incorporation sensorially than with merely representing.

REFERENCES

Blau, Herbert. 1990. "Universals of performance." In *By Means of Performance: Intercultural Studies of Theatre and Ritual*, edited by Richard Schechner and Willa Appel. Cambridge: Cambridge University Press.

Classen, Constance. 1993. *Worlds of Sense: Exploring the Senses in History and Across Cultures*. London: Routledge.

——. 1998. *The Color of Angels: Cosmology, Gender, and the Aesthetic Imagination*. London: Routledge.

Kirby, Michael. 1995. "On Acting and not-acting." In *Acting (Re)Considered: Theories and Practice*, edited by Phillip B. Zarrilli. London: Routledge.

Logue, Christopher. 1984. *War Music: An Account of Books 16 to 19 of Homer's 'Iliad'*. London: Penguin.

Lury, Celia. 1998. *Prosthetic Culture: Photography, Memory, and Identity*. London: Routledge,

Michalko, Ron. 1998. *Mystery of the Eye and the Shadow of Blindness*. Toronto: University of Toronto Press.

Millar, Susanna. 2000. "Modality and mind: convergent active processing in interrelated networks as a model of development and perception by touch." In *Touch, Representation, and Blindness*, edited by Morton A. Heller. Oxford: Oxford University Press.

Mirzoeff, Nicholas. 1999. *An Introduction to Visual Culture*. London: Routledge.

Phelan, Peggy. 1993. *Unmarked: The Politics of Performance*. London: Routledge.

Shipley, Thorne. 1995. *Intersensory Origin of Mind: A Revisit to Emergent Evolution*. London: Routledge.

Vesty, Rob. 2000. Personal interview (5 March) with author, London.

13

A DOUBLY "ENVIRONMENTAL" SENSORIUM
Omaha Magic Theatre's *Sea of Forms*

Maya E. Roth

Upon entering a small converted storefront theatre for *Sea of Forms,* Omaha Magic Theatre (OMT) audiences encountered a sea of white styrofoam, nearly a foot high in many places. For the 1986 premiere and in subsequent runs (1987, 1989) of this experimental multimedia performance, popcorn and shell bits covered the floor, extending from wall to wall; styrofoam animal sculptures hung from the ceiling; large and small blocks of styrofoam created walls, shelves, and touchable icons. The physical world of the theatre was "totally transformed by the styrofoam sculptural installation" (Terry and Schmidman 1986–87–89). Because audience seating clusters (mats, swivel seats) were positioned throughout the space, everyone walked through that styrofoam, smelled it, touched it before, during and after "the play."

Created by Megan Terry and Jo Ann Schmidman in collaboration with visual artist Bill Farmer, three composers, a textile designer, and cast members during an intensive workshop period, *Sea of Forms* placed considerable emphasis on developing sensory awareness and interconnection. I return to *Sea of Forms* now because as an audience member and later a performer in its second run with OMT, I found that it successfully engaged the "other senses" for audiences. It did so in part as a trademark strategy of 1960s experimental performance and subsequent *avant-garde* theatre, so committed to creating a living (read *corporeal*) performance experience for audiences. Like the 1960s US experimental dance-theatre scene that Terry and Schmidman helped to shape (both were founding members of the Open Theatre, led by Joseph Chaikin), this production incorporated environmental staging to deconstruct Western bourgeois boundaries between art and politics, performer and audience, self and other. In its particularity, *Sea of Forms* provided an antidote to more "invisible" consumptions – from the toxic contamination of human and natural resources to commercial appropriations of open space. Through its theatrical staging *and* its ecological metaphysics, in other words, *Sea of Forms* doubly inflected environmentalism. In this discussion, I focus on the variety of sensory ways that this production sought to bring audiences to their bodies and to an interconnection with space, others in the space, and nature as a way of heightening ecological conscience.

Sea of Forms was developed in Omaha, Nebraska, over a several-month workshop period in 1986. Building on a community-based model for devising socially engaged musical performances and creative community that Schmidman and Terry had used with success for several years, including for *Goona Goona* (about domestic violence, 1979), *Kegger* (about teenage alcoholism, 1982), and later for *Walking Through Walls* (about personal and social empowerment, 1987), OMT invited community volunteers to participate in a series of creative workshops and theme-based discussion forums.[1] The multidisciplinary workshops were thematically focused on environmental issues and "healing the Earth." Participants ranged in age from 14 to 80, with occupations ranging from student to engineer, server to musician, artist to educator. While the Artistic Director's and playwright-in-residence's creative roles often overlapped, typically Schmidman led workshop participants in *avant-garde* performance training and improvisational sound/movement structures, while Terry observed, taking rehearsal photographs and notes on the lively group discussions that followed, guided by questions or ideas that she or Schmidman posed. At critical junctures, Terry would bring in snippets of text, which she wrote most evenings, inspired by the process. Then Terry and Schmidman, long-time life and creative partners, would devise discrete performance segments guided by organizing motifs such as performance ritual, family ancestors, consumer culture, mythic forms, playing in space – elements they later shaped in time and space, like a moving, dynamic puzzle that transformed from one scenario to the next. All community or company members who participated in the full workshop process then performed *Sea of Form's* premiere, which benefited from a depth of investment and ensemble ethic fostered by the process's intensive exchange.

Fundamentally, *Sea of Forms* was a performance encounter. Within OMT's *oeuvre* of theme-based multidisciplinary performance works and Terry's acclaimed earlier playwriting (*Calm Down Mother,* 1965; *Viet Rock,* 1966; and *Approaching Simone,* 1970), *Sea of Forms* stands out for engaging the audience to an exceptional degree by modeling, and cultivating, embodied sentient consciousness. It was to this integrative, experiential emphasis in performance that *Sea of Forms* owed its popularity and its lasting influence on those, like myself, who encountered it.

SENSORY PLAY

Changing the environment is the most obvious mechanism by which OMT sought to initiate an awakened sensory engagement for audience members no less than for its performers. Audience members (sixty maximum) were encouraged to arrive half an hour early to explore the environment; the likelihood of pre-show audience exploration was increased by scheduling the play's start time for 8:30 pm, at least twenty minutes later than standard theatre time. House staff provided personal welcomes to audience members to explore the installation throughout the performance space and to choose their seats arranged within it. The styrofoam world was enhanced by minimalist ("mysterious" yet "peaceful") sound compositions, atmospheric lighting, and textured walls, which also invited exploration. Some audience members frolicked amid the moving styrofoam forms as they might in piles of leaves, soft snow, waves, or bubble tents; others handled the iconographic objects and moved slowly from sculptural form to form, choosing a favored place in the performance world after relocating to various spots. Still others stepped gingerly through the space with grins or unease.

Regardless of audience members' approaches to the multidisciplinary performance installation, the styrofoam crunched beneath their feet, excess from corporate packaging – familiar and de-familiarized both. It was at once curiously beautiful and playful, a sea of styrofoam in a 100' × 20' × 15' space. It was also vaguely disconcerting, having to move or settle amid this mass of synthetic packaging that takes centuries to break down in the biosphere.[2] That popped under the weight of contact. That refused to stay neatly contained in space – styrofoam bits clinging to clothing and feet, piles spilling from here to there, pieces going home with people, reappearing for days. Both the pleasures and displeasures of the styrofoam experience were heightened by audience and performer corporeality, by their tactile contact – sympathetic and/or direct.

Making the theatre environment a playland, reminiscent in ways of childhood sandbox games or sensory bubbles, evoked physical memories, sensory presencing, I want to suggest, and also kinesthetic fantasies. "You don't so much attend it as immerse yourself in it," wrote theatre reviewer Joan Bunke. "It's an imaginative experience, as advertised: A fanciful sculpture and performance adventure" (1986). For *Omaha World-Herald* reviewer Steve Millburg, "the spell began as I walked through the door to find the theatre full of eerily lighted Styrofoam sculptures, some on the floor and some hanging in space. ... Covering the floor was a thick layer of those little Styrofoam thingies that are used for packing... like a foamy sea. I kept wanting to dive in. They'll let you do it, too" (1986).

Although twentieth-century Euro-American actor training devoted considerable attention to the development of actors' awareness and expression of secondary senses like smell, taste, touch, and, in experimental theatre, spatio-kinetics, relatively few Western theatre performances devote focus to developing *audience members'* sensory employment and expression.[3] In this aspect, *Sea of Forms'* unguided interactive pre-show anticipated the sensoriums more recently popular in science museums (e.g. the San Francisco Exploratorium) or entertainment/sensory discovery centers (such as Entros, Stephen Brown's 1990s "intelligent amusement park" and bar in Seattle). One strategy for sense immersion is to impede sight and visual stimuli because of their dominance in our perceptual orderings. In contrast, *Sea of Forms* heightened audience perception of secondary senses (touch, sound, spatio-kinetics more than smell and taste). By softening sight instead of blindfolding or blackening it (as often done in live sensoriums or haunted houses), this performance sidestepped the risk of (blinded) fear, and, moreover, interrupted the privileging of individualized experiential encounters over social ones. *Sea of Forms* intensified "secondary" sensory experiences and presented them in the co-presence of layered sights and sounds, thereby conjuring an interactive ecosystem in balance. In so doing, the performance emphasized shifting interrelations among people and diverse forms in a dynamic environment.

While in performance *Sea of Forms* was visually striking, imaginatively so, and also acoustically layered, it successfully highlighted touch and spatio-kinetics.[4] Audience members became participants developing sensory relationships to and in a dynamic cohabited space. This is to say that the pre-show opening, and the performance itself, activated people's sensory (and thus psychic) awareness of their relationships to space, in space, and with each other. When performers were in the space – moving through exact places where audience members earlier had been actively engaged – a physical remembrance or connection was invited, intensifying spatio-kinetic relationships and identifications. Furthermore, during the performance itself, audience members chose whether and where to sit, stand or lie down: "If you wish to sit on the floor you may. If you wish to stand you may. And please be prepared to move when the play seems to warrant your moving," guides the program note (1986–87–89).

Like the open improvisational time for audiences prior to performance, the program note's open environmental framing ("move as you wish") heightened what I want to identify as a kinesthetic sense for audiences. This kinesthetic sensitivity was made more concrete when any audience member(s) moved, for one person's movement accented all their changed relationships; even small bodily movements registered to others because packing bits shifted, gently rustling. As for so many of Terry and Schmidman's transformational theatre structures, *Sea of Forms'* performer-characters, meanwhile, actively engaged in ongoing spatial transformations and reorientations to each other and to the audience once the play began, gravitating toward different areas of the performance space, and, as if in different sensory worlds, sometimes quite abruptly. Audience members' experiences of these spatial reorientations and flows, already palpably intensified by their own earlier primary sensory focus on space and touch, was gently reinforced by the sound of styrofoam moving, by the visible patterns made in the styrofoam, and by their own redirections to follow the play.[5]

This is to say that *Sea of Forms* accented the dynamic role of space itself in performance and, indeed, in lived experience. In phenomenological terms, the pre-show cultivated intentional awareness of the (localized) environment and an emotional relationship to it. Making space the single most important organizing element for its themes and audience reception, this performance valued space and place as prominently as people. Theatrically, its "thematic space," to apply Gay McAuley's all-inclusive term for theatre space, performance space, textual space, and fictional place, was of an interactive ecosystem contaminated by consumer debris but ripe for creative transformations (McAuley 2000).

When the performers first entered the theatre space, in a procession, they too began by discovering the styrofoam world, directed to bring their "creature senses" – heightened smell, sharp eyes, aural acuity. One performer seemed to emerge from the styrofoam sea as if it were primordial ooze, the fluidity of unsettled bits evoking the ocean; another crawled; another scrambled and then paused as if on hind legs. If the first rounds of entrances were audience members' explorations of the styrofoam (playful and/or quiet, sensorily attuned and largely reading as "human"), the second rounds of entrances were performers' amplified sensory exploration and sensitivity to their shared world (alternately playful, spiritual, animalistic, and largely reading as "in tune with nature").

The waves of performer entrances further highlighted the space and, moreover, drew attention to motion and the flow of energy within space. The use of space for *Sea of Forms* highlighted its presence and endowed it with energy flows, making it feel alive rather than neutral or invisible, casting it as organic rather than empty.

The sea of styrofoam highlighted socio-spatial relations, making them not only visible and audible but tactile: for during much of the performance everyone was physically connected in and *to* the space. As in a pond or swimming pool, the space was defined as not only shared but also continuous and tactile, so that a ripple near one person shifted others' experiences. Meanwhile, the sense of participation and connection was not wholly positive in the styrofoam world, even with all its creative transformations. Somewhere, sometime, sensory experience or critical remembrance prompted that the natural world evoked by the installation (mounds of snow, seafoam, animal and human forms via the sculpture and performances) is increasingly contaminated by industrial and consumer waste. Developing spatial relationships and sensory-kinetic perceptions – of people in their bodies, of people to space, and of our spatial relationships to each other – helped this performance to invoke an embodied appreciation of our interrelation(s), an integrative perspective vital to environmental health. If we are all connected, the performance implied, if we grasp the dynamic materiality of ecosystems, of cohabitation and ourselves as embodied beings, the consequences for environmental hazards are both personal and social, spiritual and bodied, political and scientific. *Sea of Forms* eased into this ecological sensibility by awakening sensory perceptions, by emphasizing intrigue, delight, and wider experiential connection to the world and others.

ENVIRONMENTAL PRAXIS

The alternative theatre movement during the 1960s in the USA sought to foreground encounter, often using a revisioning of spatial and tactile physical relations as key vehicles.[6] While the metaphor of touch was not new to Euro-American theatre, broadly conceived, and had been central to the practice of modern dance, still these theatrical experiments initiated another model of performance to the West (marked white), one based less on presentation and instead more explicitly based on experiential encounter. These *avante-garde* performance traditions sought to heighten, and more concretely to access, the metaphor of touch, which has enjoyed prominent currency for centuries, expressed by the phrase "to touch the audience" or "it moved me deeply." (These experiments were trying to tap the sense of participatory community and holism perceived as lost or absent in Western societies.)

Nearly thirty years ago, Richard Schechner suggested ways to talk about the spatio-sensory dynamic of environmental theatre. In his influential study *Environmental Theater,* which used The Performance Group's work as a model, Schechner wrote of "an actual, living relationship between the spaces of the body and the spaces the body moves through" (Schechner 1973: 12). Unsurprisingly, a theatre that builds on "the assumption that human beings and space are both alive" may invite an ecological ethos, where systems are interconnected and fluid, supporting diversity and interrelationship simultaneously. Environmental theatre, wrote Schechner:

> encourages give-and-take throughout a globally organized space in which the areas occupied by the audience are a kind of sea through which the performers swim; and the performance areas are kinds of islands or continents in the midst of the audience. The audience does not sit in regularly arranged rows; there is one whole space rather than two opposing spaces. The environmental use of space is fundamentally *collaborative* ... The design encourages participation; it is also a reflection of the wish for participation.
>
> (*ibid.*: 39)

Schechner's model of a "successful environment" for environmental theatre creates "a feel ... of a *global space*, a microcosm, with flow, contact, and interaction" (ibid.: 30).

The ecological sensibility implicit in Schechner's description of environmental theatre space operated explicitly in *Sea of Forms*. The spatial design organized the space as a fluid whole, with islands of audience amid a uniquely *tactile* sea and with shifting routes of performance and audience exchange; audience and performance sites were organized in relation, spatially mapping a sense of dynamic and constant relation. More uniquely, *Sea of Forms* created an activated, full space where multiple "forms" emanated natural, cosmic, and social energies in interaction – humans in a range of relations, animals, objects (sculptures, styrofoam shells, musical instruments, microphones, angelic totems, and amplifiers). The space itself – as an ever-changing, active, and interactive presence – became both intriguing and palpable. What I am approaching here is a way to talk about how *Sea of Forms* created a sensory mapping of space based less exclusively on visual and auditory assessment than on tactile and energy, experiential ones. While OMT created highly imagistic theatre with *Sea of Forms*, in many ways akin to group performance art, they were also firmly committed, as they describe in *Right Brain Vacation Photos*, to "total theatre," where each element, and therefore each sense, "is as important to the whole as any other element" (1992: 54).[7]

The "wish for participation" that Schechner described in *Environmental Theater* fueled OMT's performance making and its politics. Rather than hitting audiences with sensory overload or an awakening by sensory assault, *Sea of Forms* invited audiences into transformed consciousness. Terry and Schmidman understand this as central to their feminist theatre. If touch and spatio-kinetics, each reliant on co-presence and proximity, played primary roles in developing ecological sensibilities in this performance, others of the senses helped to create embodied insights as well. The music, much scored and some improvised, was nearly constant, often intoxicating, for example. In a small space, surround sound, synthesizers and the power of nine voices singing softly or full-out from different locations throughout the space could sink into audience bodies, reverberate in their bones. At other times, audience members hummed with performers, grinned and shimmied shoulders, tapped their feet, indicators of the corporeal presencing and interactive community enabled by the performance.

Breath too brought audience members to their bodies – and then to each other – in key moments. Less than five minutes into the performance, all the actors began chanting in harmonics for many moments, working with breath, sound, and repetitive rocking motion to create a resonant, meditative environment where the heartbeat slows and senses flow one into the other.[8] "Seemingly floating in the styrofoam packing material that covered the floor, the cast performed a multi-part, polyrhythmic chant aimed directly at the medulla oblongata," wrote Dan Prescher in his 1986 review. The performers resonated sound qua sound throughout the space, evoking a spiritual-religious practice, creating an aural chamber in their bodies, the theatre, and others, thereby loosening Cartesian boundaries between bodies, time, and space, even as individual voices emerged distinct from the group. The script underlined the sensory interconnections built by breath, rhythm, and organic patterns: "I don't want to insult your interior uniqueness," one performer intones, text weaving in and out of others' sustained sound, "Yet our breathing repeats" (Terry and Schmidman 1986–87–89: 4). This embodied aural experience helped to stimulate both presence and reflexive attention, endowing the language with deeper meaning.[9]

By layering a meditative and sensorily full space, OMT sought to create a multi-dimensional, interrelational sensitivity to physical and metaphysical environments.

"You must learn" to look with clear eyes to "see each droplet of rain on the grass" and also to "see dimly" in order "to see things that are dim – visions, mists and cloud people," as one performer said, her voice reverberating in direct address to the audience, the script quoting there from Jamake Highwater's *Dance: Rituals of Experience* (*ibid.*: 12). Through metaphors of experience and sensorily rich environments based on breath, touch, space, and sound, the play encouraged audience members to practice a different map of sentient relations. The performance guided participants toward simultaneous perception of their own bodies and the "one body" of the world. This embrace of double perception, inspired by Daoist and Native American traditions, circulated openness to recognizing all things as interrelated. It brought the audience into the same "present" and open mode as moving-meditation and performance forms as varied as chi gung, tai chi, contact improvisation, and stage combat, which use the techniques of "soft eyes," spatio-kinetics, and embodied breath in order for practitioners to become more present in their own bodies while, paradoxically, opening to energy beyond their bodies (to others moving and to dynamic space); in this sentient meditative mode evoked by *Sea of Forms*, peripheral vision is possible and heightened readiness to act is joined by calm (a state not unlike the reflexive phenomenological attitude where I perceive and am aware of perceiving, feeling the fluid connection with the world and consciousness formed though experience). "I see me in that tree," says Seven; "We are not separate you from me," says Four, using a round of rhymes to reinforce the shared web of relations (*ibid.*: 41). Using the verbal/textual to reinforce the sensorial, the performance sought to stimulate a deep sense of organic patterns because perceiving interconnections – to nature and to others – sustains ecological conscience.

Terry and Schmidman's script, rich in sensory images, interweaves humor and open address, spiritualism, and scientific awareness. Examples of the latter include a catchy, smart song about genetic cell behavior; key thematic focus on the "lizard brain" of evolutionary memory; songs and chance lines that track technological advances and their promise; and key performance moments that pose pollution's toll as a tragedy ripe for creative responses.[10] "If you listen with your soul and all your surfaces," says Three, and if you "hear from within while enveloped by breath, fur or pine needles," continues Seven later, then one can feel a part of the "expanding universe" where "living is fuller because we are more than … us," completes Four, imagining a meaningful, sentient life (*ibid.*: 20).[11] This approach to environmentalism, which links spiritualism and science, is juxtaposed to a consumer culture where "I cannot distinguish myself from what I've bought," as one performer jauntily confessed to the audience, his body covered with chunks of Styrofoam (*ibid.*: 24).

Sea of Forms was in many ways a multidisciplinary, experiential, postmodern performance filled with wit and creative collaboration. It was also, in some respects, part environmentalist community performance ritual. While many Earth-friendly community performance rituals – from Anna Halprin's now international *Circle the Earth* dance rituals (yearly since 1981) to the Rainbow Family Gathering's annual *Circles for Peace and Healing* (beginning 1972) to the 1986 (and then 1996) Harmonic Convergence rituals celebrating the start of the "New Age of Peace" for people and the planet – were performed in nature, consciously placing humans in the "great cathedral" outdoors; *Sea of Forms* was performed in a storefront space filled with styrofoam as if to say, Americans must feel the interconnectedness with nature even while in urban places, and we as a heterogeneous community must transform the growing clutter of our lives into creative redress of both social and natural spaces. Undoubtedly, its setting hailed a more ideologically diverse audience, involving not only believers and self-identified environmentalists but also creative consumers and skeptics seeking entertainment at a funky downtown theatre.

EMBODYING ECOLOGICAL CULTURE

In *Staging Place: The Geography of Modern Drama,* Una Chaudhuri recognizes ecology as a recent thematic trend in contemporary theatre, situated in relation to the last century's ongoing exploration of dramatically changing relationships to nature (through technology, urbanization, and modernism). She suggests that towards the end of the twentieth century, many works – from Maria Irene Fornes' *The Danube* to Laurie Anderson's *United States* to Tony Kushner's *Angels in America* – were critiquing toxic contaminations of nature and, ultimately, ourselves. *Sea of Forms* invited similar emphasis, although beginning from a place, somehow, of hope. It sought to create ecological consciousness through humorous critique and, as much, through community, interactively cultivated for the audience through sensory contact, environmental theatre's ethic of collaboration, performance ritual, and play. The performance not only creatively accented cohabitation and ecological subjects but also actively practiced ecological sensibilities: the styrofoam, after all, was not only great fun, not only a palpable reminder of our wasteful material accumulation in the environment (and how we must live with what we have wrought, inevitably), but also a demonstration of creative *re-use*, a hallmark of the environmental movement.[12]

A post-show encounter again invited audiences to explore the space and to interact with performers, who returned still in costume. This interactive time facilitated community, as well as a return to play. Some who had been too tentative to walk in the central performance space pre-show waded through the reshaped piles of styrofoam then. If the pre-show facilitated immersion into the transformed space, the post-show facilitated incremental return to the world outside, giddy, entertained or inspired. There was laughter and conversation. Several audience members attended *Sea of Forms* multiple times, contributing to its sold-out success and subsequent runs. When they returned, these repeat viewers led others in encountering the environment. If the performance in ways crafted a semi-ritualized experience open to animism and social engagement in its quest for environmental perspective, it also succeeded as fun, as adult play and creative encounter.

One needs a sensorily rich conceptual vocabulary in order to understand how *Sea of Forms* worked as a doubly environmental sensorium. An illuminating passage from *Sea of Forms* suggests that real growth takes place in spaces where "feelings reign over words, perceptions over image. It is here in this world of feelings, not subjects, that the real growth takes place – half down into the mud – half up into the blue" (Terry and Schmidman 1986–87–89: 36). More than emotions, the "feelings" that *Sea of Forms* emphasized were the senses creatively engaged, cultivating a sentient consciousness where feeling and thought join. The senses carried this performance, as well as the play's spiritual politics, at every level, for they embodied ecological metaphors, awakening holistic perspectives. Interactive encounters with space and others heightened corporeal presencing, fostering integrative perceptions of self and the world. Perhaps because they believe "guilt doesn't make people change" even if it makes them uncomfortable, that instead of guilt about environmental waste and hazards, Omaha Magic Theatre's *Sea of Forms* structured a rich sensory world where people felt connected, psycho-physically and imaginatively (*ibid.*: 40).

REFERENCES

Bunke, Joan. 1986. "Playful theater in Omaha *Sea of Forms.*" *Des Moines Sunday Register*, 14 September.

Chaudhuri, Una. 1997. *Staging Place: The Geography of Modern Drama.* Ann Arbor: University of Michigan Press.

Highwater, Jamake. 1996 [1978]. *Dance: Rituals of Experience.* Oxford: Oxford University Press.

McAuley, Gay. 2000. *Space in Performance: Making Meaning in the Theatre.* Ann Arbor: University of Michigan Press.

Millburg, Steve. 1986. "*Sea of Forms* spins a spell of fun from moment audience walks in." *Omaha World Review*, 7 September.

Prescher, Dan. 1986. "Challenging *Sea of Forms.*" *Metropolitan*, 17 September.

Schechner, Richard. 1973. *Environmental Theater.* New York: Hawthorn Books.

Schmidman, Jo Ann, Sora Kimberlain, and Megan Terry, eds. 1992. *Right Brain Vacation Photos: New Plays and Production Photographs 1972–1992.* Omaha: The Magic Theatre Foundation and Megan Terry.

Terry, Megan and Jo Ann Schmidman. 1986–89. Unpublished manuscript and archival notes, *Sea of Forms,* Omaha Magic Theatre Archive. Berkeley: Bancroft Library, Special Collections, University of California.

——. 1987. *Sea of Forms.* Directed by Jo Ann Schmidman, composed by Joe Budenholzer, Mark Nelson, and John J. Sheehan, sculptures by Bill Farmer. Omaha and Grinnell University, Iowa: Omaha Magic Theatre, September–October.

NOTES

1 Omaha Magic Theatre (OMT) was one of the longest-running experimental and feminist theatres in the USA, lasting 25 years (1972–1998). In addition to developing new works in collaboration with visual artists and composers, it staged American *avant-garde* classics. Its full archives are housed at the University of California.

2 Scientists have recently developed packing shells that biodegrade more quickly, including peanut shells made of cornstarch substances. In 1986, this had not yet hit the US market; in 2006, this more environmentally friendly packaging remains the green alternative to the norm.

3 When I identify spatio-kinetics as a sense, I am building on non-Western disciplines of martial arts, for example, and from twentieth-century dance and theatre training. Grotowski, viewpoints, Michael Chekhov technique, and contact improvisation all offer techniques for developing relationships to space and people moving through it in order to activate sensory awareness and creative theatricality. Jamake Highwater also discusses a kinesthetic sense, based on muscular nerve receptors, when discussing dance and "primal cultures" (1996: 24).

4 *Sea of Forms* featured live and pre-composed music, audio and voice effects (e.g. a Harpo horn, vocorder, and "this is not my voice" vocalizations that sounded like whales), as well as incidental sounds. Some of these contributed to its humor, others to its production charisma. Since focus on sound as dialogue and/or music is a more familiar source of signification in performance, I am choosing to examine less-discussed aural aspects that were crucial to

the performance's underlying sensory ecology. Meanwhile, "serious musicals" were OMT's signature genre. Terry's *Viet Rock* (1966), which was the first rock musical and the first protest play about the Vietnam War, helped to imagine the "serious musical" format that she and Schmidman featured at OMT.

5   Rarely in my experience did audience members move radically from one area to another during the performance. Here I am drawing from repeat experiences with the play in production during its 1997 run.

6   For instance, the Living Theatre, the Open Theatre, the Performance Group, and Anna Halprin's San Francisco Dancers' Workshops.

7   "Theatre is text, directorial image, light, music, dance, design and architecture. Theatre is also the sound of footsteps – and silence. Each of the disciplines, which together are theatre, serve the production, the whole, as it is performed for an audience" (Schmidman *et al.* 1992: 54).

8   OMT's company members warmed up with a rigorous hour-long breath-based series of physical exercises prior to each rehearsal and performance, making them adept at creating resonant space.

9   The dual meanings of "aural" apply: related to hearing and with a sensitivity to auras.

10 Educational study guides for the production emphasized environmentalism and scientific discoveries, for example. One passage from the script employed for discussions was: "What is worse than fear of death? Falling ... from grace...? ... A big concrete block is dropped in the water. The chemicals we dump here have killed the green and brown and red plant life and all the tiny one-celled creatures who lived here. Some fish adapt to concrete. They move into this new hangout and interior decorate" (*ibid.*: 37).

11 NB: Terry often designated roles by numbers rather than names, refusing gender and cultural codings. Often a single numbered part was divided across performers during rehearsal, which reinforced OMT's emphasis on pastiche and experimental ensemble performance. In the quoted section, the effect was choral.

12 The Three R's of the environmental movement are often referred to as Reduce, Reuse, and, third best, Recycle.

14

TANGIBLE ACTS
Touch performances

Jennifer Fisher

Touch performances pose a unique challenge to conventional visualist aesthetics. They dissolve the separation of artist and audience and conceptually frame the proximal interstices. Often, the beholder in effect co-creates the piece as visual apprehension gives way to the immediacy of kinesthetic involvement. The distinct relational aesthetics of touch in turn confers an affective texture that can range from rough to soft intensity, from cool to agitated engagement. In this chapter, I will focus on performances by artists that function as tactile experiments in pain, pleasure, desire, healing, power, and knowledge. Each enactment embodies specific socialities of contiguous touch whether through gestures of greeting and relationship, kinesthetic therapies, ritual aggression, libidinal play, extra-rational knowledge, or the provocation of spatial boundaries.

Before the Enlightenment, allegorical representations of touch were typified by depicting the absence of vision, portraying blind individuals engaged in the haptic exploration of objects. The theme of blindness continues in the Futurist artist F.T. Marinetti's pivotal experience during the First World War, which inspired his 1924 manifesto, *Tactilism*. One night, crawling through the darkness of an artillery dugout, he collided with cold, steel bayonets, sharp-edged mess tins and the bristly heads of sleeping soldiers. So entranced was he by the range of sensations that even after finding his sleeping pallet, he remained awake and obsessed with "feeling and classifying" the vivid experiences that he would eventually proclaim "a tactile art" (Marinetti 1971 [1924]: 109). What is remarkable is that, at its root, *Tactilism* is strikingly performative. Marinetti's experience of tactility occurred while in motion, activating his entire body as a sensing apparatus and engaging the space between himself, other people, and surrounding objects. In positing tactilism as an aesthetic form, Marinetti recognized that touch, like any of the senses, is rooted in human physiology, yet it simultaneously bears cultural capabilities that can be cultivated with training, discipline, and practice. To develop tactilism as a tenable artistic practice, Marinetti formulated exercises to enhance and refine the perceptual dimension of feeling. He distinguished and codified modalities of tactility: on the one hand, *contiguous* touch involving the apprehension of cold, smooth, lukewarm, irritating, warm surfaces and contexts; and, intriguingly, on the other hand, *affective* touch – involving being "touched" by feelings of excitement, sensuality, wit, will, certainty, or abstraction. Marinetti's prototypical tactile work, *Sudan-Paris,* a table laden with a variety of objects and texture, required the audience to interact performatively with its surfaces. Travel between the African and European continents was evoked by the haptic translation of landscape, climate and culture into a "touch-scape." Materials portraying Sudan were, in his view, crude, greasy, rough, sharp, and burning; the Mediterranean Sea offered slippery, metallic, cool, elastic sensations; and Paris was rendered as soft, delicate, warm and cool, artificial, and civilized (*ibid.*: 110–11). Despite its troubling colonialist stereotypes, *Sudan-Paris* provides a proto-vocabulary of tactility's diverse affects.

Tactilism not only bears aesthetic characteristics and significations in its own right, it also holds a more radical capacity to decenter sight from the eyes altogether. Marinetti advocates "a visual sense born of the fingertips" that exceeds two-dimensional surface texture (*ibid.*: 112). Such tactile synesthesia invests sight throughout the body. In Marinetti's words: "The epigastrium [upper abdomen] sees. The knees see. The elbows see."[1] Touch, he proposed, is also the means by which some people sense and view the interior of bodies – an interoceptive ability apparently functioning without the mediation of X-ray technology. In the aesthetic of tactilism, touch supplants vision in the privileging of the five senses and holds powers available to be tapped and explored. Marinetti defined the ontology of tactilism in relational terms, as preconscious perception that discerns feeling as knowledge as distinct from intellectual cognition:

> When we feel a piece of iron, we say: This is iron; we satisfy ourselves with a word and nothing more. Between iron and hand a conflict of preconscious force-thought-sentiment takes place. Perhaps there is more thought in the fingertips and the iron than in the brain that prides itself on observing the phenomenon.
>
> (*ibid.*: 112)

In this regard, Marinetti articulates a prescient understanding of the neurophysiology of touch. It is the tactile modality of proprioception that can qualify the ways in which the interstices between people are intensified, where the spaces of proximity become charged.[2] This dislocation of contiguous knowledge from the certain meanings of spoken discourse locates touch as a first-order kinesthetic event, one that is irreducible to language.

As a communicative act, then, touch, in effect, incorporates the social interface as it dissolves the boundaries between subject and object. Acts of touching, as cultural events, presuppose affective encounters – the relation between "being touched" and "being moved." Touch performances propose qualities of feeling that impact powerfully and ideologically. In this regard, Terry Eagleton's (1990) recuperation of the aesthetic revivifies it as a category of cognition in its experiential, relational, corporeal, and sensorial capacities. Eagleton's aestheic ideology is incorporated in the bodies and habits of human subjects in modalities of power ranging from the coercive and the hegemonic to the emancipatory. Considering the specificity of the regime of the senses, then, it is the manner of touch that carries specific ideological bias. There is a politics inherent in how touch is enacted and perceived. Coercive deployments of touch typically rely on the pain end of the pleasure–pain continuum – e.g., the incontrovertible effects of force or torture. In turn, tactile hegemony would pertain to how we *ought* to touch – social conventions of touching or not touching – whether firmly shaking hands or refraining from touching one's genitals in public. And finally, emancipatory touch encompasses a range of touch-generated epistemological "shocks" that, in Walter Benjamin's terms, fracture habits of rationality to enable other kinds of knowledge: those becomings of touch such as the *coup de feu* kiss or the spontaneous healing. The performances I will discuss below all engage touch by producing enlivened zones of tactile intensity, often impacting skin to skin. Within this sensory morphology, performances featuring gestures of touching other human beings enact particular affective socialities and close-range transference. Yet, while often intimately implicating the audience, these performative touches exceed the codes of personal relationship.

TOUCHING BLIND

As much as performance is staged as a visual spectacle, contemporary artists have simultaneously played with the "invisibility" of touch to interrogate technologies of vision. Valie Export's performance *Tapp und Tastkino* (Touch Cinema, 1968), with Peter Weibel, was performed as an actionist guerrilla street action. Deploying a megaphone like a sideshow shill, Weibel enticed passers-by to insert their hands into an awkward cardboard bra worn by Export. This makeshift device – a miniature proscenium – allowed participants to feel her breasts and featured the candid texture and warmth of her flesh. The beholder's hands caressed her breasts in semi-enclosed darkness, an act of sexual freedom, perhaps, but obscured to the eyes even as it was realized in public. Wearing a wig, Export resembled a mannequin. Timed with a stopwatch, the touching was limited to a moment or two. For Export, the piece pivoted on the dissociation of touch and vision. Her intention was to reverse the cinematic experience of watching sexually provocative images of women by providing the opportunity to touch the real thing in public view (Mueller 1994: 17–18). First performed in Europe after the events of May 1968 and amid a climate of sexual liberation, this performance confronted voyeurism with sensory impact. Rather than presenting herself as an object on view, Export retained agency throughout the piece. Acts of touching were framed to deliberately confront social prescriptions governing patriarchal ownership of women and, in the case of women participants, incite homophilic acts.

A visual barrier was also utilized in Marie Ange Guilleminot's performance, *Le Paravent* (Wind Shelter, 1997), where it was the audience that was touched, but sightless to a distinctly non-sexual massage. Performed in the context of the city-wide Münster international sculpture exhibition, weary art viewers sat in chairs circling a twelve-paneled, two-meter-high teak enclosure and inserted their aching feet through apertures to receive treatment by a reflexologist, invisibly ensconced within. As participants sat facing the screen's immediacy, parts of their bodies disappeared into a realm of highly charged tactility, yet facial identities and reactions remained unknown to both the masseuses and their subjects. While initially resembling the 360-degree structure of the nineteenth-century panorama, *Le Paravent* actually inverted this technology of vision. While the panorama affords an overall view, the orientation of Guilleminot's installation was deliberately partial, available only from the outside of the enclosure. In turn, the submission of a body part to an extended, relaxed sense of time and the politics of a soothing action were important to the work's politics of trust that characterized the bonds between artist, artwork, and beholder.

PERILOUS TOUCH

Pleasure and pain lie at polar ends of the tactile continuum. Significantly, neither pleasure nor pain is retained in memory. Just as women forget the agony of labour, lovers can recall only fragments of ecstasy. The boundaries of tactile pleasure are culturally specific and somewhat mutable, especially given the complex satisfactions of sado-masochism, for example. Yet pain is a sensual indicator that, in no uncertain terms, conveys the limits of the body both cutaneously and kinesthetically. "Ouch!" serves as an alarm that wakes up mental and psychological faculties and brings the immediacy of present awareness. In the history of art, portrayals of touch are the most diverse of all sense representations, and they defy representation by a single attribute. Premodern allegories of the senses frequently depict touch as a mytho-logical being reacting in pain to a bird's peck or scorpion sting – moral cautions to the excesses of the flesh (Nordenfalk 1985, 1990). Here, anguish, the opposite of the caress, achieves mythical status by conferring a specific acuity to experience. In the contemporary context, performance artists have enacted excruciating actions upon their bodies with similar mythical affect: Stelarc suspended himself by hooks through his flesh, Orlan executed graphic plastic surgeries, Gina Pane repeatedly slashed her arm with a razor blade, Ron Athey painted with bleeding wounds, and Chris Burden crawled over broken glass. These performances foreground acts that rupture the protective dermis that renders the body discrete. Such performances enact a kind of aesthetic fakirism. As visual spectacles that stage pain they share with medieval penitent rituals the idea that an ethical ideal – art in this case – supersedes any personal discomfort.

Yet another group of pain performances evolve in more interactive terms where the artist deliberately places his or her body at risk and opens themselves to torment inflicted by the audience. For example, Chris Burden's *Back To You* (1974) presented the artist stripped to the waist, lying on a table in a freight elevator. A sign in the elevator invited the audience to push ⅝-inch pins into his body. He endured the puncturing of his skin on his stomach and foot by a member of the art audience while others watched via a live video feed (Ayers and Schimmel 1988: 65). For *Rhythm 0* (also 1974), Marina Abramovic announced that she would be totally passive in a room with paint, feathers, whips, knives, even a loaded gun, and that the audience could do with her whatever they wanted for six hours. Interactions escalated to intimate touching, the cutting of her skin, and eventually, to placing the gun to her head with her finger wrapped around the trigger. A fight broke out as observers intervened (McEvilley 1983: 52). These performances stage the artist as the willing subject of potential abuse and confer upon the audience the agency to induce pain.

Within the genealogy of at-risk performance, Yoko Ono's *Cut Piece*, first performed in Japan in 1964, is particularly striking because its tactile politics have expanded in performances over a forty-year span. In each performance, Ono entered a theatrical stage, formally dressed, and placed sewing shears on the floor. She assumed a kneeling posture, her eyes fixed on the audience. The audience was invited, one at a time, to cut off a piece of clothing, which they were allowed to keep. Throughout its forty-minute duration Ono remained motionless, sometimes wincing as the scissors grazed her skin. By the end of the performance, she was left holding whatever clothing remained to her nakedness. Conducted entirely in silence, the piece was loaded with anxious affect, of intimacy hinging on threat and pain. The mood and motives of this piece have shifted significantly according to its location and historical context. During early performances in Japan, participating audience members removed fewer clothes but were more violent, as in Kyoto in 1964, when a man threatened Ono holding the scissors over her head. She responded by remaining still in her posture, placidly resistant to this display of aggression. In a London performance from the same period, all but shreds of clothing were savagely cut off. In the 1965 New York performance, some of Ono's male Fluxus colleagues expressed the view that *Cut Piece* was too "hot" and "emotional." Ono has elaborated on this: "They couldn't quite pinpoint it but something was disturbing them. There was a feminist sensibility that surfaced in that piece. I think it was hard for them to watch" (Ono 1994: 37). Ono's intention was deliberately provocative: to create an intimate situation in order to confront specific ontologies of racial and gender chauvinism. At the opening of Ono's retrospective at the Museum of Modern Art in Oxford in 1997, *Cut Piece* took place in the charged atmosphere of a media event. The unruly crowd was distinctly *interested* in Ono's celebrity status as the widow of Beatle John Lennon (Stiles 1992: 42–5). Given a broader cultural curiosity and her extreme vulnerable circumstances, bodyguards in the front row were ready to intervene if a participant got too aggressive with the scissors. Importantly, in the post-9/11 context, the motivation for a 2003 performance of *Cut Piece* in Paris shifts from anguish and outrage to a more heart-focused meditation. Ono remarks on the work's new affective resonance in her artist's statement:

> Following the political changes through the year after 9/11, I felt terribly vulnerable – like the most delicate wind could bring me tears. … Some people went to Palestine to act as human shields. That really touched me. … *Cut Piece* is my hope for World Peace. … When I first performed this work, in 1964, I did it with some anger and turbulence in my heart. This time I do it with love for you, for me, and for the world. Come and cut a piece of my clothing wherever you like the size of less than a postcard, and send it to the one you love. My body is the scar of my mind.
>
> (Ono 2003)

Here Ono foregrounds touch in terms of a potentially liberating mediation of corporeal and emotional states. The piece consciously invokes the tangibility of affectively sensed proximal engagement. Ono's explanation of the Japanese concept of *kehai* is evocative of the quality of presence. She explains: "*kehai* [refers to] when you're in a room, sitting and you sense a person behind you. … A certain vibration that is just beyond tangible, obvious reality. That's the kind of thing I was interested in bringing about" (Ono 1994: 39). The sense modality of *kehai* evokes the proprioceptive experience of energized space and the relational enactment of aesthetic experience.

The kinesthetic enactments of *Cut Piece,* as with *Back to You* and *Rhythm 0*, intensify the zone between artist and audience. Tensions surface as people decide whether or not to participate. Notwithstanding the actual gender of the artist, the deliberate relinquishing of will presents a passive or "feminized" subjectivity. While these iconic tableaux acknowledge the implicit danger for those within patriarchal regimes of vision, the artists sustain the role of victim, hero, and renunciant simultaneously within the assumed conceptual contract (Watson and La Frenais 1991: 15). Kristine Stiles has insightfully acknowledged the "destructive side of creation" in such pieces that collapse "the presumed neutrality of the ubiquitous object and the distinct observer"(Stiles 1992: 35). Conducted within a climate of peace activism that spans 1960s radicalism, emergent feminism, the Vietnam War and the World Trade Center attacks in New York city, Abramovic, Burden, and Ono enact a conscience of nonviolence that encompasses potential brutality. They frame and intensify the zone of transgressive proximity at the confluence of the artist's will and the audience's ethics.

HELPING HANDS

The hand plays an iconic role in active touch, and several performances have engaged the space between individuals through the use of hand gestures. Mierle Laderman Ukeles' monumental performance *Touch Sanitation* (1979–80) utilized a palpable hand signal: the ritual handshake. For eleven months, Ukeles traversed New York city to shake the hand of approximately 8,500 sanitation workers. With each handshake, Ukeles expressed respectful acknowledgment: "Thank you for keeping New York city alive." With outstretched hand, Ukeles emphatically extended a gesture of affiliation and commonality with sanitation labourers. This handwork comprises part of Ukeles' series of "maintenance art" works, which center on the live system of hands-on service activities: "This is an artwork about hand-energy ... the touch, the hand of the artist and the hand of the sanman. I want to make a chain of hands ... to hold up the whole City" (Ukeles 1995 [1979]: 183). As a meditation on tactile contiguity, *Touch Sanitation* extended into a living web of relationships. Adopting her art making to the schedules of the workers, she organized a series of "sweeps" of the fifty-nine sanitation districts of the city, where she would follow the workers on their routes (Morgan 1986: 48). To engage the piece, each removed his or her glove to "press flesh" with the artist. She shared the occupational hazards of exhaustion, nausea, and bronchitis as a consequence of her proximity to garbage (Morgan 1982: 72). While some workers were initially suspicious of her, Ukeles ultimately became a kind of hero of the sanitation department and has occupied the unsalaried position of "artist in residence" for the New York Department of Sanitation since 1977. *Touch Sanitation* confronted social stigmas that alienate manual labourers by considering them as untouchables, extensions of the garbage they handle. The aesthetic bonds of the handshake ritual affirmed Ukeles' empathy with municipal workers whose taken-for-granted activity keeps the city clean and safe. The handshake recalled political campaigns, award ceremonies, and inaugural events. This resounding gesture actualized Ukeles as a feminist agent, homemaker, and artist in relation to a class of labourers where maintenance service was feminized, even if performed by men. This tactile performance focused attention on the conditions affecting sanitary workers as it honoured them within a living structure of relationships.

Diane Borsato's performance *Touching 1000 People* (1999) shares with Ukeles an interrogation of the thresholds and networks of affable sociality. But distinct from Ukeles' handshake, Borsato flew below the radar of the face-to-face ritual, deliberately remaining invisible to those whom she touched. Inspired by psychological research that has found that even seemingly innocuous tactile contact tends to improve the well-being of individuals, Borsato's artistic proposition was to intentionally uplift the mood of an entire city by anonymously imparting a loving touch (Borsato 2001: 64; Figure 14.1). This performance involved surreptitiously touching

Figure 14.1 *Touching 1000 People* by Diane Borsato (with photographic assistance from Dean Baldwin), Montreal, 1999.

a pool of 1,000 strangers in the city of Montreal, often in subtle ways that they may have been only unconsciously aware of. Borsato targeted selected individuals by chance (in the manner of Sophie Calle, who stalked a man on a business trip) or deliberately transgressed comfortable interpersonal space (similar to Vito Acconci, who followed people in the street or deliberately stood too close in a museum). Borsato's performance likewise enlivened the boundaries of public and private spheres. But while Acconci and Calle suspend contiguity, Borsato broke this taboo to actually touch her subjects.

Touching 1000 People deliberately challenged Borsato to perform evasive social choreographies. She found that individuals display distinctly different senses of spatial entitlement. As a young woman, it was more challenging for her to touch teens and finely dressed women and easier to touch the elderly and men. The nature of the context also pertained to the challenge of touching strangers. It was more difficult to touch people in the formality of museums and easier among the distractions of supermarkets. As distinct from the incidental contact that one might experience in maneuvering through the city, this unidirectional action required intentionally "reaching out." Borsato set herself the goal of touching thirty people or so a day, which she tallied on a list beside her bed at night. If she was short she would make up the difference the subsequent day (Borsato 2002). The actual impact of Borsato's tactile transgressions – notwithstanding their benevolent intentions – is a provocatively affective conceptual experiment.

RECOVERING TOUCH

The use of touch in art has long risked being denigrated as "touchy-feely" in critical discourse. Such judgments reveal a pervasive uneasiness concerning the tactile; it seems easier to reject the seeming earnestness of touch as ludicrous. Western culture is heir to sense hierarchies that, since Aristotle, have privileged the distal senses of sight and hearing over the proximal senses of touch, taste, and smell. Where vision affords an all-knowing transcendent perspective, touch implicates the beholder in often unpredictable ways. More strikingly, anxieties about touch reveal uneasiness about embodiment itself, especially because it is a reflexive mode of tactility that perceives corporeal awareness. To vilify the regime of "the touchy" and "the feely" is also to ignore the essential role of tangibility to spatially imbued climates of mistrust, excitement, or possibility.

The touch performances of Praxis – the collaborative duo of Delia Bajo and Brainard Carey – carry such an in-your-face sincerity. Like those of Ukeles and Borsato, touch is ordained one person at a time. Praxis' two-and-a-half-year performance *The New Economy* (1999–2001; Figure 14.2) involved the intimate care of strangers. A sign on the door of their East 10th Street storefront studio greeted passers-by with the invitation: "Welcome, free hugs." The performance engaged a non-pecuniary exchange with intimations of succour in the form of hugs, foot washings, the application of a band-aid with a kiss, or gifts of one-dollar bills. While it began before 9/11, the tenor of gravity in New York city following the Twin Tower attacks conferred a resonant context on the piece, which came to prominence at the

Figure 14.2 *The New Economy* by Praxis, 2001. Courtesy of the artists.

2002 Whitney Biennial (Danto 2002: 32). In a traumatized civic culture, offering an embrace, administerting to psychic or physical wounds, or engaging in libation rituals provided an antidote to shock. Offered to a shaken populace, such simple acts, however small or seemingly undemanding, alleviated anxiety and provided assurance. A single hug may not have gone far in solving complex emotional struggles, but the kinesthetics of opening the arms into an embrace did shift habitual defenses and carried a politics of tactile consolation that contributed to a climate of recovery.

Significantly, each of Praxis' gestures are acts of connecting that, in the moment of contact, make it difficult to sustain an analytical frame of mind. These ministrations recall portrayals of Christ's laying on of hands to heal the blind. Participants have expressed the feeling of sacredness, and some have even asked the artists if they are a church (Carey and Bajo 2002). The rite of tactile benediction – of art world *cognoscenti* and neighborhood homeless alike – is not dissimilar to the hugs given by contemporary Indian saint Mata Amritanandamayi (also known as Ammachi), whose tactile *darshan* involves embracing up to 8,000 people a day. As with such beings, it is the practice of service rituals that are intimate, but not personal in any sustained sense, that the artists wished to cultivate. Likewise, foot washing, another offering by Praxis, is an act of reverence and devotion practiced in biblical times and still today in South Asia. Praxis found that Americans tended to resist requesting an act of such humility, but if the artists entreated them directly, they would always accept.[3] The foot-washing performance asked participants to soak their feet in a basin of warm water. One foot at a time was lathered with a luxurious soap, massaged, and then dried with a fluffy towel. The foot-washing had a distinct kinesthetic impact, which, Carey explains, "plants the participant in their seat. It leaves them grounded, very much there, and opens their speech. They talk more" (Carey 2002). Throughout the performance, Bajo and Carey quietly asked participants, "Who are we?" or "What is it we do?" queries that opened a dialogic creativity (Carey, cited in Lightly 2002). As distinct from artistic assertions that fixate on notions of discrete identity or talent, art, for Praxis, is created at the moment of relational action. This artistic ideal is intentionally continuous with Joseph Beuys' concept of "social sculpture," whereby ephemeral enactments transform quoditian life (Singer 2002: 175). Praxis' nascent tactile economy opened people in striking ways pertaining to the capacity of touch to focus present awareness and its role in the therapeutic rehabilitation of trauma. People felt safe enough to expose themselves, hugging on for a long time or pulling up their shirt to receive a band-aid for a broken heart. Such gestures melted alienated social protocols of urban living, and the most requested actions were hugs and band-aid application.

IMMERSIVE TOUCH

The visceral engagement of body-to-body contact has been explored in performances that open the audience to being acted upon in a more certain, even forceful, manner involving diverse tactile modalities of pressure, weight, and temperature. Such performances characteristically constrain the beholder's body temporarily in ways that may evoke feelings of apprehension or pleasure, through close sensing of the other bodies as warm or fresh, soft or sweaty. In addition, they compel the beholder to assume specific postures, or to engage their vestibular systems, impacting the tactile modalities of balance and gravity.

The position of the performer to the audience was crucial in *Imponderabilia* (1977) by Marina Abramovic and Ulay, a performance that emphasized the physicality of the artists. Nude and standing face to face in the main entrance to a gallery, the two artists forced visitors to make a choice: which artist to face as they rubbed against their flesh to enter the gallery. This work intensified the spatial interval between the artists, implicating the spectator physically in the artists' then romantic relationship. The energy between them was invisible yet palpable as their eyes remained locked in a mutual gaze (Abramovic 1998). As people touched the artists' naked bodies, cultural, libidinal, and emotional boundaries were tested.

In turn, Vienna-based artist collaborative Gelatin, comprising Florian Reither, Ali Janka, Wolfgang Gantner, and Tobias Urban, invite the audience into intense physical proximity with other bodies that typically combined contiguous touch with tactile modalities of weight and gravity. For *Human Elevator* (1999), a performance staged in Los Angeles, Gelatin secured thirteen body builders to a vertical framework. Participants entered at ground level and were swiftly hoisted thirty-three feet to the roof of an apartment building. People expressed elation and enjoyment at the experience of being lifted, which was described by Gelatin as having the visceral quality of a "burp." The performance required the audience to surrender vestibular control and to trust the group to sustain them against the grounding force of gravity. The pressure of being enclosed was calming, and of being lifted by strong arms exhilarating.

Contrasting the dynamics of ascent in *Human Elevator,* Gelatin's *Schlund* (2001) presented a more abject and libidinally charged descent through what the artists described as "live meat" (Tischer 2001a). Eighteen obese actors were recruited to act as "human scaffolding." Strapped into a structure in Munich's Bavarian Theatre, their corpulent bodies were stripped nearly naked and lavishly oiled. The word *Schlund*, "throat" in German, carries a sinister fairytale signification of being devoured (Tischer 2001b). Gelatin's fascination with viscerality simulates the experience of being slowly swallowed in a bottomless gullet. Participants began their slide from the top of the humanoid canal and slithered slowly down with the bulges and folds of warm, greasy flesh. The slippage afforded extreme close-up views of thighs, groins, and bellies, as well as direct contact with a variation of skin surfaces, from the hairless to the hirsute, from soft flesh to rough. This carnal slide carried sexual resonances as well, in the manner of being invaginated, infantilized, rebirthed by flesh. Women were encouraged to go topless, and some experienced being groped by the more opportunistic components of the human cylinder. The intention of the artists with *Schlund* was to create in the beholder a state of sensual dissolution, of becoming liquid as contrasted to a solid sense of self (Tischer 2001b). The medium of immersive massage instilled a sense of strongly affective, precognitive abjection as distinct from having the visualist distance to judge offense. It presented a rare opportunity for immersive body-to-body contact that was qualitatively different from a sexual experience of penetrating or being penetrated. The tube running through the collective body operated more like an alimentary canal. The artists presented a collectively enacted cannibalistic continuum where distance gave way to viscous surfaces. *Schlund*'s encompassing, or digestion, of one hundred and fifty people enacted what Margaret Morse (1994) calls an "oral logic" of introjection, of being surrounded or eaten by the other, of being assimilated and transformed by the host. The contiguity of adjacent skin dissolves subject and object distance, eye to eye, skin to eye, skin to skin. As the artwork engulfed the audience, they we warmed, frottaged, and even at times fondled.

The gravitational plunge has characterized many of Gelatin's performances, which have extended to throwing themselves in the canals of Venice as the Austrian representatives for the 49th Venice Biennale. As a striking coincidence, Gelatin's show documenting *Balcony* (2000), their interventional performance at the World Trade Center, was slated to open on 11 September 2001 at the Leo Koenig Gallery in lower Manhattan. This exhibition documented Gelatin's intervention on the façade of Tower One. During March 2000, Gelatin outwitted the security systems of the Port Authority by installing an external balcony on the ninety-first floor, a gutsy action that had involved wearing harnesses, unscrewing aluminum moldings that held the window in place, using suction cups to remove the glass, and ultimately outfitting a cantilevered balcony large enough to hold one person. After the terrorist attacks, the artists fell under the suspicion of the Port Authority for transgressing WTC security and strangely revealing that there was no security protocol on the *exterior* of the towers.[4] Vertigo, the sense modality of vestibular proprioception governing balance and gravity was, it turns out, presciently confronted by the artists in order to realize *Balcony*. Since the catastrophe, a feeling of vertiginous implosion has resonated at ground zero.

The corporalities of touch performances are complex. Touch is both visible as an actual gesture and invisible, sensed as corporeal positionality. While I have focused on tactile enactments, these touch performances do not terminate at the skin. Susan Buck-Morss (1992) has described the synesthetic system as the extension of the nervous system beyond the body. I would like to suggest that such a synesthetic system is perceived by the tactile modality of proprioception in discerning the performative context as a volumetric or "charged" space. Proprioceptive awareness is particularly important in engaging the nervous system, the vestibular system, and the sense of volition to perceive how the body experiences itself and others in space, in the sensing of location, vertigo, mood, and climate.

The tactile performances I have discussed here share an emergent affect as artistic responses stemming from contexts of political instability, whether during the 1970s in the context of the Vietnam War, or in the post-9/11 situational anxiety and escalation of the Middle East crisis. Just as the immediate after-effects of catastrophic events create a momentary stillness, manual contact gives pause. During a collective mood of epistemological shock, the corporeal embodiments of touch are immediate and tend to bring cognition into present time. Both the fragility of the body and its necessity become evident. Tactile art stands as a caution to the escapist disembodiment promised by virtual worlds, to the actual consequences of deleting the body, which sufficiently mesmerized by visualist phantasmagoric effects may be compelled to self-destruct. But positing touch as an alternative sense hierarchy is not the point. Rather, the conjunctions of tactility and visuality in the performances discussed here present a relational aesthetics of touch that can elaborate the energies and volitions inherent in contiguity and conjuncture. Tactile affect and haptic sensorial mediation necessitate a more synesthetic conception of the senses. As contiguous touch occurs between performer and audience, detached perception dissolves, and possibilities materialize for mutually dynamic encounters in real time and space. In contrast to the visualist legacy, which carries a logic separating subject and artwork, a haptic aesthetic engages knowledge emergent in proximity, undeferred presence, and the in-between spaces of becoming.

REFERENCES

Abramovic, Marina. 1999. Interview with the author and Jim Drobnick. Amsterdam.

Ayres, Anne, and Paul Schimmel. 1988. *Chris Burden: A Twenty Year Survey*. Exhibition catalogue, Newport Harbor Art Museum.

Borsato, Diane. 2001. "Sleeping with cake and other affairs of the heart." *The Drama Review* 45, 1.

——. 2002 Interview with the author, 23 May.

Buck-Morss, Susan. 1992. "Aesthetics and anaesthetics: Walter Benjamin's artwork essay reconsidered." *October* 62, Fall: 3–41.

Carey, Brainard. 2002. Cited in Jen Lightly, "Block Island artist in the Whitney Biennial." *Block Island Times*, 6 April. Digital edition.

Carey, Brainard and Delia Bajo. 2002. Interview with the author, 3 June.

Dewan, Shaila K. 2001. "Balcony scene (or unseen) atop the world: episode at Trade Center assumes mythic qualities." *The New York Times,* Metropolitan Desk, 18 August.

Danto, Arthur. 2002. "The show they love to hate: the Whitney Biennial 2002." *The Nation*, 29 April: 32.

Eagleton, Terry. 1990. *The Ideology of the Aesthetic.* Oxford: Basil Blackwell.

Fisher, Jennifer. 1997. "Relational sense: towards a haptic aesthetics." *Parachute* 87, 4–11.

Marinetti, F.T. 1924 [1971]. "Tactilism." In *Marinetti: Selected Writings,* edited by R.W. Flint, 109. New York: Farrar, Straus and Giroux.

McEvilley, Thomas. 1983. "Marina Abramovic/Ulay." *Artforum*, September.

Morgan, Robert. 1982. "Touch Sanitation or shaking off the material act." *High Performance*, Fall.

——. 1986. "Touch Sanitation and the decontextualization of performance art (1979–80)." *Kansas Quarterly,* Spring.

Morse, Margaret. 1994. "What do cyborgs eat? Oral logic in an information society." In *Culture on the Brink: Ideologies of Technology,* edited by Gretchen Bender and Timothy Druckery. Seattle: Bay Press.

Mueller, Roswitha. 1994. *Valie Export: Fragments of the Imagination*. Bloomington: Indiana University Press.

Nordenfalk, Carl. 1985. "The five senses in late medieval and Renaissance art." *Journal of the Warburg and Courtauld Institutes* 48.

——. 1990. "The Sense of Touch in Art." In *The Verbal and The Visual: Essays in Honour of William Sebastian Huchscher,* edited by Karl-Ludwig Selig and Elizabeth Sears, 109–20. New York: Italica.

Ono, Yoko. 1994. "Instructions in the martial arts: Yoko Ono in conversation with Robert Enright." *Border Crossings* 13, 1: 37.

——. 2003. Artist's statement, *Cut Piece* performance, September 2003, at the Ranelagh Theatre, Paris; presented by the ARC/Musée d'Art moderne de la Ville de Paris. www.e-flux.com

Phillips, Patricia C. 1995. "Maintenance activity: creating a climate for change." In *But is It Art?* edited by Nina Felshin. Seattle, Bay Press.

Singer, Debra. 2002. "Praxis (Delia Bajo and Brainard Carey)." *Whitney Biennial 2002*, New York, Whitney Museum of American Art and Harry N. Abrams.

Stiles, Kristine. 1992. "Unbosoming Lennon: the politics of Yoko Ono's experience." *Art Criticism*, 7, 2: 42–5.

——. 2000. "Cut Piece." In *Yes: Yoko Ono*, exhibition catalogue, edited by Reiko Tomii and Kathleen M. Frello, 158. New York: Japan Society and Harry N. Abrams.

Tischer, B. 2001a. "Schlund, hot, love: the post-orgasmic fat art of Gelatin." *Art Hustler,* http://www.theposition.com/takingpositions/arthustler/01/04/09/gelatin

——. 2001b. "The post-orgasmic fat art of Gelatin." *The Position* www.the position.com/takingpositions/arthustler

Ukeles, Mierle Laderman. 1969. *Manifesto! Maintenance Art: Proposal for an Exhibition*, unpublished photocopy.

——. 1979 [1995] "Unpublished Letter Concerning the Handshake Ritual." Cited in Patricia C. Phillips, "Maintenance activity: creating a climate for change" in *But Is It Art?* edited by Nina Felshin. Seattle: Bay Press.

Watson, Gray and Rob La Frenais. 1991. "The poetry of the personal, in conversation with Yoko Ono." *Performance* 63: 15.

Woods, Randy. 1991. "The art of waste transfer." *Waste Age*, August.

NOTES

1 The epigastrium is the part of the abdomen immediately above the stomach, which interestingly, here, evokes the idea of "gut feeling." Marinetti predicts that tactilism will "render great practical services by preparing good surgeons with seeing hands and by offering new ways to educate the handicapped," anticipating the haptic interface and tele-operated surgery (Marinetti 1971 [1924]: 112).

2 Touch is a key component of the haptic sense – from the Greek *haptikos* – which encompasses touch, kinesthetics, and proprioception. The terminology of the nascent field of haptics is so mutable that diverse fields, including psychology, medicine, brain research, robotics, virtual reality, critical theory, and aesthetics, have defined the term in radically different ways. In the context of art, I have defined a haptic aesthetic that, in addition to contiguous touch, encompasses physical comportment and perambulation (see Fisher 1997).

3 Surprisingly, no one wanted the dollar bills, and even the East Village homeless didn't return for the money (Bajo and Carey 2002).

4 Evidently fearing legal and political repercussions, the artists have deleted mention of the *Balcony* project from their website and have subsequently denied that it actually happened. Gelatin's limited edition book *The B-Thing* documents the project with grainy photographs taken from a hired helicopter, showing a figure dressed in a white jacket out on the balcony (see Dewan 2001).

Part IV

CASE STUDIES

15

PERFORMERS, SPECTATORS, CANNIBALS
Making sense of theatrical consumption

Kerrie Schaefer

This essay undertakes a performance analysis of the Sydney Front's *Don Juan* in order to re-evaluate the significance of Brecht's notion of culinary theatre for contemporary performance. The analysis examines how seduction operates as a principle of performance to enable a range of challenging encounters between performer and spectator. The Sydney Front's seduction of the spectator elicits the figure of the cannibal signaling the entrance of a charged mode of consumption onto the stage. The spectacular display of cannibalism in performance takes place in the context of a discussion of the efficacy of political theatre in "the society of the spectacle" where the audience has been transformed into consumers. In this discussion, the figure of the cannibal acts as a limit term articulating "the horror" of the modern world in which there are evidently no checks on consumption. While questioning whether we are at the limits of our capacity to consume, the figure of the cannibal also illuminates the need for the practice of restraint in the midst of a culture of excess. Thus, the figure of the spectator-cannibal revitalizes thinking about the contemporary mode of the culinary in terms of political and ethical performance.

In seven years as one of Australia's leading experimental theatre companies, the Sydney Front[1] created seven major performance pieces: *Waltz* (1987), *John Laws/Sade* (1987), *The Pornography of Performance* (1988), *Photocopies of God* (1989), *Don Juan* (1991), *First and Last Warning* (1992), and *Passion* (1993). In this body of work, the Sydney Front staged a relentless interrogation and playful manipulation of theatrical conventions, inciting *Guardian* theatre critic Betty Caplan to remark "never was the line between high art and bullshit so finely drawn."[2] In 1989, the Sydney Front released an artistic statement articulating the group's carnivalesque aesthetic:

> Our work is about excess, about a gesturing that goes far beyond that necessary for any reasonable discourse. The superabundance of our work has the paradoxical aim of releasing the spectator from false complicatedness. We continually collapse our own rhetoric and bring the focus back to the body's fleshy organs. By thus returning to where meaning is embodied, we aim to protect ourselves and the spectator from the terrorism of grand abstractions that cannot be lived out.
>
> (*25 Years of Performance Art in Australia* 54)

Despite its mischievously overblown style, the Sydney Front's artistic statement identifies the focus of the company's theatre of excess as the performer and spectator conceived as sites of embodied meaning and relational significance.

A brief summary of performances representing the Sydney Front's short but significant history demonstrates various stages in the company's conceptual development of the relationship between the performer and the spectator in live performance. In *Waltz*, the performers executed a series of extreme physical actions in an attempt to exhaust the spectator's appetite for spectacle. In *The Pornography of Performance*, the performers offered up their bodies to the gaze *and* touch of the spectator, making tangible the spectator's desire for living flesh. Ushered into the performance space by a company member, spectators were encouraged to place their hands through small, round holes cut into tall, cylindrical objects, several of which were placed about the performance space. Standing inside each tube was a naked performer. In *Don Juan,* the performers changed tack and required that the spectator place his or her body on the line. In the penultimate scene of the performance, the Sydney Front bribed[3] an audience member to take off his or her clothes and to stand naked on stage for two minutes. The performers then disappeared leaving the naked spectator standing in the middle of a circle of spectators. In *First and Last Warning,* a sign at the box office announced a two-tier ticketing system dividing the audience into first-class and standard spectators. First-class spectators were ushered to seats away from the action and there served champagne and *hors d'oeuvres*. Standard spectators were required to undress and change into black nylon slips given to them by Sydney Front performers (male and female spectators were separated, initially, by a red velvet curtain running the length of the performance space). When the curtain fell and the performers appeared they were also wearing black nylon slips. For the duration of the performance, the performers shared their costume, the performance space, and some key performance actions with the standard spectators (including the construction of a wall made out of cardboard boxes to obscure the view of the performance space from first-class spectators). In *Passion*, the performers failed to appear at all. The performance script for *Passion* – a set of written instructions for the audience to perform – was delivered to an audience member chosen by a small girl in a Holy Communion dress. *Passion* proved to be the Sydney Front's ultimate production. Ongoing experimentation with the principle of seduction in performance, where the anti-productivist logic of seduction is closely aligned with reversion and disappearance (see pp. 5–6), led to the dissolution of the company itself in 1994.[4]

Production of *Don Juan*, the subject of this essay, marked a significant change in direction for the group prompted by the varied responses of European and UK audiences to *The Pornography of Performance*.[5] The performers discovered that while highly literate theatre critics and other savvy spectators were able to recognize the playful use of boundaries between high and low, some audience members were unable to do the same, which is to say that *The Pornography of Performance* seemed to actively produce voyeurism in some audience members, who perceived pornography where the performers were aiming to encourage self-critical awareness of the pleasures of theatre spectatorship. *The Pornography of Performance* forced the Sydney Front to rethink their mode of audience engagement. The result was evident in the company's 1989 artistic statement (earlier) and an accompanying list of creative themes and concerns:

Theme 1: seduction: a game of identity for adults ("mastery of the strategy of appearances, against the force of being and reality").[6]
Theme 2: sacrifice: the one magnificent gesture that would put an end to games once and for all, every night, again and again.
House Style: the body's lurid bruises veiled and revealed by an ornate theatricality.
Ideal Spectator: one who would surrender to us for one night, and think better of it in the morning.
Overwhelming vice: a stifling need for control.
Redeeming virtue: a passionate skepticism.

(25 Years of Performance Art in Australia 54)

These themes were preserved in the production of the Sydney Front's *Don Juan*. In an extraordinary gesture matching the mythical libertine's roaming infidelities, the Sydney Front poached the theme of seduction from the legend of Don Juan[7] and employed the dynamics of seduction to interrogate the relationship between performer and spectator in live performance. In an interview, a company member elaborated on the Sydney Front's shift in strategy:

> In *The Pornography of Performance* we didn't challenge the roles between the performer as exhibitionists and the spectators as voyeurs. In *Don Juan* we play with this relationship throughout the show. We take the idea of seduction in the Don Juan myth and apply it to the theatrical relationship between the actor and spectator.

(Waites 1991: 7)

Publicity for the show further underlined the group's new orientation. A flyer advertising the performance carried the headline: "Extreme seductiveness is probably at the boundary of horror (Georges Bataille)." Bataille's cryptic remark was immediately clarified by the Sydney Front's direct declaration of intent: "Having allowed the public to fondle our bodies in *The Pornography of Performance*, the members of the Sydney Front now intend to redress the balance. *Don Juan* is a fevered speculation on operatic excess, sex, desire, and seduction."[8] In the creative work space of rehearsal, borrowed elements from *Don Giovanni* were recombined in a mix with inter-textual and other (non-text based) materials taken from a diverse range of sources.[9] The Mozart and da Ponte opera, remixed yet still recognizable in sound, became the *medium* of seduction in the multimedia performance piece *Don Juan*, drawing the spectator inexorably into a game of escalating stakes.

In a review of the Sydney Front's *oeuvre*, Jane Goodall queried the appropriation of the writing and ideas of French philosopher and essayist Georges Bataille by an Australian experimental theatre company. As a constitutive set of themes, seduction, excess, and horror derive from the intricate entanglements of a historical, European, *avant-garde* literary discourse. This early twentieth-century literary discourse is far removed from Australian theatre practice in the late twentieth century. However, rather than suggest a case of misappropriation, Goodall examines the way in which Bataille's "excremental philosophy" resonates with a performance ensemble working in a post-colonial context:

> To claim this non-status [as the supplement or excess] is to refuse a whole repertoire of ready-made positions which, whilst they all express opposition to colonialism and cultural imperialism, are all the same defined by the very forms of cultural logic which they seek to defeat. Engagement in "identity politics" almost inevitably means

engaging in nationalist or essentialist rhetorics which mimic those of imperialism itself. The Sydney Front have developed a mode of performance which interrogates the dynamics of the actor-audience relationship in a way that ruthlessly ironizes the quest for identity.

Seduction as a principle of performance allows for a whole range of baroque evasions of identity and identification.

(Goodall 1993: 33)

The Sydney Front's seduction of the spectator begins on the margins of the performance of *Don Juan*. At the box office, the spectator purchases a theatre ticket and is given a black plastic party mask. Sometime later, with the audience (some of whom are masked) milling in the courtyard outside the entrance to the black box performance space, the double doors of the theatre are thrown open to the resounding tune of two full orchestral chords. In Mozart's opera, the chords announce the arrival of the avenging stone statue come to dine with Don Giovanni at his impudent invitation. At the performance space, the same musical phrase provides the signal for the audience to enter, underlining the theme of the performers taking revenge on the spectators. On the threshold of the theatre, the spectator exchanges his/her theatre ticket for a small plastic glass of red or white wine.

Upon entry into the performance space, the spectator faces a less disarming challenge in the form of the Sydney Front performers occupying the audience seating. Seven performers dressed in white wedding dresses, their faces and upper bodies powdered ashen-white, are scattered throughout the audience seating. The seating structure is barricaded with wooden boards entwined with barbed wire to prevent audience access. A row of wooden barriers on the floor of the performance space forces spectators to walk in single file in front of the seated performers. As the audience slowly files into the space, they assemble on the opposite side of the barriers, face to face with the ghostly brides. These figures of frustrated desire fix odd spectators in greedy stares. They feverishly write notes in small black books taken from under their seats, pointing at spectators and whispering to each other inaudibly against a soundtrack of gibberish barely recognizable as Mozart's opera played at twenty times its normal speed. Thus, the Sydney Front's Opening Scene[10] initiates the spectator into the grotesque world of seduction.

As I have argued elsewhere,[11] the front-on, face-to-face physical arrangement of performer and spectator establishes an encounter of two-way gazes that is of the order of a challenge. Baudrillard, a critical source in the rehearsal process, has characterized a challenge of this order as seduction. He states.

In seduction we are not dealing with a new version of universal attraction. The diagonals or transversals of seduction may well break the opposition between terms; they do not lead to fused or confused relations but to dual relations. It is not a matter of a mystical fusion of subject or object, or signifier or signified, masculine and feminine etc., but of a seduction, that is, *a duel and agonistic* relation.

(Baudrillard 1990: 105, italics in original)

The Sydney Front may have poached the theme of seduction from the legend of Don Juan, but it is Baudrillard's notion of seduction that they put into play in performance. As Victoria Grace argues in her feminist reading of Baudrillard's work, his use of seduction is in opposition to, and a process of critique of, conventional constructions of the predatory male seducer or *femme fatale* and accepted readings such as the Freudian one (Grace 2000: 141). Baudrillard's theoretical works critique the productivist logic common to the major discourses of modernity. His theory of seduction is developed strictly in this context and is therefore best understood as a mode of action that operates outside of and as a foil to the forces of productivity, which perpetuate belief in power, truth, reality, sex, sexuality, and/or identity. As Grace states: "where production is literally making something appear, bringing it into the realm of the visible or perceivable (or even performing, as in a theatre on a stage), seduction is that movement that removes from the realm of the visible, that vaporizes 'identity' and is marked by ambivalence. Seduction is about reversion and disappearance" (141). The attributes of seduction are play and gaming, challenges and duels. As seduction cannot take on the terms of power directly, it plays on the surface appearance of things, denying them their truth and turning it into a game (the secret). Through this game play, seduction thwarts all systems of power and meaning. It is the triumph of seeming over meaning.

Employing the sense of the term meant by Baudrillard, the Sydney Front put the tactic of seduction into play in *Don Juan*. The performers actively exploit the two-way play of looks between spectator and performer, and performer and spectator, laying down a playful challenge to the self-identical "I" – eye – of the spectator. In making direct eye contact with the spectator, the Sydney Front performers construct a relationship that is "a dual and agonistic" encounter. Baudrillard characterizes such an encounter, "where looks alone join in a sort of dual/duel," as "a tactility of gazes ... a duel that is simultaneously sensual, even voluptuous, but disincarnated – a perfect foretaste of seduction's vertigo, which the more carnal pleasures that follow will not equal" (Baudrillard 1990: 77). While the encounter of looks across a safe distance may be felt as a delightful tension, as Baudrillard suggests, in theatrical terms the agonistic nature of this challenge is amplified. Drawn out of the dark and into the light, the spectator's journey is from anonymity and immunity to identification and vulnerability. That is, in the Sydney Front's *Don Juan* the spectator is shown negotiating the agony of acting within the theatrical frame under the "obsessive and lugubrious eye" (Bataille 1985: 17) of the performer. This horrible seduction of the spectator, unsettling a secure sense of identity, is explored further in subsequent scenes.

At the end of the Opening Scene, one performer leaves the barricaded seating structure and ventures into the audience. He is directed by the other performers to choose one spectator, a man. This man is singled out from the rest of the audience. He is seated on a chair in the centre of the floor space directly in front of the performers. The audience around him forms a semicircle to better view the performers' verbal seduction of the man. The performers ask the man a set of leading questions from a prewritten script. For example: "Did you come here alone tonight?"; "Do you have a lover at home?"; "Are you looking for a change?"; "Do you have any un-nameable desires?" In the next moment, one of the performers from the back row of the audience seating says to the seduction victim, "I think I'd like to touch you." He stands and begins to walk down the stairs toward the spectator. At the same time, the barbed-wire-covered bar blocking the audience's entrance to the front row of seating lifts and moves upward toward the ceiling – the stage manager manipulates the mechanism that slowly raises the bar. The way is made clear for the performer to get his hands on the spectator. At this point, the other performers rise from their seats, one saying "I think we'd all like to touch you." They proceed down the stairs and onto the floor of the performance space behind the leading performer. The leading performer walks up to the Seduction Victim as the other performers fan out behind him, sizing up the spectators surrounding the seated man.

There is a significant shift between the Opening Scene, where the performer and spectator are locked in a dual encounter of looks (a duel), and Seduction Victim, where the distance between performer and spectator is dissolved in the possibility of physical contact. This shift does not represent a collapse of the performer/spectator relationship into a fleshy (con)fusion. The Sydney Front uses the ploy of "getting their hands on the spectator" to get onto the floor of the performance space, where they move the spectators to the sides, creating a corridor up the middle for the performers. In the following scene, Java Dance, the performers hitch their wedding dresses to thigh height and dance provocatively up and down the performance corridor eyeing up the spectators on either side. If seduction is "an escalation of stakes" drawing intensity purely from "the gaming, from the challenge" (Grace 2000: 157), then this chop-busting, hip-thrusting, eyeballing, lip-licking dance raises the stakes of the game. But what is *at stake* in these disorienting displacements of the spectator that constitute the game of seduction that is *Don Juan*? This is played out in the penultimate scene of the Sydney Front's performance.

The scene is called Audience Strip. It begins with the space in blackout. The audience is occupying most of the performance space in a random fashion at the conclusion of a particular sequence of scenes not discussed here. A performer appears under a spotlight in the middle of the space. He asks the audience to gather round him in a circle. He then announces that he has a request to make: "We would like one member of the audience to take their clothes off." The performer explains that the audience member will be required to stand naked for two minutes. He reassures the group that "nothing further will be required of them." A spectator steps forward.[12] The performer asks the man to remove his clothing. While the spectator undresses, the performer finds someone in the audience with a watch with a second hand and asks them to time the two minutes. When the spectator is fully undressed, the performer asks that the count begin and disappears offstage with the other performers, leaving the naked spectator in the middle of a circle of spectators. In the Sydney Front's second season of *Don Juan*,[13] the performance concluded at the end of Audience Strip. In this scene, the performers achieved their ultimate aim, which was to seduce a spectator into becoming the spectacle (at least for two minutes). At the end of the two minutes, the performers did not return to the stage, leaving the naked spectator to dress and the rest of the audience to slowly trickle away. The anticlimactic end to the performance acted as the final provocation in the Sydney Front's series of seductive challenges. Having taken centre-stage, the spectator had become the spectacle, making the performers redundant.

Returning to the question of what is at stake in this penultimate scene of *Don Juan*, arguably the naked spectator taking centre-stage represents a small victory for the untrained, undisciplined, unrehearsed, artless punter over the trained, disciplined, rehearsed, professional performer in the theatre. In "Oh for unruly audiences! Or, patterns of participation in twentieth-century theatre," Baz Kershaw undertakes a historical survey of post-Second World War British theatre that investigates, in ecological terms, the "edge phenomenon" of actor–audience interaction as a key indicator of the general health of theatre as a social and political process. Kershaw's study, broadly applicable to Western theatre generally, tells the story of "the growing dispossession of the audience, a shutting down of options in this particular ecology of performance: so that whoever the future of the theatre belonged to, by the turn of the millennium it was certainly not the punters" (Kershaw 2001: 141). Kershaw identifies two key historical stages in the cultural disempowerment of Western theatre audiences. The first stage, occurring between the 1950s and 1970s, transformed theatre audiences from patrons to clients, a process that saw spectators "unwittingly succumb to the dubious power of the professional" (141). The second stage, dating from the 1980s onwards, transformed theatre audiences from clients to customers, a process that saw spectators "submit to the dehumanizing dominance" of the capitalist commodity market (141). Kershaw links the historical shift from theatre patrons to clients to consumers to a growing acquiescence in audiences, a relinquishing of cultural power that impacts negatively on theatre's relevance to communities and democratic social processes.

A superficial reading of *Don Juan* might conclude that this Sydney-based experimental theatre company acts to counter the dominant trend of audience acquiescence. However, it seems to me that something much more invidious is played out in *Don Juan*. The apparent gesture toward 'radical democracy' is countered by the fact that the spectator's ascent to centre-stage is very carefully stage-managed throughout the entire performance of *Don Juan*. The Sydney Front's hands-on choreography manipulates the spectator into a key position centre-stage. Furthermore, the spectator's final performance is scripted. He/she is told to undress and stand naked for two minutes while another spectator with a watch with a second hand monitors the time: "nothing further will be required of you." This audience is in fact a highly disciplined and docile audience controlled by the performers, who have not been made redundant but, rather, have stepped sideways into managerial roles. The performers might appear to be absent, but they are powerfully present backstage. From this position of invisibility and immunity, they issue the spectator with an imperative to perform. Thus, rather than counter the trend of audience acquiescence, the Sydney Front plays it out to its contradictory end. They demonstrate that the moment of most heightened participation of the spectator in theatrical performance is pure spectacle. The audience attends curiously to the antics of the spectator thrust centre-stage. But whether the spectator performs or not, it is the spectacle itself that is compelling, and the audience consumes and is consumed by it.

That audiences are consumers[14] has recently become a critical focus in performance studies as scholars attempt to come to terms with the nature of the relationship between the emerging "performative society" and traditional or classical notions of theatre and drama.[15] How can theatre/drama have political purchase in the broader community and democratic processes of a society when the theatre spectator is transformed into a "consuming shopper" (Kershaw 2001: 144)? What is happening when theatrical performances begin to emulate the experience of retail shopping, confirming the spectator as "market follower, the late capitalist consumer trained like an athlete to the hectic pace of product turnover and market strategies" (Fuchs 1996: 138)? The issues arising from these kinds of questions dramatically rewrite an earlier model of theatre spectatorship and consumption, namely Brecht's notion of the culinary theatre. As Fuchs states, there has been "a shift in the central organ that shopping theatre works on in contrast to the traditional theatre that Brecht called 'culinary.' Consumption has worked its way down from the eyes, ears, and emotions to the digestive organs of the theatergoer" (131). Criticism can no longer be directed toward the distant, culturally superior spectator–voyeur because the new spectator is already down and dirty in the middle of masses avidly acquiring commodities. The problem as Fuchs outlines it is that the new spectator "like Brecht's smoker and sports enthusiast, abolishes the pedestal of the artistic event – not to gain the greater distance of dialectical inquiry, but to close the distance in what could be called *simulacrity*" (138). In contemporary culture, which, according to Abercrombie and Longhurst, is built on the mutually reinforcing values of spectacle and narcissism (Abercrombie and Longhurst 1998: 98), the theatre event is used "to project back onto the newly deinteriorized subject a mediated, improved sense of his/her own reality" (Fuchs 1996: 140).

In light of the seismic cultural shift that has occurred since Brecht's theatre days, the culinary as a metaphor with explanatory or critical power has been abandoned, left behind in the postmodern hyperspace of late capitalism. In theatre and performance studies, the ground seems to have shifted away from the culinary or alimentary toward retail, the practices of the consuming shopper arguably best representing the current predicament. This seems to me an opportune moment to recall what is perhaps a little-known paper first performed by Susan Melrose at *The Politics of the Body* conference at the Performance Space in Sydney in 1987, later published in *Spectator Burns*.[16] Drawing on the work of Bourdieu and de Certeau, Melrose argues that the problem of the efficacy of political theatre is best addressed through a "political theory of the culinary arts" as the theatre relation is subsumed by the logic of consumption:

> The theatre relation is one of difference, in controlled conditions which maintain that difference; which seeks transcendency of maintained difference through an ingurgitation, through direct and oblique two way gazes … which perform as the lips and tongue of desire. Its metteurs-en-scene choose and combine and offer bodies to be licked by the gaze, which I am seeing here … as oral, as a mouth, a play of lips and tongue, a drama of feeding.
>
> (Melrose 1988: 51)

Melrose characterizes the encounter between performer and spectator as "cannibal-eye-sation" (51). Theatre, she asserts, "always (all ways) offers bodies to the gaze, to the senses"(51), effectively binding the spectator into a relationship that "has little to do with the Aristotelian empathic projection into 'character,' and much to do with eating the raw and the live, our own kind with nosing and sniffing and ingurgitation, with sucking, drinking, swallowing, biting, digesting" (54). When the naked (raw) flesh of a spectator is offered up on a plate for the delectation of other spectators in the Sydney Front's *Don Juan*, the spectral subject of cannibalism is reintroduced to theatre and performance studies discourse.

In Maggie Kilgour's excellent essay, "The function of cannibalism at the present time", she states:

> Cannibalism is again a means of satire, a trope with which we parody more idealized myths about ourselves. At present, there is some concern with our cannibal past – not our savage prehistory, but the history of imperialism and its subsumption of "cannibal" societies – as well as our cannibal present – the modern world of isolated consumers driven by rapacious egos.
>
> (Kilgour 1998: 241)

The cannibal scene in Sydney Front's *Don Juan* is not simply an all-out attack on the insatiable appetite of the spectator turned cannibal ("the horror!"). Typical of the Sydney Front's ruthlessly ironic style, the cannibal scene in *Don Juan* is not merely a case of people eating *other* people (spectators feasting on the performer-to-be-eaten) but people eating the *self-same* or, more precisely, a member of their own (social or political) body. This scene of "endo-cannibalism," as anthropologists call it, demonstrates, in extreme, Kershaw's assertion that "the theatre experience trans-forms the audience itself into a commodity, as their bodies embody the ideology of theatre as commodity form" (Kershaw 2001: 144). Thus, in the Sydney Front's *Don Juan,* the cannibal doubles as the limit term articulating the unsustainability of dominant theatre practice where the bodies of the spectators are the commodities to be consumed.

The notion that the cannibal is the privileged threshold term of modernity is further explored by Elspeth Probyn in *Carnal Appetites. FoodSexIdentities*. She states that the "cannibal as a mythic figure is exemplary of excess: he is after all the only human being who can eat everything, who is truly omnivorous, but who practises restraint" (Probyn 2000: 99). In this formulation, the figure of the cannibal is an exemplar of the practice of restraint in excess and, therefore, "rearticulates a way of being within the increasingly senseless production of identity as cannibalisation of difference" (99). Probyn goes on to suggest that "an ethics and practice of restraint is only *possible*, and that it may be the only possibility, within a culture of excess" (99; italics in original). The Sydney Front's seduction of the spectator releases the fluid figure of the cannibal, which serves to rearticulate the contemporary mode of the culinary in theatre, which is perhaps more raw than Brecht imagined but no less focused on an "unnatural" feeding. At the same time, the performance space is, possibly, transformed into a critical space for the practice of restraint in excess.

REFERENCES

25 Years of Performance Art In Australia. 1994. Paddington, Sydney: Ivan Dougherty Gallery, University of New South Wales College of Fine Arts.

Abercrombie, Nicholas and Brian Longhurst. 1998. *Audiences. A Sociological Theory of Performance and Imagination*. London, Thousand Oaks, and New Delhi: Sage Publications.

Bataille, Georges. 1985. *Visions of Excess. Selected Writings, 1927–1939*, edited by Allan Stoekl, Carl R. Lovitt, and Donald M. Leslie Jr. Minneapolis: University of Minnesota Press.

Baudrillard, J. 1990. *Seduction*, translated by Brian Singer. London: Macmillan.

Fuchs, Elinor. 1996. *The Death of Character. Perspectives on Theater after Modernism*. Bloomington and Indianapolis: Indiana University Press.

Goodall, J. 1993. "Seduction and the Sydney Front." *Canadian Theatre Review* 74 (Spring 1993): 32–4.

Grace, Victoria. 2000. *Baudrillard's Challenge. A Feminist Reading*. London and New York: Routledge.

Kershaw, Baz. 2001. "Oh for unruly audiences! Or, patterns of participation in twentieth-century theatre." *Modern Drama* 42 2: 133–54.

Kilgour, Maggie. 1998. "The function of cannibalism at the present time." In *Cannibalism and the Colonial World*, edited by Francis Barker, Peter Hulme, and Margaret Iversen, 238–59. Cambridge: Cambridge University Press.

Melrose, S. 1988. "Beyond presence? Repoliticising theatre's bodies." *Spectator Burns. Performance/Theory* 2: 48–61.

Probyn, Elspeth. 2000. *Carnal Appetites: FoodSexIdentities*. London: Routledge.

Waites, J. 1991. "Treading a fine line. The Sydney Front and *Don Juan*: exploring the actor–audience nexus." *The Sydney Review* (April): 6–7.

NOTES

1   Formed in November 1986 and disbanded in December 1993, the Sydney Front was Andrea Aloise, John Baylis, Clare Grant, Nigel Kellaway, and Christopher Ryan. In seven years together, the core collective collaborated with a wide range of artists drawn from various disciplines, including performers, writers, composers, opera singers, performance artists, video artists, and lighting designers. As well as creating seven major performance works in seven years, the Sydney Front presented the solo performances of Nigel Kellaway in *The Nuremburg Recital* (1989) and Clare Grant in *Woman in the Wall* (1990); collaborated with video artist John Gilles to produce the critically acclaimed *Techno Dumb Show*, first shown at the 1991 Sydney Biennale; and produced several smaller performance pieces, including *The Burnt Wedding* (1988), *Water Work* (1988), *Prescripts* (1989), *Op Cit.* (1991), and *Tourists* (1991). In 1992, the Sydney Front was awarded the Sydney Theatre Critics Prize for Best Fringe Theatre Company.

   I worked with the company for just over six months in 1990/1991. I documented the entire rehearsal process for *Don Juan* and the first and second performance seasons at the Performance Space, Redfern, in April 1991 and 1992, respectively. I approach the work of the Sydney Front as a participant-observer in the performance-making process and as an expert spectator in performance. My analysis of the Sydney Front's *Don Juan* is informed by reception of various performances and by knowledge from the process.

2   *The Guardian*, 24 August, 1989. Caplan was remarking on a production of *The Pornography of Performance*. The Sydney Front toured *The Pornography of Performance* to cities in the UK and Europe, including London, Amsterdam, Copenhagen, Roskilde, Dusseldorf, Salzburg, and Brussels in 1989/90.

3   A cash amount of up to $50 was set aside each night to bribe spectators into performing naked. The Sydney Front always managed to bribe an audience member into performing naked, often for less than the $50 amount set aside. Occasionally, a bribe was not required at all.

4   The performers agreed to disband at the start of 1994 after meeting and deciding that they had nothing more to achieve as a theatre company. The group returned funding to the Australia Council for the Arts (www.ozco.gov.au), and the performers went their own ways. John Baylis was for several years artistic director of Urban Theatre Projects (see *Community Theatre: Global Perspectives* by Eugene van Erven. London and New York: Routledge, 2001) and now manages the Theatre Board of the Australia Council for the Arts. Nigel Kellaway is a mature artist still working in contemporary performance in Sydney (see http://www.realtimearts.net/rt47/scrap.html). He is currently artistic director of a performance venture known as the Opera Project and the recipient of a prestigious Australia Council fellowship. Clare Grant was artistic director of Playworks (a national organization for women writing for performance) for several years. She currently lecturers in the School of Theatre, Film and Dance at the University of New South Wales, Sydney.

5   Audience reactions to the Sydney Front's international touring production of *The Pornography of Performance* were the subject of a paper presented by founding company member John Baylis at the inaugural Contemporary Performance Week in Sydney (Sidetrack Theatre,

Marrickville) in 1990. Baylis noted that at certain venues some audience members returned night after night, queuing in front of the same booth each night. Baylis also noted that performers were propositioned for sex after shows.

6 The Sydney Front quote directly from Baudrillard's *Seduction* (p. 10) but do not acknowledge Baudrillard as the source.

7 See Tirso de Molina's morality play *The Joker of Seville and the Guest of Stone* (1630), Lorenzo Da Ponte's libretto for the Mozart opera *The Punished Libertine or Don Giovanni* (1787), or Molière's *Don Juan* (1655) in *The Theatre of Don Juan. A Collection of Plays and Views, 1630–1963,* edited by Oscar Mandel. Lincoln and London: University of Nebraska Press, 1963.

8 For the production of *Don Juan,* the five core members of the Sydney Front were joined by composer Ray Marcellino and soprano Annette Tesoriero. While Tesoriero was included in the rehearsal process with the core Sydney Front members, Marcellino worked independently of the core creative group. While the performers devised an original performance based loosely on the legend of Don Juan, Marcellino worked closely with and from Mozart's opera. In the final analysis, the performance of *Don Juan* diverges from the score composed by Marcellino. In other words, musical and performative elements in the Sydney Front's *Don Juan* are independent layers of meaning interacting in complex and often contradictory ways.

9 My unpublished PhD dissertation "The politics of poaching in postmodern performance: a case study of the Sydney Front's *Don Juan* in rehearsal and performance" examines in far more detail than is possible here the process of making *Don Juan.*

10 In rehearsal, the Sydney Front gave names to the scenes they devised: for example, the "Opening Scene," "Seduction Victim," "Java Dance," "Dick Lecture," "Thump Rump," "Pavan/Fuck Me," "Audience Counseling," and "Audience Strip". In this essay, I use these titles when discussing particular scenes.

11 See "Staging seduction: the Sydney Front and the postmodern geopolitics of theatre's bodies and spaces" in *Body Show/s: Australian Viewings of Live Performance*, edited by Peta Tait. Amsterdam: Rodophi, 2000: pp. 80–92.

12 Here I am referring to a particular production recorded on video in which a male spectator did step forward at this point.

13 *Don Juan* was reworked for a national and international tour in 1992. Before the show went on tour, it played a second season at the Performance Space. It is this version to which I am referring here.

14 See Abercrombie and Longhurst (1998: 77–98).

15 See, for instance, Baz Kershaw's "Dramas of the performative society: theatre at the end of its tether." *New Theatre Quarterly* August 2001: pp 203–11; and Jon McKenzie's *Perform or Else: From Discipline to Performance.* New York: Routledge, 2001.

16 *Spectator Burns* was a local, independently published journal on seminal issues in Australian and international performance in the 1980s. The papers from *The Politics of the Body* conference were published in the second of three issues of *Spectator Burns*. Although it is impossible to determine the extent of the influence of Melrose's paper on the Sydney Front, it is fair to say that critical concerns were shared in so far as members of the Sydney Front participated as performers and panelists in *The Politics of the Body* conference, and John Baylis was on the editorial board of the journal.

16

INDONESIAN THEATRE AND ITS DOUBLE
Putu Wijaya paints a theatre of mental terror[1]

Cobina Gillitt

A performance is an attack against the monotonous rhythms of life. An upset to the equilibrium. A blow to idle conditions. A jolt to the seething atmosphere. A scream that can also become a whisper. A stab as well as a caress. A nuclear bomb that is also a haiku.

Putu Wijaya, Indonesian (Wijaya 1997: 387)[2]

In the Balinese theatre ... everything that is a conception of the mind is only a pretext, a virtuality whose double has produced this intense stage poetry, this many hued special language.

(Artaud 1958: 62)

In my experience, a circular doubling-back manner of discussion often takes place when Western-trained theatre practitioners see, or should I say experience, Balinese-born Putu Wijaya's theatrical work for the first time. Inevitably, as if they have discovered a fabulous treasure that no one else has noticed, there is the enthusiastic comment: "Now that's the epitome of what Antonin Artaud meant by his 'Theatre of Cruelty'!" The unstageable has been staged.

Although I have performed on several tours and helped to lead many workshops with Putu[3] and his group Teater Mandiri since 1988, I still feel my proverbial hackles rise when I hear this response. Perhaps overly possessive of Putu's creative talents, I want to jump up and scream: "No! Artaud only saw a colonial exhibition of Balinese dance in Paris in 1931. Putu is Balinese. Can't you see that Putu's theatre doesn't need to be explained in terms of a Western theorist who used his subjective reading of Balinese theatre to justify a personal crusade against naturalism in the theatre? Can't you see that Putu came to it directly by virtue of being Balinese?" But is this really true? Putu's reply is that he has never read Artaud, but it is up to the audience to decide whether that statement is true or not. He considers himself a "contaminated Balinese." He claims that if he were to try to be Balinese in his work he would fail miserably, but at the same time he cannot deny his roots.

By the time Putu Wijaya (born 1944) became interested in forming his own theatre company in Jakarta in 1972, he had become disillusioned with the conventional Western model of theatre production that he had been taught at ASDRAFI, one of Indonesia's national theatre academies.[4] His studies had become an exercise in trying to become someone he was not, performing in a way alien to his Balinese upbringing and his deep-rooted concept of what constituted performance. This led him to re-evaluate not just the form and structure of theatre performance but its very essence. In fact, much of Putu's theatre looks "Western," not "Balinese" at all. But it is the manner in which he views and approaches every aspect of its production, from rehearsals to performance, that brings it closer to the Balinese models he was surrounded with as a child.

In Bali, traditional performance is regarded as a gift to society, not just as entertainment. Whether staged in the temple, town square, or home compound, performances can only be held at auspicious times on days designated in consultation with a priest. The sponsors and performers follow these guidelines, not only for the public showings but for meetings and rehearsals as well. An exception to this are tourist productions, which are on a set schedule. Nevertheless, all ritual obligations are met during these performances, particularly since they are often held in local temples and *banjar* (neighborhood association). While the performances can be entertaining for their audiences (the human community and the gods), they are ultimately intended as social therapy. Their aim is to create harmony between people, nature, and the divine: a holistic view that incorporates the seen and the unseen, the corporeal and the spiritual, the natural and the contrived.

Without consciously acknowledging any childhood influences from watching traditional Balinese theatre, Putu felt that what he wanted to do in his theatre was different from the conventional Western style he was studying. For Putu, theatre had to include ritual – a spiritual journey as well as a diversion: its "goal is not to entertain, yet it is entertaining" (Wijaya 1997: 387). This merging of a traditional view of performance with an urban, Western-influenced, concept of theatre formed the basis for his theatre company, Teater Mandiri, established in 1971. *Mandiri* is a Javanese word meaning independent or self-sufficient. Being *mandiri* and without many financial resources led the group to adopt its credo of *bertolak dari yang ada* (build from what is readily available). If it existed, the group would make use of it. If it did not exist, the group would do without or create it in another way. It was an all-encompassing attitude toward all stages of constructing a performance. At the core, the group had their bodies and personal experiences. From this, a concept was developed, then a script, costumes, set, music, etc. – a creative process in all senses of the word.

In mid-1975, following a couple of disappointing heavily text-based productions, Putu and some friends went into a field in Jakarta where the current Jakarta Arts Institute is located. Pointing to a cartwheel lying in the grass, he asked his friends to begin interacting with it, moving their bodies as slowly as possible. Soon, random people were arriving one by one and spontaneously joining in the improvisation, which was illuminated by a single headlight from Putu's scooter. The participants never talked about what they were doing, but almost thirty people began to meet nightly at 2:00am during the fasting month of Ramadan[5] and then for another three months after that.

After a short time, Putu began to shape the improvisations into performance material. He invited Nashar, an up-and-coming contemporary painter, to teach the group *tenaga dalam*, a martial art that emphasizes endurance and inner strength. According to Putu, after Nashar's involvement the group's slow-motion movements "became intense and strange," and because their rehearsals were held in the dark, it was almost like being in another world (Wijaya 1987). Gradually, the group began working with masks and building simple props to complement the scenes they were creating. Over the four-month period, they refined their improvisations into set scenes, and a performance emerged.

According to Putu, the resulting imagistic piece, entitled *Lho*, "expressed the spirit of Indonesia" (Wijaya 1988). *Lho* is a word that Indonesians often use. It expresses simultaneous feelings of surprise, gladness, disappointment, and trouble. It signifies an acceptance of the unexpected, especially during the political and economic turmoil experienced by Indonesians during the 1960s and early 1970s (Putu Wijaya Tentang Drama 'Lho'nya 1975). It is a way of life, a philosophy, a way of surviving and connecting to what is going on around you. It is "a combination of ignorance and wisdom of the people in the past to tell them how to survive this 'jungle,'" (Wijaya 1988) and a way to communicate with "*desa, kala, patra.*" *Desa* (place), *kala* (time), and *patra* (mood) are three principles of Balinese Hindu philosophy. Together, *desa, kala,* and *patra* are about adjusting to one's surroundings, both spatially and temporally, and *lho* is a method of achieving this. *Desa, kala, patra*, along with *bertolak dari yang ada*, became the two fundamental principles necessary for becoming a "*mandiri*" person.

When the audience entered Teater Arena at Taman Ismail Marzuki, Jakarta, in November 1975 to watch *Lho*, they found the theatre completely shrouded in black cloth except for a white strip hanging down the back wall (Dharnoto 1975: 4). On top of this wall sat several musicians. On the left side of the stage was a large *kentongan* (wooden slit drum) with a number of masks placed askew among various musical instruments. The actors were sprawled about the floor "as if in trance" (*ibid.*). Putu passed by each one "awakening" them. The music was thunderous. The theatre went dark.

The following is Putu's account of the performance:

> The play began with a darkened stage. In the darkness, the lighted tips of burning incense danced. Next the swishing sound of *ondel-ondel* (large body puppets made out of dried banana leaves) was heard. Suddenly a gong was struck and the stage was filled with the screams of actors entering the stage. In the next scene, lit by torchlight, a woman was raped by several men. Next there were women parading up some stairs. The women were shrieking loudly and then opened up their sarongs to reveal several small dolls coming out of their bellies. There was no dialogue. There were some monologues at one point, but they had absolutely no meaning. One actor actually left the theatre while reciting his monologue, an essay of mine called *Kentut* (Fart), so that we could hear him but not see him. At the end of the performance, all the actors exited the Arena Theatre. The audience was requested to follow. The actors then stripped naked and got into a cart, which was then pushed to the fountain in front of the theatre. Then one of the actors pushed the others into the fountain with a large stick. Several of those actors pretended to defecate in the fountain while talking about politics.

> (Wijaya 1998)

The audience reaction to *Lho* was mixed. The theatre was packed every night, but many reviewers panned it. Some picked up on the *Kentut* monologue, likening the production to a big smelly fart (Winantno 1975; Husani 1995). The defecation scene, intended as an indictment of politicians (pontificating crap), was taken by some as "Western-style exhibitionism" (see "Rendra Megecam Adegan Terlanjang Diatas Pentas" 1976). For Putu, *Lho* was meant to portray "a circus of the human condition in Indonesia" (Wijaya 1988). Life must be seen as a totality; there may be war, but there is still absurdity. Often, human behavior appears irrational. Sometimes what comes naturally is actually the opposite of what is expected, like laughing at a funeral. Putu showed this both through the forcefulness and severity of the images – the rape, the defecation – and by breaking theatrical convention by extending the performance beyond the interior of the theatre building. The audience had no choice but to get involved because the music was so deafening, the images so brutal, and because they physically had to get up and move if they wanted to keep watching.

The effect of *Lho* was totalizing. Every area within the space had been explored by the group, from the stage to the walls to the ceiling to the seating, even to the outside of the building itself. With no budget to speak of, they made use of masks, dolls, flags, sticks, gongs, ropes, music, sound, smell (from the incense), light, color, and most importantly their bodies. The success of the performance from Putu's point of view furthered for him the true meaning of what it means to be *mandiri*. His motto of "building from what is available" had been reconfirmed, illustrating that each performance should and does begin with the people/bodies involved.

However, Putu's critics were judging *Lho* by conventional theatre standards based on the national theatre academies' promotion of Stanislavsky-style naturalism. In response, Putu's first step in reclaiming his own sense of what constituted theatre was to change its name, referring to it as *tontonan* rather than *teater*. Despite its growing usage since the mid-twentieth century in the term *teater moderen* used to describe Western-style naturalistic plays, the word *teater* in Indonesia technically refers to a group or a building, not a performance event. On the other hand, *tontonan* is an Indonesian word with its root in the verb "to watch" (*tonton*). Typically, it is used to describe "shows" or "spectacles," including street performances, sports events, and other popular entertainment. It also includes rituals and performances at temple ceremonies. It is a humbling word that situates a performance away from so-called high forms, such as Western theatre and classical court dance. It suggests an event larger than what is merely happening onstage. It includes the audience as one of the performers – as part of the collective during a collective meditation. It is a word that suggests a high degree of adaptability. Putu's idea of theatre – being able to adapt to any circumstance, allowing for a large number of improvised moments, including the collective efforts of the group, encouraging audience interaction, talking to various levels of society, and setting up exaggerated situations – are all found in numerous Indonesian traditional *tontonan*.

Shortly after *Lho* closed, Putu published an essay entitled "Teater Luka" (Wounded Theatre) in the daily *Sinar Harapan* explaining what he was trying to do with *Lho*. *Luka* simultaneously means wound, open sore, or injured, but also, when combined with *hati* (heart) it means offensive – a wounded heart. *Lho*, as a piece of Teater Luka, was an offensive action depicting offensive scenes: showing what is *luka* in society by causing the audience to *luka* through sensory overload. Teater Luka rips open "neat and tidy systems" (Wijaya 1976) with abandon without prejudging the possible results:

> Experimental theatre illustrates what conventional theatre is – since people have as their goal to experiment. Non-literary theatre, for example, illustrates how literature has become king in the life of the theatre. Meanwhile, Teater Luka doesn't care what it is rebelling against or how others perceive it – it is there and has multiple interpretations in keeping with the background of its participants – its players and its director and its audience.
>
> (Wijaya 1976)

According to Putu's concept of Teater Luka, there is no one correct interpretation of a *tontonan*. The participants do not even have to agree. Nor is there an end to the *tontonan*, because it continues in the hearts and souls of the participants after it is over. There is no way to critique Teater Luka, because "this theatre is not to be discussed, but to be experienced" (*ibid.*). It is a sensory (sight, sound, and smell) event that goes beyond the intellect, affecting the audience on a visceral level. The only way to talk about the play is for all the participants (performers, director, and audience) to gather together afterwards and disclose their personal experiences in relation to the whole event.

Putu's *tontonan* begin with corporeal rather than intellectual capital. That is not to say that it is always the most important aspect of the performance, although it can be. Rather, by starting with the body, life is brought into the performance in a pure and spontaneous way. Putu concentrates on preparing the actor's body and voice for endurance. He works on breathing and group trust, but not characterization and motivation. This frees his actors to embody their roles so that they rely more on intuition than on analysis. Each of Putu's plays is virtually a monologue, written for a particular group to air its particular grievances – usually illustrating the breakdown of communication between the empowered and the powerless. Individuals who do emerge as such do so to add complexity to the situation, but not to confound it. Dialogue can be spoken by anyone on the stage. Each character is examined in relation to the whole, not as a separate entity:

> I not only portray the spirit of the individual, but also use individuals and groups of individuals as tools to draw a larger picture. ... Sometimes the actor is a character, but he is also frequently a thing, a color, or a shape in the structure of the performance.
>
> (Wijaya, quoted in Zarrilli 1989: 44)

Putu, who studied painting while enrolled at the theatre academy, treats the stage as his canvas. Each actor, light, set piece, prop, music cue, etc., has its own properties, its own color, texture, and viscosity. The strokes that Putu uses are broad, and no one stroke is more important than another. The subject of his painting is the same for the run of a particular play, but for each performance the "big picture" comes out slightly differently, depending on everything from the theatre building to the weather. These differences are not masked but are incorporated and often foregrounded in the performance. For example, in Bali if a dog should walk across the stage, an actor will make a comment about it and the dog will become part of the performance. In Teater Mandiri, if an actor is sick or forgets a line, another actor can simply step in. If the lighting operator forgets a cue, an actor will call it out. Every actor has been present at every rehearsal and therefore knows all the lines and has internalized the overall composition – not the psychology of it, but the overall desired effect.

Putu's actors are not involved in character development but rather are deployed in the service of the larger composition. He often likens his productions to a combat situation, and his actors need to be prepared for any eventuality. As soldiers, they need to be relaxed but alert, aware of the others and their surroundings, ready to improvise if necessary. Putu does not set blocking, so actors must always be conscious of the overall stage picture. Often the image feels chaotic, which only enhances the feeling of terror that Putu wants to induce in the audience. Onstage, from the actors' point of view, there is never chaos. Although they may not know where their fellow actors will move to next, they are able to anticipate it. One exercise Putu developed to train his actors is called "bats." The whole cast is asked to move with eyes closed, slowly at first, then faster and faster taking care not to touch anyone else. Using their "bat radar," Teater Mandiri actors can produce a controlled chaos while the audience is thrown off-balance.

In fact, Putu does not allow his actors to analyze their characters in relation to the overall production. He believes (and for the most part it is true from my experience) that his actors do not and cannot grasp what he is trying to say in his plays. Nor should they, for according to Putu's self-named *Teater Bodoh* (Stupid Theatre) style, which celebrates the body over the intellect, the actors need to come off as simply and uncomplicatedly as possible in order to empower the audience to rethink their own lives, which is Putu's ultimate goal:

> With Teater Bodoh, the audience is invited to re-experience something pure. The audience is touched by a problem, but not through speech. Teater Bodoh invites the audience to understand themselves. Teater Bodoh only helps show, it doesn't provide the prescription.
>
> (Wijaya 1987)

The resulting onstage chaos is reminiscent of the activity-filled traditional Balinese paintings that Putu grew up with. The correlation between his performance work and the paintings is striking. In a traditional Balinese painting, the whole canvas is filled with activity: there is no one focal point; there is no one subject. It is life in all its complexity, both happy and sad, pleasant and unpleasant, peaceful and violent. The spectator has the freedom to focus on any part of the painting and in any order he or she chooses. This style is in sharp contrast to that of another Asian tradition, classical Chinese painting, where a single subject is framed by empty space. The spectator is directed toward this single subject and is asked to reflect upon it in isolation. But in traditional Balinese paintings, there is no single path to the subject of the work. There is no single narrative. There is no perspective. Far and near appear the same. Past, present, and future are simultaneous. Like traditional Balinese painting, Putu's performances have multiple subjects; an intertwining of reality and fantasy; a blatant disregard for temporal, causal, and character unity; and no strong guidelines for interpretation. The real and the fantastic are stylistically indistinguishable. Balinese paintings and Putu's theatre can be understood as being about *both*.

Putu uses elements from traditional performance familiar to his local audiences and his international global theatre-savvy audiences to direct them toward an appreciation of unfamiliar nontraditional performance. His theatre can be characterized by this contradiction. *Tontonan* are often characterized by their layering of multiple meanings, as in traditional *wayang kulit* (shadow puppetry), where "there can be no single, intended correct response to a play, no one complete interpretation" (Becker 1979: 230). In his essay "Text-building, epistemology, and aesthetics in Javanese shadow theatre," A.L. Becker discusses how modes of reception for Javanese *wayang kulit* are similar to Sanskrit Indian *rasa* theory. Rasa theory addresses the way in which performers take into account their audience, gauging their performance accordingly. For example, for an audience educated in the intricacies of the performance, the performers will put on a more complex performance, equal to the audience's understanding. In Indonesia, *rasa* encompasses a whole range of sensations, from the physical act of tasting and feeling to a more abstract sense of experiencing. It also means to think or to believe. In Bali, the difference between a great performer who has *rasa* and a merely technically competent performer is that the former has *taksu*, a type of personal talent spirit or charisma. *Taksu* derives its energies from within the performer, from God (or the gods), and from the community.

Putu's theatre utilizes this concept of *taksu* by engaging the full spectrum of the meanings of *rasa* from the moment the audience enters the performance space and smells burning incense, sees the colorful costumes and lighting, hears the deafening sound effects, and feels the vibrations of the ear-shattering music. He uses dozens of actors, jarring images, and nonrealistic situations. The hyperstimulation from excessive sensory experience (*rasa*) literally shakes up the spectators' systems of belief (*rasa*). Putu calls this Mental Terror.

Putu's Mental Terror is "a type of mind cleansing" that "pummels the audience with a series of shocks so that throughout the performance the spectators remain in a chaotic situation from which they have no opportunity, desire, or ability to free themselves until it is over" (Wijaya 1997: 387). He toys with accepted conventions of both modern and traditional performance aesthetics to subvert expectations and to create a new stage vocabulary. Through a visual, aural, and olfactory bombardment, he wants to present his audiences with a thought, a dilemma, a complex package of potentialities that will allow them "the opportunity again to evaluate. To think. To weigh. To consider. To breathe. And then to choose" (*ibid.*: 388). Putu's *tontonan* are designed to conform (*cocok*) to each audience member's needs, to commune with individuals in the audience, rather than the audience as a single entity:

> Meaning is dependent upon the spectators' points of view. If the spectator is politically oriented, then the theatre becomes a political one in his eyes. If the spectator is consumed by a moral dilemma, the theatre becomes a sermon on morality. If the person just needs to laugh, the theatre then becomes a joke. If the person wants valuable artistry, then the theatre shows the possibilities for artistic experimentation. If the person doesn't want anything at all, theatre truly doesn't speak about anything. It becomes a collection of movement, activity, sound, dialogue, nothing more than a picture.
>
> (Wijaya 1980: 20)

Because each spectator is an individual and experiences differently, there are as many interpretations of a single performance as there are audience members. Viewing this type of work can be perplexing for the modern urban Indonesian, who has learned to compartmentalize and be "guided" on how to receive images, particularly by government systems, including education and the media. Putu's hope is that his theatrical style will terrorize his audiences into reconsidering their present state of existence and their expectations for the future (Wijaya 1997: 387–92). I have also observed that Putu's work is perplexing for Western audiences because it straddles a slippery area between Western and nonWestern theatre without identifying itself as an intercultural project. Those unfamiliar with the Balinese elements identify with the Western ones – more often than not seeing Artaud's theories realized in Putu's work but at the same time failing to acknowledge the Balinese influence on Artaud's work. Those who identify the Balinese elements by and large fail to realize that Putu is not consciously trying to recreate them in his theatre. Revisiting the beginning of this essay, I have come to the conclusion that in order to break free from this circular conundrum, my best response to the inevitable Artaud comparison is to accept that Putu's theatre is always going to be to some degree *both*. The elements that comprise *both* are not clearly defined, but it is the type of *both* that doubles back on itself and only exists in relation to the other. For example, in Balinese Hindu–Buddhist-based philosophy, it is believed that what is empty is also full, what is old is also new, and so forth. One state is inextricably connected to the other. In Putu's theatre, I have encountered a doubling back and forth between theory and practice – the seen and the unseen: a desire to stage what our senses perceive on stage in the theatre and beyond in our minds and hearts. It is related to the dialectic encountered by countless audiences watching *wayang kulit*, where at least two possible outcomes are contained within the single action. Although we know that a character will inevitably follow its *dharma*, the other potential is always there, unspoken and unrealized. Therefore, yes, Artaud is there, as much through his absence as through his invocation by an audience member whose personal reaction to the performance is integral to the whole experience. Through Mental Terror, Putu's goal is to unsettle his audience by making palpable the other potential, suddenly and violently without warning.

REFERENCES

Artaud, Antonin. 1958. *The Theater and its Double*, translated by M.C. Richards. New York: Grove Press.

Becker, A.L. 1979. "Text-building epistomology and aesthetics in Javanese shadow theatre." In *The Imagination of Reality: Essays in Southeast Asian Coherence Systems*, edited by A.L. Becker and A.A. Yengoyan. New Jersey: Ablex.

Dharnoto. 1975. "LHO: Sebuah Teater Puisi?" *Suara Karya*. 12 December: 4, 6.

Husani, Agus. 1995. "Lho … Ini Tontonan Kentut." *Harian Angkatan Bersenjata*. 4 December.

"Putu Wijaya Tentang Drama 'Lho'nya." 1975. *Harian Angkatan Bersenjata*. 21 November.

"Rendra Megecam Adegan Terlanjang Diatas Pentas." 1976. *Kompas*. 17 January.

Wijaya, Putu. 1976. "Teater Luka." *Sinar Harapan*. 17 January.

——. 1980. "Jalan Pikiran Teater Mandiri: Bertolak Dari Yang Ada". In *Pertemuan Teater 80*, edited by W. Sihombing, S. Sukirnanto and Ikranegara. Jakarta: Dewan Kesenian.

——. 1987. "Perjalanan Teater Mandiri." Unpublished ms.

——. 1988. Interview with author. Jakarta, 19 October.

——. 1991. Telephone interview with author. 13 February.

—— 1997. *NgEH*. Jakarta: Pustaka Firdaus.

——. 1998. Interview with author. Tape recording. Jakarta. 4 April.

Winantno, Ateng. 1975. "Lho, Permainan Kentut." *Suara Karya*. December 5: 4–5.

Zarrilli, Phillip. 1989. "Structure and subjunctivity: Putu Wijaya's Theatre of Surprise." In *Putu Wijaya in Performance: A Script and Study of Indonesian Theatre*, edited by E. Rafferty. Madison: Center for Southeast Asian Studies, University of Wisconsin.

NOTES

1   This essay was originally presented as a paper at the ASTR Conference, CUNY Graduate Center, Hunter College, NY, in a seminar entitled "The Performance Sensorium: The 'Other Senses' In The Theatre" on 11 November 2000. It is adapted from my dissertation

"Challenging Conventions and crossing boundaries: a new tradition of Indonesian theatre from 1968–1978," completed in 2001 for the Department of Performance Studies, New York University.

2   Unless otherwise indicated, all translations from Bahasa Indonesia to English are my own.

3   Making reference to Indonesians by name is complicated. Family names are not used throughout most of the country. In Bali, a person's full name gives an indication of caste, gender, and birth order but not necessarily the parents. What people are actually called sometimes has nothing to do with their given names. In everyday communication, people's names are even further confounded by the addition of a word marker that indicates the person's relationship to the speaker in terms of age, familial ties, and station. In fact, Putu Wijaya's given name is I Gusti Ngurah Putu, signifying that he is male, of *kesatriya* (noble) caste, and is fifth-born. "Wijaya" is a name he adopted as a young adult at the same time that he shed his caste markers. In scholarly Indonesian works, a person is either referred to by their full name or by the name by which they are commonly known. Hence, no disrespect is intended when I refer to Putu rather than Wijaya. In citing works by Indonesian writers, I have followed the convention of the National Library of Congress, which lists authors alphabetically by their last name if they have more than one.

4   ASDRAFI (Akademi Seni, Drama, dan Filem), located in Yogyakarta, Central Java, was founded in 1954. Putu attended classes there in the mid-1960s. The other main theatre academy at that time was ATNI (Akademi Teater Nasional Indonesia) located in Jakarta.

5   During Ramadan, one must fast during daylight hours, so generally people curtail their daytime activity. During the night, they can eat as much as they want in order to keep up their strength. Also, Putu found that the participants concentrated better late at night when no one else was around (Wijaya 1987).

17

ARTAUD'S ANATOMY

Allen S. Weiss

> He is this unframed hole that
> life wanted to frame.
> *Artaud le mômo*
>
> (Antonin Artaud)

The mid-nineteenth century saw a confluence of epistemological and aesthetic transfigurations that would mark European art for nearly a century: the internalization of the sublime, the liberation from representation, the hybridization of genres, the fantasy of the total work of art, the destruction of aesthetic hierarchies, and the valorization of intoxication and synesthesia.[1] Consequently, the epistemological function of the body as paradigm was radically transformed: from the early modernist fragmentations of the body (analytical Cubism, Futurism, Dada, Surrealism, and the entry of psychopathological art into the mainstream of modernism) through the psychological and philosophical acceptance of the distorted and abnormal body image (as manifested in Nietzsche's insistence of the soul as being something of the body; Freud's psychoanalytic symptomatology and the metapsychology of dreams and the claim that all ego is body ego; Jungian archetypal analysis and the role of the symbolic body; Schilder's study of body image; Minkowski's investigations into the pathology of lived time; Dubuffet's notion of *art brut*, and Merleau-Ponty's studies of the phenomenology of the lived body). These epistemological and aesthetic conditions at the core of high modernism would find an apogee in Antonin Artaud's "theatre of cruelty," only to finally implode in the dystopia of his madness, giving way to those final works that would radically transform not only theatre but also poetry and poetics in general.

BODY, NOT SIGN

"Thus when I can grasp a form, imperfect as it may be, I fix it, for fear of losing all thought." (I, 1, 24)[2] These words, written in 1923 to the editor Jacques Rivière, offer the core of Artaud's counter-aesthetic, indicating both the spuriousness of the force/form distinction and the ontological primacy of the body in pain. In response to Rivière's formalist critique and ultimate rejection of his poetry, Artaud responded:

> This scatteredness of my poems, these defects of form, this constant sagging of my thought, must be attributed not to a lack of practice, a lack of command of the instrument that I employed, a lack of intellectual development, but to a central collapse of the soul, a sort of erosion, both essential and fleeting, of thought, to the temporary nonpossession of the material benefits of my development, to the abnormal separation of the elements of thought (the impulse to think, at each of the terminal stratifications of thought, passing through all the states, all the bifurcations, all the localizations of thought and of form).

(I, 1, 28)

Such is an archetypically modernist aesthetic justification of shattered forms, logical equivocations, radical irrationalism, aleatory contingency, nonlinear temporality – attributes that will remain a constant throughout Artaud's work. Rivière responded with praise of Artaud's extraordinary self-diagnosis, claiming that his style – a writing that is "tormented, tottering, crumbling, as if here and there absorbed by secret whirlwinds"(I, 1, 34) – is remarkably successful in describing the state of his soul.

Rivière, like Artaud, fell into the critical trap of the intentional fallacy, but from the other side of the equation; the irony is that Artaud believes that his suffering authenticates his writing, but that writing is always inadequate to life; Rivière, to the contrary, believes that the writing is an exceptional expression of the illness, rendering Artaud's suffering eminently communicable, although stylistic weaknesses remain .

Writer and editor found themselves on opposing sides of what had become the incommensurable Western epistemological rift between expression and reception, between solipsistic incommunicability and communicative empathy, between radical alterity and community. Such recognition of pain indicates the Nietzschean transformation of Cartesian doubt into modernist anguish and uncertainty. However, crucial in reading these works is avoidance of reducing the text to a symptomatological index (a typical extrapolation of the intentional fallacy); for, in fact, the etiology of the malady constitutes a necessary but insufficient hermeneutic condition, always subordinate to the effects of writing. This conflict or confusion of genres and narrative positions, already evident in Artaud's *L'Ombilic des limbes* (1925; *The Umbilicus of Limbo*) offers the ontology of a labyrinthine, polymorphous, polyvalent, perverse subjectivity. For Artaud, the pure presence of the body was both the absolute site of contingency and the source of psychic energy: both the force and the form of expression are based on pain and the void. As he writes in *Le Théâtre et son double* (*The Theater and Its Double*, 1938), subjective interiority is constituted as an unsituatable, ever-shifting and incommunicable corporeal void, "a fragile and fluctuating core untouched by forms" (IV, 18), circumscribed by pain – a pain constantly and always inadequately expressed through language. On the inside there is nothing: consciousness is but a unity effected by transgression, rupture, and dispossession.

BODY AS SIGN

Artaud elaborated on this epistemology of pain in a letter (16 April 1925) of the same epoch to Max Morise, offering a critique of the Surrealist notion of revolution: "My sick mind prohibits these subterranean incursions, inter-spiritual, spatial-internal, I am perpetually at the edge of a small emptiness [*néant*], localized at a single point" (I, 2, 118). This suggests not the effects of the unconscious or of psychic automatism but rather a struggle with the inner and outer voids, with infinitesimal emptiness and incommensurable infinity – with self and God. This monstrous version of creation *ex nihilo* prefigured the polemic of *Le Théâtre et son double*, where in a rarely commented upon section Artaud takes up the issue of nothingness as crucial to his theory of language: "Every powerful feeling provokes in us the idea of the void [*vide*]. And the clear language that hinders this void also hinders poetry from appearing in thought" (IV, 86).[3] Self-reflection – and whatever poetry may follow from it – was not to be an operation of either pure cogitation or emotion founded on a mind/body split or a text/ theatre dissociation. Rather, it would become a dynamic process of perpetual mutation, transfiguration, or transformation, where the body would exist as a paradigmatic trope. For, after all, once the body becomes sign, pain would be obliterated, emptiness justified, and the limitations of individual psychology overcome. *Le Théâtre et son double* opens with an extraordinary and terrifying metaphor, where Artaud likens the theatre to the plague. Descriptions of the most excruciating pain and the most terrifying devestation of the body lead him to the conclusion that the theatre, like the plague,

> is a crisis that is resolved by either death or a cure. And the plague is a superior disease (mal) because it is a complete crisis after which there remains nothing but death or extreme purification. Similarly, the theatre is a disease (mal) because it is the supreme equilibrium, which cannot be acquired without destruction. It invites the mind to share a delirium that exalts its energies

(IV, 38–9).

Given Artaud's critique of the primacy of the written script, his theatre has long been valorized as a site of extreme expression and histrionic action, a position congruent with his earlier aesthetic of radical subjectivity authenticated by pain – a pain seemingly brought to its hyperbolic, indeed ecstatic limits in the plague-theatre. But how can this be reconciled with his calls, in the section of *Le Théâtre et son double* entitled "En finir avec les chefs d'oeuvres" (To have done with masterpieces) for the destruction of the psychological theatre? The answer is precisely in his notion of theatre as a curative apparatus – this radical theatre is to serve as a cure not only of all pain but indeed of all psychology! As such, it is the anti-Aristotelian theatre *par excellence*: cathartic not merely of all troubling emotion but of all interiority. The theatre is not to be the scenarization of the painful body or the representation of the tormented psyche but rather a device where pain (and its psychological derivatives) is overcome via the body becomes sign hieroglyph. As in the theatre of Gordon Craig and the Bauhaus before him – where the human body would no longer play a paradig- matic role – the actor's body in Artaud's "theatre of cruelty" exists in ontological parity with all other components of theatre, no longer organized according to a written script or restricted by psychologizing narrative. The body is "raised to the dignity of signs" (IV, 112), while speech is "manipulated like a solid object" (IV, 87). Body, voice, music, sound effects, lighting, costumes, décor, and staging are all to be conceived as "animated hieroglyphs" (IV, 65), a sort of *Gesamtkunstwerk* devoid of linearity, narration, representation, or closure. The theatre of cruelty thus overturns the very basis of the subjective, and ultimately Romantic, aesthetic characteristic of Artaud's Surrealist period.

The cure for the body in pain is sought in the transformation of body into sign: an ultimate extrapolation of the high modernist concern with the foregrounding of the materiality of the aesthetic signifier. But such curative "cruelty" is duplicitous, indeed contradictory: this theatre is to be nonpsychological yet paroxysmal and delirious; concrete though metaphysical; hieratic, but nonhierarchical; hyperbolically human, and archetypally sacred. The psychological double-binds of Artaud's early quest for poetic authenticity are now raised to the level of an incompatible network of stylistic opposi-tions – aesthetic double-binds, as it were. It is precisely due to such paralogisms that the theatre of cruelty is an impossible theatre. Whence the profundity that would make of it the inspiration of an incredibly diverse list of playwrights, writers, poets, dancers, and performers such as Jerzy Grotowski, Peter Brook, Tatsumi Hijikata, Carmelo Bene, Richard Foreman, Valère Novarina, Diamanda Galas, Gregory Whitehead, and Christof Migone. For ever since Nietzsche's critique of Western metaphysics, it is apparent that paradigms of cognition (and, consequently, paradigms of art and performance) depend upon the aleatory contingencies and accidents of material existence. Art becomes a matter of imperfections and accidents (in both senses of the word: the aleatory and the wound), not essences or representations. Artaud's struggle would entail the century's most extreme interrogation of interiority and its most radical critique of representation, where the decadent declension of Romantic poetics and epistemology would result in a hyperbolically modernist solipsism.

NO BODY, ONLY SIGNS

In 1937, Artaud went mad: language fled, the body was tortured, the mind ripped apart. He suffered the crushing and humiliating torments of paranoia, the shattering fragmentations and dismemberments of schizophrenia, the stultifying and alarming pressures of hypochondria, the terrifying and petrifying attacks of anxiety, and the alienating and uncanny effects of derealization.[4] He was sent from asylum to asylum until he was finally received in the psychiatric hospital of Rodez in 1943, where he stayed until his release and return to Paris in 1946. Dead to the world, for years his only form of expression consisted of an alternation between total withdrawal and violent ravings, believing himself to be bewitched and tortured by demons, until he finally received the electroshock therapy that, despite his consequent vituperative protestations, was most probably responsible for his entry back into language and communal life. From that moment on, Artaud wrote incessantly, producing a vast corpus of works of inestimable complexity and profundity, both in literary and in psychological terms.

In one of Artaud's earliest publications, *Fragments d'un journal d'enfer* (*Fragments of a Journey to Hell*, 1926), he describes his body as "the limbo of a nightmare of bones and muscles" (I, 1, 117), terms that would become emblematic of his lifelong torments and the consequent phantasmal deformations and transformations of his body. This is a body in "limbo" because it is suspended between life and death, immanence and transcendence, heaven and hell; it is a "nightmarish" body because its very form is susceptible to the machinations of both imperious libido and cruel necessity. These torments had always informed his theory of theatre: early on, in *Le Théâtre d'Alfred Jarry* (1926), he claimed that the spectator "will henceforth go to the theater as he goes to the surgeon or the dentist" (II, 22), and his life work ends, in *Pour en finir avec le jugement de Dieu* (*To Have Done With the Judgment of God*, 1947), with the imperative that man must be placed "yet one more time, but for the last time, on the autopsy table to remake his anatomy" (XIII, 104).

His body racked in pain, Artaud spent his entire life seeking cures and attempting to remake his own anatomy, as he clearly states at the very moment at Rodez that he began to overcome his madness: "The same body was remade to perfection a hundred times; it is my own" (XVI, 42). This corporeal reconstitution was necessary, for in the psycho-theological tragedy that was played out in his soul and on his body at Rodez, "The spirits took from me the soul of the plague and of syphilis and only left me a body which was not the one that I wanted to make" (XVIII, 117). Nearly each and every page of Artaud's writings – be they theatre, theory, diaries, letters, poems, or drawings – bears witness to this constant self-transformation charted out on a phantasmal body of the greatest plasticity and inconsistency. Cruelty takes on new meaning: it is both hieratic necessity and corporeal pain, the weight of totality and the pain of fragmentation, the agoraphobic anguish of the infinite cosmic void and the claustrophobic terror of the tomb, the respiratory choice between scream and suffocation (the two limits of modernist poetry: noise and silence). In this context, an "anatomy" of Artaud may be diachronically derived from the totality of his writings, with the proviso of remembering that for Artaud force and form are never to be dissociated, such that the body is always a body in pain. Thus the following fantastic anatomy is not a merely formal, sterile, predictable, and predicable Cartesian taxonomy of the monstrous formal possibilities of the human body as delineated by the imagination, but the delirious expression of the disconcerting polymorphousness at the core of human existence (and, by extension, at the end of modern theatre and poetry).[5]

Artaud was flayed, purged, screwed, unscrewed, twisted, gassed, gazified, poisoned, crushed, raped, burned, beaten, vampirized, spellbound, bled, gutted, sliced, putrified, petrified, liquefied, crucified, electrocuted, stabbed, infected, choked, sodomized, asphyxiated, decomposed. He suffered from the plague, leprosy, syphilis, cancer, cholera, parasites, crablice, microbes, constipation, suppurations, gangrene, scorbut, pustules, cysts, colic, inflammation, trembling, vertigo, palpitations, paralysis. He had a stone lodged in the brain, his scalp quivered with electricity, his temples were vitrified, his ears receptacles of deafening noise, his teeth aching totems, his bones a crushed morass and his spinal column a calcinated ruin, his sperm a mass of loam, his liver a filter of the unconscious, his spleen a filter of infinity, his stomach a painful void, his anus a birth passage, his penis sometimes a power rod, sometimes the void of a vagina, his skin a benumbed sheath, his nerves electrified, his toes sexualized, his members aflame and lost in the distance, and many other mutations and torments too grotesque to even name.[6]

Artaud lived through the ultimate contradictions, always voiding the law of noncontradiction: he was simultaneously man and woman, dead and alive, mortal and immortal, human and god. Artaud's body was now, like the theatre of cruelty before it, epidemic. In his struggle for his existence, the aesthetic contradictions that sustained the theatre of cruelty were now experienced as the psychological double-binds that structured his existence. They would soon be raised to the level of poetry.

Such is a monstrous body, in so far as monsters symbolize alterity and difference *in extremis*. They manifest the plasticity of the imagination and the catastrophes of the flesh, characterized by material incompleteness, categorical ambiguity, and ontological instability. Monsters are often indicators of epistemic shifts, and the monster that Artaud became was no exception. True monsters, like true artistic creations, are totally idiosyncratic and *sui generis*. Yet Artaud was not defenceless: he possessed arms and armor in this struggle with destiny, demons, and gods: "cuirasses, canons, blockhouses, totems, gri-gri, caissons, bars, barbed-wire, staffs, nails, studs, boxes, bricks, paving-stones, hewn rocks, gas, poisons, lightning, flames, smoke, discharges, electricity, partitions, surfaces, walls, carders, saws, gallows" (XXV, 218). But most of all, he had his writings – not just literature, but magical power objects, veritable transformers of the world. He understood that "It is what can be called the syllogistic functioning of the organism that is the cause of all illnesses" (XXVI, 157), knowing all too well that "The body that I aim at is inaccessible. It is not an idea accessible to similar ideas, desires, or otherwise; it is the result of my own effort made through daily projections of will through totems in the middle of the breath" (XXIV, 338).

His body – that mass of pain and contradictions – was ultimately unpredicable; it is rather through the magic of the word (the totem of the living breath; the power of pure volition) that the body will be made anew. "The secret of the soul is in the decorporization of a body" (XVI, 156) – not the body in the abstract but a body, Artaud's unique body, his flesh made word, the poet's body. Such is the prime act of desublimation: to realize that "the body is the first abstraction" (XV, 206) and that "beings are incarnate poetry" (XIX, 144) – the final manifestation of the theatre of cruelty was played out on his own body. But to free himself from the judgments of man and God, he needed to abolish the laws of syllogistic predication that bind humanity to grammar, syntax, logic, reason, and truth.

Is this not what is meant, most profoundly, by being a poet?[7] Must not the poet's body be other than that of men and gods? "Neither force nor element nor matter nor body, a being without needs, that's what I am, with neither sensibility nor heart nor hunger nor thirst nor sleep, a concrete and sempiternal poet's soul which I shall impose upon the uncreated world to make of it a created world" (XIX, 176). The poet must disappear behind his words. But this is not enough: contingency – that mix of chance and necessity – must be surmounted in order for the word to free itself from the weight of the world and the heavens, as circumscribed by the incommensurable distance between the null void within and the infinite void without, between self and God. This is precisely the purpose of the numerous negatory lists that appear throughout Artaud's diaries and last writings. The lengthiest is in *Suppôts et suppli-ciations* (*Henchmen and Torturations*, 1946): no spirit, no soul, no heart, no family, no families of beings, no legions, no confraternities, no participation, no communion of saints, no angels, no beings, no dialectic, no logic, no syllogistic, no ontology, no rules, no laws, no universe, no conception, no notion, no concepts, no affects, no tongue, no uvula, no glottis, no glands, no thyroid, no organs, no nerves, no veins, no bones, no slime, no brain, no marrow, no sexuality, no christ, no cross, no tomb, no resurrection, no death, no unconsciousness, no subconsciousness, no sleep, no dreams, no races, no genders, no females, no faculties, no principles, no attributes, no acts, no facts, no future, no infinity, no eternity, no problem, no question, no solution, no cosmos, no genesis, no beliefs, no faith, no idea, no unity, no anarchy, no bourgeoisie, no parties, no classes, no revolution, no communism, no analysis, no synthesis, no inside, no reserves, no exudation, no sweat, no inspir, no suspir, no zone, no irradiation, no physiology, no classes, no class struggle, no organism, no psychology, no discernment, no rank, no class, no society, no quality, no virtue, no vice, no honor, no sin, no value, no love, no hate, no sentiments (XIV, 2, 13–16).[8]

This list (like those of the torments and weapons before it), must be given *in extenso*, for such insidious listing – operating as an open-ended set of inclusive disjunctions – destroys all taxonomic and rational schemes. Neither hypotactic nor paratactic, this list entails the elimination of all possible predication. This enumeration is errant and erratic, decentering and decoding, disorganizing and detotalizing, shattering the orders of grammar, syntax, and logic hitherto symbolized by the coherent, "healthy" organization of the corporeal schema. All that remains for Artaud is a body and "blows, blows, blows, blows, blows" (XIV, 2, 16). Artaud's final task, his greatest effort, would be the ultimate transformation of that body to avoid those blows, to eliminate pain, or to create, as he succinctly puts it, "The body reduced to its simplest expression without anatomy so as not to oblige the being to pass through certain laws for nothing is yet accomplished" (XIX, 81). How does one change a body so as to become oneself?

NEITHER BODY NOR SIGN

A body perfectly adjusted to my being, to be more and more there. What hinders me? Infinity. Solution: to close oneself in upon one's present body with no other idea than to avoid suffering without any question, to burn all the metaphysical spectres of destiny.

(XXIII, 27)

This closure – an antipsychological and anti-ontotheological procedure – is the key to Artaud's last great creation, the "body without organs," enunciated in *Pour en finir avec le jugement de Dieu*. In order to protect himself from malevolent influences, in order to preclude the body's torturous distortion, dismemberment, and disappearance, Artaud closed himself off from the forms and forces of the world, from the heavens, and from his own libido. But is this body without organs empty or full? Is it but the residue of catatonia and paranoia? Does it express the microcosm of the dystopic void or the utopic plenitude of being? Or is it but another corporeal emblem of the double-bind that structured Artaud's entire life and work, expressed by the amphibological phrase "the judgment of God," such that we can never be sure about who is judging and who is judged? Camille Dumoulié offers a repertoire of possible interpretations of the body without organs: that unframed space in which human life perpetually escapes its "frame"; a new strategy of humor, imposing an ungraspable reality upon thought; a secular renewal of the gnostic ideal of the glorious body and the mystic notion of the resurrected body; the libidinal body anterior to the constitution of the imaginary; the body of pure desire; a totally literary creation, constituting the transferential body that links author and reader. However, he concludes, "So as to undo the concept, it is necessary to anticipate the concept in the gesture, the dance, of the body and the organs. There are no rules to do so; every body is master of the game, sworn to its singularity, alone capable of inventing its own lines of flight beyond the frames of subjectivity and the organism."[9] The body without organs cancels out all the previously operative contradictions and antinomies in Artaud's work and life. One might add that the body without organs is a form of resistance; it is limitlessly iconophobic and antirepresentational, especially antagonistic toward that icon of icons, that symbol of symbols, the gestalt of the well-formed human body. Obviating the intentional fallacy, it is neither physical nor metaphysical, libidinal nor psychological: the body without organs exists beyond all possible narcissistic identifications and projections.

The body without organs was enunciated for radiophonic diffusion. Throughout his life, Artaud had felt the overtones of his spoken words resonate between the vibratory pitch of his body and the echoes of his speech returned by the world. But now he suddenly experienced the disquietude created by the recorded, radiophonic voice; for this voice arrives from without, minus its usual corporeal thickness – and without the always associated pain. Via recording and broadcast technology, voice is separated from body, signifier from signified, performance from text, subject from socius, life from death.[10] Radio serves as a phantasmal prosthesis so that the body can be recreated through the "surgery" of montage. But metaphysical risk is overwhelming and the poetic stakes immense: his voice was destined to be restored as a hallucinatory presence, destined to float eternally in the limitless airwaves. The body without organs thus signals a great transformation of modern poetry, where words escape the tomb of the book in each and every instant: theatre as performance as poem as body.

NOTES

1 See Jean-Pierre Criqui, ed., "Synesthésies/fusion des arts," a special issue of *Les Cahiers du Musée national d'art modern* (Paris: Centre Pompidou, 2000–2001); and Weiss, Allen S., "Drunken space," in *Feast and Folly: Cuisine, Intoxication, and the Poetics of the Sublime* (Albany: State University of New York Press, 2002).

2 All citations of Artaud are from *Oeuvres complètes,* Vols 1–26 (Paris: Gallimard, 1976–1994). All translations are my own. Of the approximately thirty projected volumes of his complete works, over half consist of diaries from Rodez (1945–1946; XV–XXI) and Paris (1946–1947; XXII–XXVI) and his correspondence from Rodez (IX–XI and the *Nouveaux écrits de Rodez*); another four contain finished works of the final period (XII–XIV). The best translations of the last works are by Clayton Eshleman (with Bernard Bador), *Watchfiends and Rack Screams* (Boston: Exact Change, 1995).

3 Although Artaud's polemic regarding nothingness and the void must certainly be placed in the context of the history of European mysticism, it is almost certainly not without relation to contemporary philosophical speculation, especially Jean-Paul Sartre's existentialist system as expressed in *L'Être et le Néant* (Paris: Gallimard, 1943), where consciousness is equated with nothingness.

4 The best work on Artaud's madness is Maeder, Thomas, *Antonin Artaud* (Paris: Plon, 1978); see also Lotringer, Sylvère, "The art of the crackup," in Edward Schehr, ed., *100 Years of Cruelty: Essays on Artaud* (Sydney: Power Publications and Artspace, 2000), 175–200; and Weiss, Allen, "Psychopompomania," in *The Aesthetics of Excess* (Albany: State University of New York Press, 1989), 113–34. The finest anthology of writing on Artaud in English is Edward Scheer, ed., *Antonin Artaud: A Critical Reader* (London: Routledge, 2004).

5 Among the best accounts of contemporary theatre in the context of Artaud's poetic revolution are Blau, Herbert., *Take Up the Bodies: Theater at the Vanishing Point* (Urbana: University of Illinois Press, 1982); Blau, Herbert, *Blooded Thought* (New York: Performing Arts Journal

Publications, 1982); and Fuchs, Elinor, *The Death of Character* (Bloomington: Indiana University Press, 1996). The theoretical underpinnings of this epistemology are delineated in Kristeva, Julia. *La Révolution du langage poétique* (Paris: Le Seuil, 1974). Perhaps the most Artaudian of contemporary theatrical figures is Carmelo Bene; see Manganaro, Jean-Paul, ed., *Carmelo Bene, dramaturgie* (Le Centre International de Dramaturgie, 1977), and Ventimiglia, Dario, ed., *La Ricerca Impossibile* (Venice: Marsilio Editori, 1989). In October 1996, Carmelo Bene performed an extraordinary reading of Dante inspired by Artaud at the Théâtre de l'Odéon in Paris.

6 For Artaud's visualizations of the body, see Paule Thévenin and Jacques Derrida, *Antonin Artaud: Dessins et portraits* (Paris: Gallimard, 1986).

7 On the relations between Artaud's psychological states and his poetics, see Scheer, Edward, "Sketches of the jet: Artaud's abreaction of the system of fine arts," in *100 Years of Cruelty*, 57–74; and Weiss, Allen S., "Libidinal mannerisms and profligate abominations," in *Breathless: Sound Recording, Disembodiment, and the Transformation of Lyrical Nostalgia* (Middletown: Wesleyan University Press, 2002).

8 These pages of the notebooks are here reduced to a simple list for heuristic reasons, whereas in fact the vertical list of negations is interspersed by exclamations, glossolalia, etc. This list must be read in context. Furthermore, it should be noted that since the list appears in his notebooks written vertically, it may well be considered in the context of poetry, however vastly one must rethink that term. This set of negations, while perhaps not yet a poem in itself, certainly indicates the preconditions of a new poetics.

9 Dumoulié, Camille, *Antonin Artaud* (Paris: Le Seuil, 1996), 121.

10 On *Pour en finir avec le jugement de dieu* in the context of the history of radio, see Weiss, Allen S., "From schizophrenia to schizophonica," in *Phantasmic Radio* (Durham, NC: Duke University Press, 1995), 9–34. For a first-hand account of Artaud's last years, by the person who would become the editor of his complete works, see Thévenin, Paule. *Antonin Artaud, ce désespéré qui vous parle* (Paris: Le Seuil, 1993). This work is of particular interest for her account of Artaud's scansion of his own poetry and his manner of reciting the glossolalia. The major theoretical statement inspired by the body without organs is Gilles Deleuze and Félix Guattari, *L'Anti-oedipe* (Paris: Minuit, 1972); see also Gilles Deleuze and Félix Guattari, "28 Novembre 1947 – Comment se faire un corps sans organes," in *Mille plateaux* (Paris: Minuit, 1980), 185–204.

INDEX

NOTE: Page numbers in bold refer to a chapter by an author; page numbers followed by *n* refer to information in a note.

Bertolt Brecht turned to cabaret; Ariane Mnouchkine went to the circus; Joan Littlewood wanted to open a palace of fun. These were a few of the directors who turned to popular theatre forms in the last century, and this sourcebook accounts for their attraction.

Popular theatre forms introduced in this sourcebook include cabaret, circus, puppetry, vaudeville, Indian jatra, political satire, and physical comedy. These entertainments are highly visual, itinerant, and readily understood by audiences. *Popular Theatre: A Sourcebook* follows them around the world, from the bunraku puppetry of Japan to the masked topeng theatre of Bali to South African political satire, the San Francisco Mime Troupe's comic melodramas, and a 'Fun Palace' proposed for London.

The book features essays from the archives of *The Drama Review* and other research. Contributions by Roland Barthes, Hovey Burgess, Marvin Carlson, John Emigh, Dario Fo, Ron Jenkins, Joan Littlewood, Brooks McNamara, Richard Schechner, and others, offer some of the most important, informative, and lively writing available on popular theatre. Introducing both Western and non-Western popular theatre practices, the sourcebook provides access to theatrical forms which have delighted audiences and attracted stage artists around the world.

ISBN13: 978-0-415-25829-6 (hbk)
ISBN13: 978-0-415-25830-2 (pbk)

Related titles from Routledge

Re: Direction:
A Theoretical and Practical Guide
(Worlds of Performance)
Edited by Rebecca Schneider and Gabriel Cody

Re: Direction is an extraordinary resource for practitioners and students on directing. It provides a collection of ground-breaking interviews, primary sources and essays on twentieth century directing theories and practices around the world.

Helpfully organized into four key areas of the subject, the book explores:
• theories of directing
• the boundaries of the director's role
• the limits of categorization
• the history of the theatre and performance art.

Exceptionally useful and thought-provoking introductory essays by editors Schneider and Cody guide you through the wealth of materials included here. *Re: Direction* is the kind of book anyone interested in theatre history should own, and is an indispensable toolkit for a lifetime of study.

ISBN13: 978-0-415-21390-5 (hbk)
ISBN13: 978-0-415-21391-2 (pbk)